THE ART OF THE APP STORE

The Art of the App Store

THE BUSINESS OF APPLE DEVELOPMENT

Tyson McCann

WILEY

John Wiley & Sons, Inc.

The Art of the App Store: The Business of Apple Development

Published by
John Wiley & Sons, Inc.
10475 Crosspoint Boulevard
Indianapolis, IN 46256
www.wiley.com

Published by John Wiley & Sons, Inc., Indianapolis, Indiana

Published simultaneously in Canada

ISBN: 978-0-470-95278-8
ISBN: 978-1-118-22112-9 (ebk)
ISBN: 978-1-118-23534-8 (ebk)
ISBN: 978-1-118-26007-4 (ebk)

Manufactured in the United States of America

10 9 8 7 6 5 4 3 2 1

For general information on our other products and services please contact our Customer Care Department within the United States at (877) 762-2974, outside the United States at (317) 572-3993 or fax (317) 572-4002.

Wiley publishes in a variety of print and electronic formats and by print-on-demand. Some material included with standard print versions of this book may not be included in e-books or in print-on-demand. If this book refers to media such as a CD or DVD that is not included in the version you purchased, you may download this material at http://booksupport.wiley.com. For more information about Wiley products, visit www.wiley.com.

Library of Congress Control Number: 2011939653

To CG, J, and L.

ABOUT THE AUTHOR

TYSON MCCANN is a game designer, producer, user experience, and social media consultant with experience at major game companies including Sega, 3DO, the Tetris Company, Fisher-Price, and Funcom. His broad experience includes educational software, casual and social games, and hard-core video and computer games on everything from mobile devices to current generation consoles and PC. Along with design and production on a few iPhone titles, in 2010 he was part of a team that released a top-grossing, multiple award-winning iPhone multiplayer action game.

ABOUT THE TECHNICAL EDITOR

JOSH COLDIRON is a cross-media designer who has worked on several IOS games across all apple mobile devices, including the "Hall of Fame" award-winning "Archetype." His experience ranges from producer and level design, to leading quality assurance and localization. He has practiced successful use of social networking as a marketing tool for IOS apps, as well as for his own business. Before IOS development, he was art director in the print field for various publications. He currently works alongside Villain developing new IOS titles.

CREDITS

ACQUISITIONS EDITOR
Mary James

PROJECT EDITOR
Kevin Shafer

TECHNICAL EDITOR
Josh Coldiron

SENIOR PRODUCTION EDITOR
Debra Banninger

COPY EDITOR
Kim Cofer

EDITORIAL MANAGER
Mary Beth Wakefield

FREELANCER EDITORIAL MANAGER
Rosemarie Graham

ASSOCIATE DIRECTOR OF MARKETING
David Mayhew

MARKETING MANAGER
Ashley Zurcher

BUSINESS MANAGER
Amy Knies

PRODUCTION MANAGER
Tim Tate

**VICE PRESIDENT AND
EXECUTIVE GROUP PUBLISHER**
Richard Swadley

**VICE PRESIDENT AND
EXECUTIVE PUBLISHER**
Neil Edde

ASSOCIATE PUBLISHER
Jim Minatel

PROJECT COORDINATOR, COVER
Katie Crocker

COMPOSITOR
James D. Kramer,
Happenstance Type-O-Rama

PROOFREADER
Nancy Carrasco

INDEXER
Robert Swanson

COVER DESIGNER
Ryan Sneed

COVER IMAGE
© Brian Santa Maria / iStockPhoto

ACKNOWLEDGMENTS

I AM VERY GRATEFUL to Kevin Shafer for his fantastic editorial assistance, competence and professionalism, as well as to Mary James, Mary Beth Wakefield, and all those involved at Wiley for this opportunity. To Josh Coldiron for keeping the references to past projects in check and being a logic gatekeeper. To Dane Baker of Villain for his reaching out and asking me to tag along on his company's initial whirlwind journey. To MunkyFun for having the skills to develop a hit iOS app as if they'd been doing it for years. To developers, colleagues, and those I've been fortunate enough to work with for helping me continue to grow in software development, and as a professional. And infinite thanks especially to my family and my wife, Melissa, for being so patient and supportive. I owe you unconditionally, big time.

CONTENTS

INTRODUCTION

WITH ROUGHLY HALF A MILLION active apps available for download and a current pace of 20,000 new apps approved every month (according to 148apps.biz), the iOS App Store has been without doubt a phenomenal success. From its launch in 2008, it's seen *exponential* growth both in revenue generated and apps created, and it continues to flourish.

You may have heard the early success stories of lone programmers making thousands per day in revenue off of experimental apps. From then on, it wasn't long before larger sums of money were being thrown at app development from more major players and venture capitalists, and it's been that way ever since.

Though the App Store is showing no signs of weakening, it is becoming increasingly top-heavy. For example, depending on your niche, the top 20 percent of apps may do well in terms of numbers of downloads, but as you'll see later in the book, after that, the numbers drop significantly.

The type of success that many developers aspire to (such as the success of the "Angry Birds" application) is relatively unique, but there is still great opportunity in the App Store frontier, and lessons to be learned from both success stories and failures. Trends are shifting greatly from old business models to new, and, in this book, you will find them covered in detail.

WHO THIS BOOK IS FOR

Because the App Store houses dozens of categories and hundreds of new apps each day, the big question (especially for new or up-and-coming developers or publishers) is *how can I ensure my apps stand out from the competition and make a profit?* Consider this book a handy guide for finding the answer to that question.

You do not need a Harvard MBA to read this book — far from it, in fact. Although this book is filled with statistics and some curves, they are all easily explained. Business models are about pricing, marketing, and positioning your app within its niche, something everyone will have some familiarity with. Whether you are a developer, publisher, or entrepreneur trying your hand at iOS development, this book will teach you the ins and outs of ensuring that your app has the best chance at sitting at the top of your niche.

WHAT THIS BOOK COVERS

Although this book makes references to the current state of the App Store (some of which will become outdated as the App Store evolves), it is designed to be read as a business guide for finding your niche, assembling a team, developing, and marketing an app at any time, now or in the future.

Here is a small checklist of some of the important topics covered:

➤ Current and future trends in the App Store

➤ Methods of competitive research

➤ App development costs

➤ App Store business models and customer expectations

➤ Assembling a development team and outsourcing

➤ The stages of app development (including soft launch and post release)

➤ Marketing your app

➤ Social network integration within your app (including Facebook, Twitter, Game Center, and more)

➤ Effective ways to maximize social media in your marketing campaign

➤ Post-launch maintenance and support options

If any of these are of interest to you, then you should definitely be reading this book.

HOW THIS BOOK IS STRUCTURED

Though this book was designed to be read sequentially straight through — especially for the new developer or publisher — each chapter by itself covers a complete aspect of development. So, by all means, you should feel free to skip around as desired, depending on your current interests and stage of development.

If you're either an experienced developer with an existing team, or already at some stage of development on an app, you may still find it useful to browse through some of the chapters you already feel comfortable with, to find potential additional tips and advice that may make development more efficient for your team.

Following are the topics covered in this book (in order of presentation):

➤ Chapter 1 provides an overview of where the App Store currently is with regard to trends and business models.

➤ Chapter 2 provides outsourcing information and expectations for costs.

➤ Chapters 3 and 4 go in-depth into methods of competitive research and managing customer expectations.

➤ Chapter 5 is all about the stages of development, as well as useful production and project-management strategies.

➤ Chapter 6 is an expectation checklist of sorts for things you should pay attention to in order to maximize user engagement once you're ready to begin.

➤ Chapters 7 and 8 go in-depth into the business models of free, "freemium," and premium apps, providing tips for lite versions, ads, and much more.

➤ Chapter 9 covers some of the useful approaches and guidelines Apple has developed for app and hardware design to achieve its highly respected status. This chapter also covers design approaches to iPad app development.

➤ Chapter 10 is all about social networking, from implementing Game Center and other social networks, to Facebook Connect, to maximizing your viral channels in your marketing campaign. It also covers the importance of metrics and split testing. This is an important chapter not to be missed by anyone.

➤ Chapter 11 covers soft-launch preparation and feedback, post-launch support, how to scale your app for updates, and even touches on cross-platform support. At the end of the chapter, you will find a great list of marketing and promotion techniques.

➤ To end the book are two appendixes. Appendix A focuses on recommended reading, and Appendix B is a valuable online reference tool for nearly all aspects of development.

WHAT YOU NEED TO USE THIS BOOK

This book can be read as a non-technical guide, without the need for supplementary software to get value from it. However, when you begin developing for iOS, (iPhone, iPad, and so on), you will need a Mac, typically running the latest Mac OS for the latest version of iOS (currently in iteration 5). Anything from a Mac Mini to MacBook Pro will work.

If you're just planning on testing or reviewing builds, and not being part of programming, a Mac isn't required, but you should eventually own one of the devices your app is being planned for, so you can see for yourself how new versions of your app are progressing prior to release.

You may also want to get started reading up on Apple's Developer Portal (developer .apple.com), where Apple offers everything from helpful guides for getting started, to downloads of the iOS Software Development Kit (SDK).

As well as reading up, if you're sure you'll be developing an app, be sure to enroll early for the iOS Developer Program (developer.apple.com/programs/ios/), because this is where you will get access to the App Store for either yourself as an individual developer, or your company, where you can add additional members of your team.

CONVENTIONS

To help you get the most from the text and keep track of what's happening, we've used a number of conventions throughout the book.

> *The pencil icon indicates notes, tips, hints, tricks, and asides to the current discussion.*

As for styles in the text:

➤ We *highlight* new terms and important words when we introduce them.

➤ We show keyboard strokes like this: Ctrl+A.

➤ We show filenames, URLs, and code within the text like so: `persistence .properties`.

➤ We present code in two different ways:

```
We use a monofont type with no highlighting for most code examples.
```

We use bold to emphasize code that is particularly important in the present context or to show changes from a previous code snippet.

ERRATA

We make every effort to ensure that there are no errors in the text or in the code. However, no one is perfect, and mistakes do occur. If you find an error in one of our books, like a spelling mistake or faulty piece of code, we would be very grateful for your feedback. By sending in errata, you may save another reader hours of frustration, and at the same time, you will be helping us provide even higher quality information.

To find the errata page for this book, go to `www.wrox.com` and locate the title using the Search box or one of the title lists. Then, on the book details page, click the Book Errata link. On this page, you can view all errata that has been submitted for this book and posted by Wrox editors. A complete book list, including links to each book's errata, is also available at `www.wrox.com/misc-pages/ booklist.shtml`.

If you don't spot "your" error on the Book Errata page, go to `www.wrox.com/ contact/techsupport.shtml` and complete the form there to send us the error you have found. We'll check the information and, if appropriate, post a message to the book's errata page and fix the problem in subsequent editions of the book.

> *Because many books have similar titles, you may find it easiest to search by ISBN; this book's ISBN is 978-0-470-95278-8.*

P2P.WROX.COM

For author and peer discussion, join the P2P forums at `p2p.wrox.com`. The forums are a web-based system for you to post messages relating to Wrox books and related technologies, and to interact with other readers and technology users. The forums offer a subscription feature to e-mail you topics of interest of your choosing when new posts are made to the forums. Wrox authors, editors, other industry experts, and your fellow readers are present on these forums.

At `http://p2p.wrox.com`, you will find a number of different forums that will help you, not only as you read this book, but also as you develop your own applications. To join the forums, just follow these steps:

1. Go to `p2p.wrox.com` and click the Register link.

2. Read the terms of use and click Agree.

3. Complete the required information to join, as well as any optional information you wish to provide, and click Submit.

4. You will receive an e-mail with information describing how to verify your account and complete the joining process.

> *You can read messages in the forums without joining P2P, but in order to post your own messages, you must join.*

Once you join, you can post new messages and respond to messages other users post. You can read messages at any time on the Web. If you would like to have new messages from a particular forum e-mailed to you, click the Subscribe to this Forum icon by the forum name in the forum listing.

For more information about how to use the Wrox P2P, be sure to read the P2P FAQs for answers to questions about how the forum software works, as well as many common questions specific to P2P and Wrox books. To read the FAQs, click the FAQ link on any P2P page.

1

A Brief History of Time in the App Store

WHAT'S IN THIS CHAPTER?

➤ Understanding the evolution that has led to the current App Store market

➤ Learning how four simple touch controls have led to a large leap forward for usability

➤ Finding out what's needed for an app in today's modern App Store

On July 11, 2008, Apple's App Store launched with roughly 550 apps for the iPhone — in total. Today, the App Store has roughly 500,000 apps, and is seen by savvy developers and entrepreneurs as a potentially very lucrative market that has no intention of slowing down.

Assuming that you can make your app stand out from the other apps in your niche (or even create a new one), and take advantage of the latest trends as they're really just taking shape (such as the social media wave that is discussed in Chapter 10), you have a good shot at launching a product that earns enough revenue to make it worth developing.

Because the exact intent and goal of this book is to help you develop an app that finds its audience in a competitive market, it makes sense to kick things off with an introduction to how the App Store became what it is today. Thus, this chapter enables you to see the trends that shape today's App Store market.

TIME IN A TABLE

Table 1-1 provides you with a concise view of the evolution of the App Store over the past few years.

TABLE 1-1: Evolution of the App Store

YEAR	MONTH	EVENTS
2008	July	Over just the first three days, the number of available apps shot up more than 40 percent to 800. The number of downloads in this time was 10 million. In an early interview with the *NY Times* on launch day, Steve Jobs was quoted as stating that 90 percent of apps would cost less than $9.99 (www.nytimes.com/2008/07/10/technology/personaltech/10apps.html). Little could he guess just how right he would be.
		Early metrics by Medialets (www.medialets.com) indicated that the average price for an app dropped from $4.65 that initial Friday to $4.25 by Sunday, nearly 10 percent. Paid apps also saw a similar decrease. So, it wasn't just an influx of free apps that caused the swing, but classic undercutting was taking place in a competitive market. It was a trend that continues to this day.
		Another interesting finding from the same report showed another developing trend. Free apps were garnering 25 percent more reviews than paid apps. Not only that, reviews tended to be more positive, by a quarter of a star. That's nothing to sneeze at in a 5-star rating system (especially considering that Apple rounds the ratings to the nearest half percent).
	August	According to Jobs in an August 2008 interview in *The Wall Street Journal*, within one month, the number of downloads reached 60 million, the top 10 developers earned an amazing $9 million, and the total app receipts were $21 million (http://online.wsj.com/article/SB121842341491928977.html).
		The speed at which the early App Store was growing, its software being adopted, how well it was being received by users, and the iOS being developed for, were phenomenal. That said, it wasn't without its launch problems.
		Soon after launch, *Macworld* interviewed early developers who had a few quibbles with the system. In particular, they claimed there was not a finite reasoning method for approving apps, and that their ability to adjust quickly to market fluctuations was diminished because of Apple's monthly (and not real-time) sales reports.

YEAR	MONTH	EVENTS
	September	Despite any negative feedback, there was no slowing down. In this month, Apple reached 100,000 downloads with more than 3,000 apps available for download. In addition, Apple maintained Jobs' launch price point of 90 percent of the apps costing less than the $10 barrier.
	October	During the late part of October, the number of downloads (200,000) and the number of apps available (7,500) nearly doubled from the September totals.
2009	April	In early 2009, the App Store reached the half million download barrier and had more than 15,000 apps. On April 23, 2009, the 1 billionth download took place, while at the time 35,000 apps were available in 19 categories. According to `Fiercedeveloper.com`, a researcher broke down early iPhone download use and found that nearly two-thirds of all iPhone users downloaded at least 16 to 20 apps. That's a huge adoption rate.
	July	On the one-year anniversary of the App Store, 1.5 billion downloads had been recorded from both iPhone and iPod Touch (iPad came out in April, 2010), with more than 65,000 apps, and more than 100,000 developers signed up for Apple's developer program.
	September	Apple reaches the 2 billion download mark with more than 85,000 apps available.
	November	Along with more than 100,000 apps now available in the App Store, Pinch Media (who created software for app developers that, at the time, extrapolated from more than 10 percent of all downloads) released some interesting findings. The ratio of paid to free apps was 9,300 to 71,000. Further, it found that the average app in the top 10 percent received roughly 75,000 downloads, while the average app in the next 10 percent only got a little over 9,000, and from there the next 10 percent averaged just below 4,000. Pinch Media stated that more than 50 percent of all paid apps were downloaded less than 1,000 times. This equates to a very top-heavy market with "successful" apps being in the minority.

continues

TABLE 1-1 *(continued)*

YEAR	MONTH	EVENTS
	December	By the end of 2009, according to Neilson's "App Playbook," the adoption rate had doubled from April totals, at roughly 37 apps downloaded per user.
2010	January	Available apps reach 120,000, and downloads reach a new milestone at 3 billion.
	March	For the first time, the Books category takes the lead over Games, and there are more than 150,000 apps available in the App Store. (The Games category has since retaken the lead, and currently maintains an only marginally higher percentage of active apps.)
	April	This is a big month for Apple. Not only does the App Store reach 4.5 billion downloads with more than 200,000 apps available, the iPad (Apple's first tablet) launches with more than 5,000 apps available. The iPad goes on to sell more than 1 million units with more than 12 million app downloads in its first month. Further, a similar pattern of top categories for the iPhone ensues, with Games, Entertainment, then Books being the iPad's top three categories.
	September	The total of available apps reaches 250,000, and the total number of downloads hits 6.5 billion. This month, Apple also finally released documentation on some of its submission policies. The "App Store Review Guidelines" for iOS apps was a list of all Apple's conditions for submitting an app, among them the now-infamous "fart" reference: *"We have over 250,000 apps in the App Store. We don't need any more Fart apps. If your app doesn't do something useful or provide some form of lasting entertainment, it may not be accepted."*
	October	The number of downloaded apps reaches 7 billion, and the number of available apps reaches 300,000.
	November	Apple's Hall of Fame appears, highlighting 50 apps Apple claims are the "best of the best."
2011	January	More than 350,000 apps are available, and more than 10 billion apps have been downloaded.
	June and Onward	In June, Apple claimed there were more than 425,000 apps available for download, with more than 14 billion downloads. By September, the count will be roughly 500,000 apps and counting.

> *Chapters 3 and 4 take a look at the current non-linear trends, in addition to even more statistics.*

To appreciate this phenomenal growth, it may be helpful to take a visual look at the general trend of apps downloaded versus apps available in the current App Store. Figure 1-1 shows data points taken from Wikipedia spread roughly over a three-year period. It is interesting to note that the trend of downloads versus available apps is roughly similar, which means that, overall, the market isn't getting too oversaturated with apps. Otherwise, the amount of downloads would not be keeping pace. It may also be that Apple's approval controls are working.

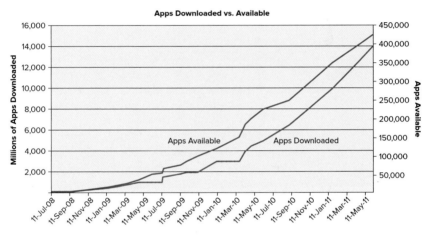

FIGURE 1-1: The trend from the first three years of apps downloaded versus apps available shows that apps and demand are keeping pace

Now let's look at the evolution of the modern App Store from a more user-centric perspective.

THE EARLY APP STORE

When the App Store first launched in mid-2008, it was like the first primordial soup from which certain life forms are thought to originate. It was a volatile place with app prices in extreme flux, and huge numbers of early adopters.

Developers had already released more than 600 apps that took advantage of the iPhone device in exciting new ways, providing both monetary incentive and creative ideas to new developers. Figure 1-2 shows what the iTunes App Store looked like on launch.

FIGURE 1-2: Looking at the App Store on launch in July, 2008, note the abundance of white space, lack of the "App of the Week," and the absence of a Books category

Novel Uses of the Touch Screen

The iPod Touch and iPhone's touch screen was a giant step in the evolution of interface control for several reasons. Sure, the Nintendo Wii started the trend when it announced its novel "Wii-mote" motion controller in 2005 that provided yet unseen interactivity for home consoles. But for mobile devices, tablets, and indeed future touch devices yet to come, credit for navigation protocol will typically go to Apple's first touch devices.

When you begin to create your app, the more naturally the app is integrated with the device it's hosted on, the better feedback and reviews you'll get from your customers. To that end, and as a primer for what's possible using these touch screens, Table 1-2 shows the four main ways the features seen in the original iPod Touch and iPhone are part of today's user expectations in a touch device.

TABLE 1-2: iPod Touch and iPhone Touch Screen Features

FEATURE	METHOD	PRACTICAL USES
The Pinch	Drag two fingers together to zoom in, and spread fingers out to zoom out.	Image manipulation. Game world zoom (two-dimensional or three-dimensional). Web navigation (zoom to fit needs). Documents (zoom to fit needs).

FEATURE	METHOD	PRACTICAL USES
The Swipe (or Flick)	Swipe (or flick) a single finger in any direction, then let go. It can be very similar to, and used in conjunction with, the "drag."	Navigate "pages" of information, such as the home app layout on any current iPod/iPhone/iPad. Usually requires some indication of where you are, and how many total pages there are. Many games and apps have adopted the home screen swipe approach in everything from help screens to flipping through screenshots or charts. Games especially use the swipe or flick as the most basic of controls, or for interactivity purposes. A variation of the swipe for some games is when you hold down a single finger to first "drag" an object, which then may be launched or let go. There are virtually unlimited uses for the swipe. Smooth scrolling through long web pages using the built-in browser, documents, or lists of items within apps.
The Drag	Hold a single finger down and drag to manipulate an area or object on screen to get a desired effect, then let go when finished.	Moving objects (interface or otherwise) from one place to another place in apps or games. The iPod/iPhone/iPad can also separate the screen into multiple hotspot areas (for example, vertically down the center), so that your left and right thumbs (or fingers, as the case may be) can drag in either area to accomplish different tasks. This is often seen when there are two joysticks for certain games, one on the left and one on the right. For example, in a three-dimensional (3D) first-person shooter game, the left stick could be used for moving your character on the horizontal plane, and the right stick used for aiming the camera (your view) all around.

continues

TABLE 1-2 *(continued)*

FEATURE	METHOD	PRACTICAL USES
The Tap	Swipe (or flick) a single finger left or right, or in any direction.	This is the most simple and globally used of the touch controls, and can be used for almost anything the imagination is capable of coming up with. But it is almost always used for buttons, to activate/interact with/select/toggle "interactable" objects/areas on screen, and placing objects.

Each of the four touch-screen control mechanisms shown in Table 1-2 has helped with innovating user experience design, and has had a huge influence on the way people interact with apps and games. This, combined with the phenomenal user adoption rate of the iPhone and touch screens in general, has virtually locked these in as being standards in interface design for many years to come.

Not mentioned in Table 1-2 is the Double Tap, where you simply double-tap the screen to perform an action. While this is often used to "reset" photos or viewpoints from a zoomed level, it is less intuitive than the other more natural touch innovations because of it being somewhat arbitrary. It is, therefore, used only as a last resort, or in special circumstances in games/apps.

A few other innovations for the iPhone such as the accelerometer (tilt mechanism) and newer gyroscope were also not described in Table 1-2. These have less to do with a touch screen than additional control options. When combined with a touch screen, however, even more exciting options for interface design become available.

In store for the future of touch devices are all sorts of multi-finger gestures. Apple is already at work patenting as many as it can. There may be a few multi-finger gestures that are naturally intuitive and, thus, destined to become instant classics (for example, putting at least three fingers down and rotating to rotate an image or object, or perhaps a multi-finger swipe down or zigzag to erase or close). Perhaps even further in the future on new generations of iPhones you might see 3D motion recognition using a built-in camera (similar to the Kinect by Microsoft), where touching a two-dimensional (2D) surface is no longer a feature, but rather a limitation. However, that's getting a little ahead of the game.

With unlimited invention possible in these four mainstays of touch screen controls, it can be easy to overcomplicate apps in the drive to keep them fresh and new. Let's take a look at why innovation goes hand in hand with simplification.

Simplicity Succeeds While Complexity Fails

Apple was built on simplicity and intuitive user experience (as you will see in Chapter 9), and so it's not surprising that signature apps built into the devices help paved the way for others in terms of what to expect and what can be done. In essence, Apple's push toward simplicity, combined with the quick adoption of the device from people who've come to expect a certain usability with the brand, has helped to push this mentality to the forefront of app development.

With the fierce competition of the App Store, not only must your app be innovative to a certain extent to be acknowledged, but if it isn't also intuitive and easy to learn, then (except in rare cases where the niche is still unsaturated) it simply won't have the longevity to succeed or outlast the competition.

There's another reason why simplicity is key for this device. Simplicity caters to the casual user, and that's typically where the big money is, but it comes with a disclaimer. No matter which audience you're going for, even highly niche or technical, keeping it as simple as possible will always broaden the range of people that can adopt it.

THE MODERN APP STORE

As you'll see in Chapters 3 and 4, today's App Store is all about capitalizing on certain trends (social comes to mind), finding new niches, and providing users with an experience that seems fresh and new.

With any new market, it takes time for it to take shape, and it's now been around long enough that the trends are clear. Saturation has been reached in most of the categories (not over-saturation, mind you, just enough that proportionately few new ideas are coming through when compared to small evolutions of current ones), and there exist trends, formulas, and models for success for almost any new app.

One such trend many developers are finding themselves following — sometimes because the market has pushed them there — is that of trying to keep pace with competitors who are offering everything you are, and trying to do it better. Figure 1-3 shows the current App Store interface in iTunes (which will undoubtedly evolve further).

FIGURE 1-3: Looking at the modern App Store interface, note the better use of space, a drop-down category bar, and better featured apps at the top, where it is highly desirable to earn a spot

The Slow March Toward Complex Apps

A complex app doesn't have to mean that it's difficult to learn. It can mean full-featured or even an app with a lot of content (such as a game that rivals current home console offerings in terms of length and content). In this sense, it can mean just that it may be more difficult to develop than something more focused in its feature set, or simple.

Most apps in new niches do start out more simplistic and focused, but that's not how it ends for saturated niches. For the sake of argument, let's assume that's true. If so, how and why does the evolution from simple to complex take place?

The answer is that as competition continues to heat up for the App Store, many apps are finding it difficult to succeed while being great at one thing, and instead must compete against apps that are great at many. This type of competition typically leads to battles of who can provide the most value for the least cost, at least in established niches. After all, from a consumer standpoint, why go through the hard work of finding three different social apps, each an expert at one thing, when you can find one that does them all mostly effectively? Then, later, it gets even easier for the consumer when he or she can find a competitor that does all the great new features plus a few more, all slightly better. And so the trend continues.

But as technology improves and oversaturation in a particular niche takes place, or is dominated by a few tough-to-outmaneuver competitors, the seeking out of new niches ensues. Then, on success, the cycle of the slow march toward complex apps continues forward in this new niche.

Feature-rich apps that have Facebook Connect or other social integration and viral mechanisms in place are now the norm for almost any app that aims to succeed (see Chapter 10 for more on this). And other third-party applications such as "OpenFeint" and the "Plus+" (pronounced "plus plus") network have become the norm. In September 2010, Apple's Game Center (which is better integrated into Apple's API) was launched. Similar to "OpenFeint" and "Plus+," it is also a free app where people can invite friends, see new games, compare scores, and much more.

With the rise to complexity, it becomes a necessity, in this case, to "keep up with the Joneses" just to compete. That's not to say it's *tough* to compete — far from it — but a new developer should keep in mind that there are certain standard features (described in this book) that current users have come to expect, and new ones that will appear in the future.

As a final overview of today's App Store, let's take a look at how niches in the App Store have evolved over time to become what they are today.

How Niches Have Changed from the Early App Store

With the incorporation of frequent upgrades of hardware starting with second-generation iPhones, iPod Touches, and iPads (which continue to this day), new apps are naturally going to be taking advantage, forcing existing niches to evolve, and creating new ones. Yet, it's not only new hardware that forces this evolution, but also App Store policies.

In June 2009, with the release of iOS 3.0, the App Store first allowed in-app purchases with paid apps. By mid-October 2009, the App Store's policy against free apps having the same capability was lifted, and a new business model instantly sprung up. Offering the best of both worlds to developers — that free apps were downloaded more often, and that in-app purchases could provide a constant source of revenue, even with existing users — many free apps were ready to launch with this new feature almost immediately.

Since then (as you'll especially see in Chapter 4), in-app purchases are now a large part of the most successful business models of a great percentage of top-grossing apps — often found at the very top of specific categories. A few niches, of course, are relatively untouched by the policy change, but the trend is unavoidable.

In addition to this, other innovations have sprung up and been quickly adopted. On the gaming front, friend tracking and competitive plug-ins like Game Center quickly became popular. From a developer standpoint, you can take advantage of interactive ads that don't take you out of the app, but provide sources of revenue for free apps (see Chapter 7). In-app marketing techniques such as strategic placement of in-app purchase links or cross-selling your own apps have become a bit of a science (see Chapter 8).

With all these tools, Apple's main categories have generally stayed mostly the same, but niches within them have taken advantage of technology, new policy, innovation, and have evolved into being more complex and socially engaging.

As a final piece of motivation to end this chapter, keep in mind this nugget that comes directly from Apple's "App Store Review Guidelines" for iOS apps: *"If your user interface is complex or less than very good, it may be rejected."* In other words, in the sea of complexity that is the App Store, make yourself a sleek, evolved, and big fish (since they eat all the little ones).

SUMMARY

In this chapter, you learned (or maybe reinforced your existing knowledge) about the amazing growth of the App Store, as well as some of the key innovations and evolutions it has seen over the course of a few years. Undoubtedly, it will continue to change and flourish into the future, in ways unexpected. Though educated guesses will make their way into later chapters, this book attempts to nullify being pigeonholed into how just to succeed in this market, but aims to focus on those traits of a good App Store business that will give you an edge in any future market as well.

Things to come in forthcoming chapters such as competitive analysis, finding a niche, knowing customer tendencies, and how to develop apps with niche and customer expectations according to your business model will help in future-proofing your app business.

In Chapter 2, you learn what it actually costs to develop an app in the current market, along with how best to start planning work for your team.

2

Setting Your Goals, Costs, and Expectations

WHAT'S IN THIS CHAPTER?

➤ Understanding how to overcome the desire to create versus complete

➤ Discovering how to benefit by taking on tasks "in house"

➤ Understanding the role of outsourcing

➤ Understanding outsourcing deliverables

➤ Figuring out how to hire the right talent

➤ Discovering what it really costs to develop an app

➤ Understanding both your fundamental and optional costs

➤ Learning how to keep expectations in check

You should now have a good overview of what the App Store is all about, so it's time to start getting into the planning of your new app. You may well have a great idea already (or two, or a hundred...), but how much do you think it will cost to bring that idea to fruition? Is it a complex app relative to others in its niche? Does it utilize your programmer's art, or will you have to outsource? Questions such as this will be answered in this chapter, and provide the best launching point for taking action on your new ideas.

Speaking of ideas, before you begin, you should be aware of a common pitfall for individual or small team app development that's known as *Hero Inventor Syndrome*. You won't find it in the latest DSM (the manual for psychological disorders), but experience has shown that this prevalent pitfall can significantly increase the time it takes to bring an app to market.

CONFRONTING THE "HERO INVENTOR" SYNDROME

Before the team at Villain launched their first game, "Archetype," they got a lot of smaller projects off the ground, each with grand dreams of breaking the Top 100. The design framework was worked out, schedules were made, milestones created, and the first of the contractors were contacted, all in an effort to follow the latest trends — or at least some killer ideas.

In a common work week, the team would be gung-ho for one project, only to have an idea pop into one of their heads by the weekend that they wanted/needed to pursue — always ASAP — and, thus, the next week would see the previous week's work postponed. Needless to say, planning new projects in this way broke older schedules that hadn't even been given the chance to be assigned yet.

Inevitably, the question would occur at some point in the week, "You know that game/app named blah-bleh-bloop? Well, what if we took x, did y to it, then blended in z…" and dollar signs appeared yet again in the eyes of the team. The gist is that planning an app is easier said than done. Schedules, ideas, and even grand designs do not an app make.

Everyone wants to have that one design or idea that he or she turns into the next "Angry Birds," but we can't pursue them all. That's the pitfall — the need to constantly create and ideate, but never actually take action.

Benefitting by Doing It Yourself

When you finally decide to take the plunge, it is advisable to start by making a list of what assets you have in terms of production capability, and where you're lacking. How much you can do "in-house" or all in one place largely determines the overall cost, notwithstanding external marketing pushes near the end of development.

For example, say you have an artist friend who is willing to help out with assets for a cut of profits (also known as *revenue share* or "rev" share), or you've been referred to a somewhat fresh programming team that want to prove themselves and will charge less if you go with them. Essentially, to lower costs, you decide to manage production from your end instead of paying a full-featured development studio to carry it all.

As a matter of fact, many of these teams do little more than provide a method to outsource to their own workhorse teams, with internal project managers to coordinate it all.

> *With "Archetype," the Villain team went with both in-house help and outsourcing to a more full-featured team. Because the team decided on a tight production schedule that required a competent programming team to pull off advanced three-dimensional (3D) and multiplayer support, the team outsourced to a relatively new team in the San Francisco Bay Area that took over all project management of the code and art for a reduced rate. What the team at Villain did was essentially merge two key producers/designers into the flow of the development team, especially regarding level and combat design, then quality assurance (QA), and eventually the implementation of localization (which is how to get it into other languages). It was a competent, but small, core team overall, with not a lot of experience yet on iPhone app design, which helped keep costs down on a more ambitious title.*

Outsourcing

With easier collaboration methods such as Skype and other communication/ project management tools, as well as faster asset/code turnaround than used to be possible with things like Software Development Kits (SDKs), outsourcing has fast become a viable and efficient manner to cut app and game development costs.

This section examines the ways an app developer can outsource (Figure 2-1 shows one of the most popular outsourcing tool in the U.S.), and provides some tips for finding help.

FIGURE 2-1: The easiest way to find outsourcing in the U.S

Few developers are capable of doing everything in-house — project management, production, design/level design, programming, art, audio, QA, and so on. Therefore, an important early consideration to be made is what you can achieve in-house, and what you'll need to farm out, or *outsource*.

One half-truism that comes with a caveat is the belief that you can dramatically cut app development time with more people working on it. Though, to an extent, this is true from a production standpoint, more people involved also means significantly more complexity with project management, budgeting, and bringing the different parts of the app together.

With asset development such as art, audio, and animation, these things are typically easier to generate in parallel than things like code features or new systems for your app. For programming, it's best to stick to one small team or programmer so that you're not dealing with the complications from merging and coordinating code implementation from multiple sources.

Outsourcing Assets

Typically (at least in game development), it is fairly common to outsource two types of assets — much (or all) of the art and also audio — because games are fairly heavy in each. Fortunately, if you're lucky enough to be dealing with a utility or non-game app, the required quantity of both of these diminishes greatly (relatively speaking), as does the cost.

So, what exactly is an asset that can be outsourced? *Assets* are each individual file for every piece of art, animation, and audio (be it music or sound effect, sometimes called *sfx*) in your app or game. For example, if you were doing a role-playing game, you might have several static screens (to keep costs down) for the story intro, then all the player character art, non-player characters, objects and items (which could be hundreds or thousands), background scenery, special effects, icons, maps, main and sub interfaces, sounds, animations, and thematic music.

As a general rule of thumb, the more of a "game" your app is, the greater amount of art and audio you'll need, with art usually being the much, much bigger expenditure.

Let's look briefly at each of these types of assets.

Outsourcing Art

With art, you'll first want a general scope of what you need from the designer so that you can get a proper quote. If it's a 3D game, you'll need 3D assets, so you'll need artists who can deal with exporting from programs such as Maya and 3D Studio Max. These artists are usually proficient in modeling, characters, and texture work. Figure 2-2 shows a textured 3D model from the Rocket Launcher in "Archetype," which was eventually exported into polygons for use in the game.

FIGURE 2-2: 3D model of a weapon from "Archetype"

For two-dimensional (2D) user interface (UI) work such as what is shown in Figure 2-3, another type of artist is needed — artists who are good at drawing and positioning layouts. These artists will usually work in tandem with the designer (more typically near the beginning of development) to streamline menu progression, functionality, and layout, sometimes according to the designer's initial spec.

FIGURE 2-3: Example UI from the game "Archetype"

In some instances (for example, if your app is a simple business or utility app that relies on much of the core iPhone standard UI art), the iOS programmer has access to the full set of standard graphical user interface (GUI) elements straight from Apple for use in any app. This could be a way to cut costs, but obviously there wouldn't be much except for functionality to set your app apart from the rest. So, it better be good if this is the direction you're planning on.

Another option some developers have taken (mainly to opt out of art outsourcing) is to put an artist hat on a team member who normally wouldn't be an artist (such as the programmer). This often occurs for a team that can't afford an artist, and settles for creating more "crude" hand-drawn art. Although this was (and sometimes is) highly popular in certain cases (for example, "Doodle Jump"), and it can certainly cut costs, ensure that you have a solid reason for going with this.

The hand-drawn style has somewhat worn thin after all with the resurgence of independent (indie) game development (that is, those without a big budget doing as much as they can). Don't be dissuaded from using that style if your budget or vision merits. But if your budget allows, you'll likely make a bigger impression by hiring a real artist, even for a unique "crude" hand-drawn style.

Finally, for conceptual work, typically at the beginning of development and prior to asset generation, an artist will be needed who specializes in the look/feel of the world, the backgrounds, characters, and sometimes weapons, which the 3D artist would render after being approved.

Sometimes any type of artist can function as a concept artist, but there are specialists out there who do excel in the field. These artists are usually more proficient in traditional drawing and painting methods than the others, as opposed to working mostly in the digital medium.

Figure 2-4 shows the first concept character art from a casual matching game, "Matchlings," which is full of unique characters. Initially, the Villain development team had a vampire, and it was working okay, but all of the characters were male-oriented, so the team felt the need to change a few to females to better appeal to a general audience.

FIGURE 2-4: Concept art for "Matchlings," an early game by Villain and its second to be released

CONCEPTING FOR A 3D FPS

For "Archetype," production outsourced to both a team of 3D artists for modeling the various weapons and textures, and 2D artists for things like GUI work and other 2D elements (such as the all-important logo). Production also outsourced to an outfit that could do conceptual work in the beginning for things like the look/feel of the world, and the look of the characters and weapons.

continues

continued

The game's intro was one of the later items produced, and, in fact, a significant portion of game art for in-game elements was complete before an intro was ever commissioned. When the team got to the computer generated imagery (CGI — basically pre-rendered advanced 3D graphics with great lighting and animation) intro, they had another go-round with concept stuff from that studio before they started production.

Outsourcing Audio

Audio assets come down to what UI elements you desire (typically standard button presses, swipe and gesture sounds, scrolling, and so on) with any other unique interactive elements. Typically, for good gameplay and general interface design, any action the user can do will require feedback in the form of something visual (a highlight or other indicator) and a sound effect file (sfx). This is especially true for current touch devices, because, since they lack tactile response, feedback can only be delivered via graphic or sound, as opposed to the click of a button or vibration of a controller.

Then there's music. Should you have an intro theme that loops? Should you have several tracks for different levels? How long should they be, and should they repeat? All this requires is a general indication of scope (again, typically from a designer) before setting out to get quotes. These days, it's usually enough to hire an audio engineer, and he or she will have several different libraries from which to pull and export the sounds in the format that you need — for a cost, of course.

Finally, there's voiceover (VO) work. If you have a game with VO, you're possibly talking anything from simply recording a team member's best John Wayne impersonation to paying Screen Actors Guild (SAG) fees for premium talent. Well, recording from a team member not only ups morale and is usually highly funny (at least to the team) until it gets amazingly annoying, but it is also a good way to get in placeholder assets until the real talent can be had — which sometimes is never. This method happens to be popular, for obvious reasons, within indie game development.

> *The music and sound in "Archetype" was done by a company Villain first used for a smaller project. The development team ended up liking that company's work, and so tasked it with the main theme for the game (which ended up an appropriately thematic, epic, impending doom-like march). Along with music, Villain had several sounds for weapon fire, pickups, other interactivity, and UI notifications. For when the player was awarded medals, VO was considered, but didn't make the cut because of time schedules and because, though cool, Villain simply didn't think of it as a high enough priority.*

Outsourcing Your Programming

Let's face it. Most small developers with a big idea will be in the need of a programmer or three, depending on scope, who aren't on the payroll. You should be warned, however, that this is where your budget gets a big bite taken from it. Fortunately, with iPhone development really taking off in the past few years, you should have little trouble finding a team willing to take on your app and, for whatever their reasons (which are important), work with you on cutting a deal.

To be able to find the right help, you must have a basic understanding of the scope and features of your app. For example, here are a few features worth considering for a short *feature/concept document*:

➤ Does it need 3D graphics?

➤ Does it need to connect to Facebook, Twitter, and so on?

➤ What kind of social features/sharing will it have/require?

➤ Does it use advanced motion controls like the iPhone gyroscope, or the accelerometer/tilting?

➤ Does it need to manipulate or access your music collection? (For an example, check out "Planetary," a neat iPad music app that does this in a very interesting way!)

➤ Does it have multiplayer capabilities?

➤ Does it need its own physics engine? (For an example, see "Angry Birds.")

➤ Will it need to access the Internet from within the app?

➤ Does it have high-score lists?

➤ Does it access your mail?

➤ Do you need to be able to draw?

➤ How about chat?

In this document, you should lay out a bulleted list of features you require from the following:

➤ The iPhone/iPad core functionality (such as possible controls and existing device programs you'll need access to)

➤ All the functionality you need it to be able to do from within the app

With your feature/concept document in hand, you'll be able to quickly gather quotes from competing sources and make a judgment call as to who to go with.

Outsourcing Design

Not everyone can program, but it's true that everyone is indeed a designer. It will be very tempting to try to cut costs here by throwing together a "specification" document and hope that the programmers can make enough inferences from vague descriptions to properly execute the vision. But it is strongly recommended that you hire an expert, because your killer app's core functionality and user experience depends on the design.

Ideally, you'll want to use someone who can come up with functional (and intelligent, but creative) designs, communicate effectively with clear documentation using flowcharts and the like, and be able to creatively (and quickly) iterate on team feedback. A good designer can handle the math for you, making it easier on the programmers, in addition to the design of most of the entire user experience (including controls, interface, flow, social features, and other elements that go into an app).

It's likely that you already have a million-dollar idea or more that you're kicking around, and have already jotted down some (or a lot of) info, maybe even specifics about certain features of your app. This is a time when you'd hire a designer to flesh out the experience according to the vision, while ensuring that you don't have any user experience hang-ups along the way. The outcome should be a package of the design in a nice document, ready for programming.

At other times, you might only have the idea, and simply need it fleshed out. If you don't already have a designer in house, a good choice you might consider hiring would be freelance game designers.

Avoiding the Pitfalls of Going It Alone

There is one clear way to avoid many of the pitfalls you might otherwise encounter during your journey, and it can easily be summed up with these words: *Find the right talent*. It cannot be overstated that you'll need to get good at evaluating outsourced talent based on cost, portfolio, communication, and location.

Let's briefly fast-forward and assume that you've acquired the services of reasonably capable people who, under most conditions, would do an average to great job. To deliver an exceptional app, you will *also* need these things:

➤ A capable project manager/leader/decision maker (which can be included in the list of acquired capable people)

➤ Efficient communication tools

➤ An online project-management collaboration framework (usually shared by outsourcers)

➤ A reasonable development schedule/plan

As far as a project manager, it is highly recommended that you take on this duty yourself, or already have one or two people in mind for various main tasks. This is because this position isn't usually outsourced, unless you're paying for a full-featured development team.

For communication tools, Villain hadn't yet jumped on the Skype bandwagon as a whole, but instead used Gmail (an online collaboration tool), and Gmail's built-in chat when appropriate. Nowadays, you should have a free Skype account (www.skype.com) or other similarly featured chat/messaging client. Being able to share your screen and send files, as well as instant chat and video calls, make Skype indispensable as a communication device.

For the team at Villain, because the company was paying for a team that could handle most of the art, QA, and all of the programming within the company, Villain had its own project leader who was in constant touch with the development team to work out scheduling and deliveries. In turn, the Villain team managed everything that wasn't covered by the outsourced team, including localization, some QA (everyone was involved in this), combat and level design, audio, CGI animation, other outsourced scheduling, and marketing. In the end, it was largely a collaborative effort with the outsourced team and CEO, and Villain's own team.

Appendix B provides more information on useful tools.

Other highly recommended team collaboration and communication tools are available that take the place of dedicated project-management-only programs like Microsoft Project and are used by an entire team. Online full-featured project management tools such as BaseCamp (www.BasecampHQ.com) can handle everything from multiple projects, file sharing and repositories, milestone creation and tracking, message posts and replies, e-mail alerts, task tracking, to-do lists, and much more — all in one place. They're typically super simple to use, and will help keep everyone on the same page. Most of these are not free, but relatively inexpensive, and come with monthly pricing plans.

Finally, from the project manager, you'll need a reasonable plan that reflects the scope of the app, as well as outsourcing intangibles, and merges them into a typical development timeline.

Chapter 5 provides more information on plotting the stages of development.

As shown in Figure 2-5, in the end, there's going to be an optimal solution for each outsourced component in terms of how cheap or expensive, how good the outsourcing resources are, and how fast they can work. Assuming the general principle that the cheapest is usually less experienced and not the fastest, and the most expensive is usually at least effectively experienced, the optimal solution for your project is likely somewhere in the center, near the peak of the bell curve. For example, as you elect to go with higher-priced talent along the curve, you will eventually reach a point where expenses outweigh the benefits. Conversely, if you go too low along the curve, chances become higher that the talent will not be able to complete the task on time, or as intended.

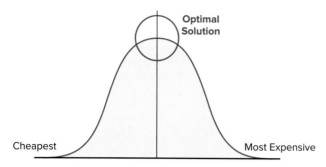

FIGURE 2-5: Optimal cost solution for hiring outsourced talent

TOP THREE TIPS FOR FINDING THE RIGHT OUTSOURCED TALENT

Following are a few tips for ensuring that you avoid the major pitfall of not having the right talent:

> **Always ask to see a portfolio** — Whether you are working with artists, programmers, audio engineers, or designers, you'll want to first tell them what your app is about in a nutshell, and then see their closest and best representative work to your future design. For programmers, stay away from those who have no or relatively little experience programming iPhone apps. It may cost less per hour, but will be more costly in the long run, both in terms of money and time. For programming teams, play the games or apps they've contributed to, while specifically asking which parts they worked on to see if it is up to your standards.
>
> In the end, if you're still on the fence, it's always a good idea to ask for references and follow up with them. Work-for-hire sites such as Elance (www.Elance.com) or Guru (www.Guru.com) have ratings and feedback you can browse, further filtering the pool to narrow your choices.

> **Gauge their communication effectiveness** — How quickly do they respond? Do they seem like they understand the vision? Are they professional in demeanor? How well can they speak your team's native language? You'll sometimes be able to find exceptional talent with very little speaking ability in your language, but generally, the more complex your app is, or for example, the less visual documentation you have available, raises the need to communicate any ideas or designs with them, and thus the better their grasp of your language should be.

> **Negotiate the rate** — Did you find someone promising, but who is out of your budget? Don't be afraid to ask for a slightly lower rate (because of your tight budget), or, failing that, potentially trade for a share in revenue. Sometimes this can actually save you quite a bit of money, but there's the chance they may not be willing to go this route. Still, it is done. In any case, to get your business it's very likely they can find some way to do the job for somewhat

less than the quote (5 percent to 15 percent isn't unreasonable to request, depending on the job), and they often bid with this in mind. Just be sure to have a number in mind that sounds fair. Asking for a discount isn't always as good as just asking, "Can you do it for X amount?" Then, if they decline, you would still have some room for a follow-up amount, whereas a simple "no" to the general discount question pretty much closes the negotiation.

At the very least, unless there's exceptionally high demand for their services at the time, you'll often come away with a better deal, even if it means negotiating in some type of small sacrifice on your own (such as scheduling, or without optional feature X, Y, or Z).

Whomever you decide to work with, ensure that you have a proper non-disclosure agreement (NDA) in effect. Basic versions can be found on the Internet and tailored to your needs, but, of course, using your own lawyer to prepare one would be the safest.

CONSIDERING YOUR FUNDAMENTAL COSTS

Unless you have iPhone programmers willing to do the work cheaply, and are coming up with a rather simple utility or business app, developing an *exceptional* iPhone app is expensive — probably more so than you might think.

In the early days of the App Store, you didn't see huge companies creating apps for hundreds of thousands of dollars, and releasing the apps with the backing of a big marketing budget. You had independent developers cobbling together apps on their own, and occasionally making huge amounts of money.

The ironic thing is that, while apps have become way more expensive to develop over time, the prices of the apps are still at their initial plateau of $0.99, and occasionally more (albeit sometimes way more for those rare niche apps). There's still the hope for huge profit for any endeavor, and surprise hits will always appear from nowhere to dominate the charts for a time and spawn copies. But you need the right combination of features, usability, and release buzz to drive a success.

So, how much does it cost in 2011 to make an app? According to a Stack Overflow (www.stackoverflow.com) forum answer by Craig Hockenberry (the developer of "Twitteriffic," shown in Figure 2-6, and available at www.twitteriffic.com), this popular social media app would have cost upward of $250,000 to create, had the owners not done the estimated 1,100 hours of programming on their own. This was at their quoted rate of $150 per hour. As it was, design cost them $34,000, using existing code cost $20,000, and other project management and QA expenses were around $16,000. The bulk of the time, however, was spent on the coding, at an estimated 60 hours per week over 9 weeks.

FIGURE 2-6: "Twitteriffic" would have cost roughly $250,000 to develop

Of course, you can sometimes find programming for much less. Villain actually got a good deal on a foreign team's first job for $25 per hour for its initial game prototype ("Matchlings"). It is safe to assume that many teams are available on Elance, Guru, or oDesk (www.odesk.com) who might do something similar.

Not all apps will have such a high budget, and, as mentioned earlier, it really depends on scope, time, and talent. But to do a sophisticated full-featured app for anything less than $50,000 to $100,000 is wishful thinking. If this is out of your budget, you'll either need people willing to profit-share and work for "free," raise money, go with cheaper and potentially less-capable developers, or scale down the necessary programming (in other words, scope) and/or art required, because those are typically your two largest expenditures.

Lest the price still seem too daunting, you should be aware of one last thing before learning about the specifics of each cost area. A "simple" game or app with similar features to something else on the market, but enhanced with your own twist, *can* be made for as little as $4,000 to $10,000 for outsourcing the entire job. However, now that heavy-hitter companies with multiple titles are dominating several App Store categories, it will be more difficult as a rule for an app like that to penetrate the Top 100 or Top 200, which is the sweet spot for revenue generation and maintaining the buzz.

Programming

Unless you have access to or are a great programmer willing to program for little to nothing, chances are you're going to be spending the bulk of your development cost on *programming*. Prices vary based on experience, location, and name recognition, but you can expect anywhere from $25 per hour at the low end (usually overseas) to $250 per hour at the other end.

With most projects, a contract will typically have several development milestones with built-in contingencies should one party or the other fail to fulfill obligations. For most projects, payment is usually made on evaluation of major milestones. Monthly is a common milestone time period, but depending on how fast the schedule is, it can be faster. This is not to say teams won't have various interim builds to evaluate, but major milestones are spaced farther apart.

> *Though it is not possible to quote the exact budget of "Archetype," some general expectations can be shared. For an advanced multiplayer 3D game including using an existing engine (that will need to be licensed), the cost can run in the hundreds of thousands of dollars, most likely in the lower hundreds. This is if you outsource to an external team. For in-house development, it's possible to do it for less, so some thought might be put into whether you should/ could hire contracted permanent employees in this case.*

Factoring in UI/UX for Game/App Design

If you want to help keep the big costs of programming down (and why wouldn't you?), you're likely going to want to hire a good *game/user experience* (UX) designer to put together a functional document — especially for business apps that depend mostly on functionality and can't rely on heavy graphics and visual effects to pick up the slack. Any design talent should be familiar with good UI and current iPhone standards in terms of UX, as well as how to design for capacitive touch options like gesturing.

Not unlike programming, design talent typically charges by scope and detail required. Therefore, for a small one-off document for a simple app, you might be able to hire a capable designer for as little as $1,000 to $2,000. But with experience and a good portfolio, it can end up being much more, even in the tens of thousands of dollars for a dedicated designer on a bigger-budget contract.

For any game that requires time to make levels (such as a role-playing game, or anything in 3D), the cost for level design can be up to $5,000 and onward for the project, again dependent on scope.

So, what should you ask for in a designer? You'll typically want these deliverables:

➤ Initial collaboration on design to get the scope and vision

➤ Optional but good-to-have items (that is, some competitive research on similar apps to ensure that you're not overlooking features or planning on unneeded ones)

➤ Initial rough draft of the design document for approval, minus some specifics pending approval

➤ Final milestone version of the document with all the specifics

➤ Sometimes (such as for a complex app), gameplay/UX follow-up with the team on early build(s) to ensure that the design is functional and the intent is being achieved

Factoring in Art Design

Like the other necessities, what you spend on *art* varies widely with scope and talent. As mentioned earlier in this chapter, you could potentially need up to three different types of artists for various tasks, and anything from next to zero total art required (but always a good App Store icon!) to mountains of it.

Art is usually not optional, and the style you choose can sometimes make or break your game/app. This is why competitive research is handy up front to help define current standards in your niche (if one exists), and to help you differentiate.

Once you have the style you're aiming for, get the quotes. For something like a triple-A 3D app, you could spend upward of $50,000 or more for the total art package (not including CGI animation). This would include 3D modeling and textures for exporting into a 3D game, concept art, as well as UI, 3D particle effects, and other in-game art. At the other end of the spectrum, for something similar to the popular vertical scrolling action game "Doodle Jump" (shown in Figure 2-7), assuming it was professionally done and not for free by the programmer, it might be had for as little as $3,000 to $5,000, depending on scope.

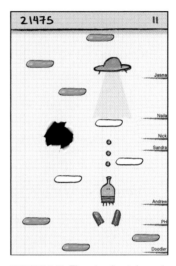

FIGURE 2-7: The simple style and hand-drawn art of "Doodle Jump" keeps art costs lower

CONSIDERING YOUR OPTIONAL COSTS

Programming, design, and art are your three necessary costs. Some might question whether design is completely necessary, preferring the scribbles-on-napkin or fast-iteration approach. Though there is some merit to this when dealing with simple apps, any well-developed, complex interactive app requires a great amount of design planning and forethought, or else you're taking huge risks with scope, budget, and time.

Audio Costs

Audio isn't always needed (for utility or business apps), and, fortunately, when it is, royalty-free libraries of sounds and songs are available on the Internet (search for "royalty free sounds" for a decent list). Reasons against this approach might be that the quality isn't always there, legal restrictions sometimes exist for particular sounds/songs, and it can be difficult/time-consuming to wade through all the muck on your way to finding a gem.

With that being said, some amazing, under-utilized audio engineers and composers are available for hire, and these people will create all your sounds from scratch, or know how to find them quickly and modify them to fit your needs.

Expect (non-VO) audio to range from $500 or so for a simple game with a few core sounds, to $5,000 or more for a full game. When VO work is required, audio costs can skyrocket. Sometimes it can be more than $10,000 for good talent per actor, again depending on what's needed and the type of talent you need.

Special Effects Costs

Special effects are considered to be any pre-rendered CGI you need for introductory movies or other story devices. These are usually anywhere from 20 seconds to a minute or longer (for full non-app games), and can get extremely expensive. Mostly, only games deal with this, and then only if they want a knock-out intro to the experience.

Shop around, because ranges can greatly vary. Special effects companies charge mostly by the time needed, how much concept/approval work is involved, overall quality desired, time required for delivery, and factor in their past portfolio as well. For example, for the exact same specification (60 seconds of CGI total, split in two 30-second movies at various times), you might get back quotes ranging from $20,000 to $200,000 or more from a triple-A studio, depending on from whom you get bids.

Aside from programming or potential marketing costs, CGI can be another top expense, so be sure your game/app needs it. Most apps won't be dealing with this, and, in fact, you can often get a lot of mileage by making use of your in-game engine for cut-scenes.

Shortening your required movie times can, of course, result in much lower bids. But don't be surprised if even a 10-second CGI quotes for more than you would think. On the flip side, sometimes the end result establishes your game/app as uniquely polished, and you shouldn't be dissuaded if this type of polish is what your app needs.

> *In the case of "Archetype," the game had virtually no story (just a sci-fi theme) and only a pretty slick menu system for navigating into and out of the multiplayer gameplay. The development team felt the best way to bring something that made players more attached to the world, in addition to extra polish, was a short CGI intro story.*

You might also be aware that audio (especially VO), in addition to CGI, can eat up a lot of memory (which is precious in apps for speedy initial download times). So, that may be a consideration as well. To save space, these things can be compressed a bit, but the tradeoff is that quality may suffer.

Localization for Foreign Markets

If you're planning on making your app available in other languages (see Chapter 5 for more details), which can often offer more visibility for your app in areas of less competition, the process rests partly with programming (for implementation), and partly with project management/production (for translation). The cost for programming should be included in your contract, and the cost for translation can actually be quite low, but time-intensive. It is worth noting that if your app is text-heavy, rendering your text in an actual font rather than images (for example, including graphic buttons with customized text in a game) can use less art resources and be easier to manage.

You can find many capable translators on Elance for any language, and their rates vary greatly, but are sometimes surprisingly low (such as $0.08 per word). Expect to pay in the range of $300 to $1,000 for a relatively small word count (less than 1,000 words) when translated into a few different languages, and upward of $5,000 to $10,000 or more for a larger game or app with thousands of words.

Don't forget, you'll not only need the game translated, but you'll need your App Store description and all update notes to be translated as well.

Quality Assurance/Testing

Even if your app has the best coders, there are bound to be bugs (errors), and lots of them, especially early on. *QA* (which entails methodically testing your app for bugs and crashes related to user experience, graphics, audio, text, gameplay, and performance) usually can be handled in-house by one or two people dedicated to the task (sometimes the project manager/producer). For general feedback and reporting of severe issues that are encountered, you can also include friends and family who play as much as you can get them to.

Occasionally, you'll want to outsource QA, but (typically) only for complex apps with many different user experiences, modes, or required hours of play. The more complex your app is, the greater the chances for crashes to occur (as shown in Figure 2-8), and those should be considered the bane of every app's road to good ratings.

When you do need dedicated QA (for example, when porting to another device and testing all its features, or during a particularly large batch of new features being implemented), costs are usually not too much of a concern for the overall budget, and can be had for up to a few thousand dollars, depending on scope.

To give a sense of perspective, for a relatively large role-playing game to be released on multiple console platforms in addition to PC, quotes from dedicated full-service companies might surprise you. It can be hundreds of thousands of dollars for full testing during

FIGURE 2-8: Crash errors need to be completely eliminated prior to release

the few months prior to release. But, of course, that kind of testing would rarely be required for most apps.

The exception, however, would be if you're doing a social simulation game such as CapcomMobile's "Smurf's Village," as shown in Figure 2-9. Many hours are spent on complex games such as this.

FIGURE 2-9: Titles like the popular "Smurf's Village" are high-budget, complex games that require significant QA

Public Relations and Marketing

The area of *public relations and marketing* is all about finding the right outlets to promote your app, and then establishing your brand in the eyes of the users as something they'd want to own/buy.

> For "Archetype," because it was a multiplayer game using dedicated servers, the Villain team needed to "stress test" the game to see how much load it could take before crashing, or before performance was inhibited. Because the team was building simultaneous localized versions in 12 languages in preparation for release, it was decided to release a few weeks early in a market with fewer potential users than the U.S. in order to gather player feedback and other data, then quickly address issues prior to the main launch. In this case, Villain went with the Portuguese market, but it could have easily been another. In the end, it helped for a more secure and polished launch with fewer complications.

With today's buzz and hype capable of being spread through social media channels faster than traditional outlets, concentrate your efforts there. Positive website exclusives and reviews are a given, as well as any Facebook and Twitter buzz.

The goal will be to hopefully have earned enough hype when the app is launched to perhaps get Apple's attention (even if not right away), and get Apple to feature it as one of its Apps of the Week.

> *The "Archetype" team went solely with a post-release effort, although things were set up prior to release so that the hype was started and maintained in heavy doses beginning from the first day. Because of the release of the Portuguese version, a few popular iPhone sites like TouchArcade (www.touchⒶrcade.com) caught on to the release early, and published an article or two as a preview to get the ball rolling. But the timing for that worked out in Villain's favor, because the buzz was fortunately generally positive, and helped fuel the hype and mystery for the U.S./global release.*
>
> *What helped in the case of Villain's "Archetype" was having two unique features that hadn't been done yet, and appeared to be anxiously awaited by a segment of the hard-core action community — smooth five-versus-five team-based gameplay on 3G devices for a relatively low price, and a dedicated full-featured "Death Match" progression system that didn't involve micro-transactions, as one of Villain's competitors did. In other words, once you bought the game, you got a lot of value without needing to spend anything more in order to "keep up." These two things, along with the positive buzz of "Archetype" having "come from nowhere" in particular, helped propel early reviews and word of mouth.*

Though traditional game companies can spend millions, your marketing budget can be successful for as little as next to zero to $2,000, if you go the social media route externally, and then use extra money to build social features directly into your game/app (if possible) so that they keep paying dividends.

Advertising Costs

Advertising can mean anything from shooting/editing a movie to become "viral" on YouTube, through social media ad campaigns, to high-cost solutions such as exclusive daily/weekly ads on high-profile websites that are getting millions of views per day.

These days, it's almost a no-brainer *not* to go with print advertising, unless you have a huge excess in your budget. Print is still very expensive, and can't reach out to or convert nearly the amount of people any reasonable social media–driven or targeted web advertising plan can.

It's also a bit of a conundrum whether to spend a lot on one-off advertising (that is, ads that are there, and then gone), versus spending a proportionally equal amount of money adding viral social features directly into your app. If you don't plan to have any social outlets built-in (for example, posting scores on Facebook Walls, or otherwise sharing with friends), then paid advertising becomes more important to drive initial customers your way in hopes of converting them into paying customers.

If you decide to go this route, posting a feature ad on prominent websites for any length of time can cost upward of several thousand dollars for each.

MANAGING YOUR EXPECTATIONS

Thus far in this chapter, you've been introduced to quite a lot of information to digest, such as procuring outsourced talent, determining how much this is actually going to cost, starting to think about your overall plan, and wondering how it's going to all come together.

Just remember, if you have an idea, there's a way to get it done, whether or not it ends up as grand or full-featured as you first envisioned. Cut back if you have to. Refine the design so that the core features stand out. And, if you ensure that it's as polished as it can be, most anything can have a chance.

The purpose of this chapter is to give you a reasonable expectation of the overall scope and cost of doing an app. As mentioned, depending on scope, time, and execution, that can mean anything from $5,000 to hundreds of thousands. Just plan accordingly.

The App Store as a Crowded Zoo

As you'll read in Chapter 3, the App Store is a chaotic, crowded, and exciting place — and growing all the time. Before you start production, it will be vitally important to do your competitive research and ensure that your planned app's core features haven't already been usurped by a competitor — unless you can do them better, and perhaps that's your plan.

By mid-2011, roughly 20 main categories and more than 400,000 active apps appeared in the iPhone App Store, with books, games, and entertainment totaling roughly 40 percent of the entire store (see `www.148Apps.biz`). This all shows that if you're developing in one of these categories, chances are you'll have some competition, even on iPad, as shown in Figure 2-10. Start planning early for how you're going to tackle features your competitors may already be working on, and you'll have the best shot for succeeding in the nearly standing-room-only App Store.

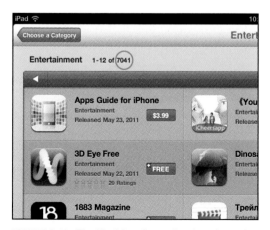

FIGURE 2-10: The iPad App Store showing signs of congestion

Unless you have a solid foundation for a development plan, succeeding in the App Store may end up meaning much less if you're way over budget to begin with.

Planning for Cost Overruns

Apps nearly always cost more than initially planned, and usually take longer than expected. Sometimes it's because of feature creep or polish, but most times it's because of an initial failure to account for all elements that go into development, as well as the hours required to get it done — an easy thing to do. Let's face it, green-lighting a project is also easier when the people with money think it's going to be less work/cost/time than they might imagine, and, therefore, initial estimates tend to fall on the low side. Add to all this the fact that Murphy's Law — if it can go wrong, it will — nearly always shows up at some point during a project, and it's no wonder budgets eventually become bloated.

Scheduling with an Iron Fist

The best way to ensure that your team stays on track is to keep everyone informed about the plan. What this means is that everyone knows in general what the others are working on, when the pieces will be put together, what the next steps are ahead of time (at least a week or two), and how that fits into the overall plan. This helps to prevent lapses in workload, and identifies potential bottlenecks for deliveries.

The development process is like a marathon, an ongoing slog with little rest until Beta, then a final push to the finish, regardless of whether it takes two weeks or a year. As in a marathon, maintaining flexibility for unforeseen events or changing conditions is key.

SUMMARY

This chapter covered a lot of material, from the benefits of staying focused and taking action, to outsourcing needs, through detailed costs and expectations. You should now be prepared for the next two chapters, which include thoroughly getting to know the App Store and your competitors, as well as honing in on expectations of your potential target demographic within the genre/category.

Researching the App Store Market

Reliable App Store metrics can be difficult to find. Apple releases precious few statistics — except the good ones as they relate to App Store growth or market share — and whatever else you can find is spread wide over the Internet. Fortunately, there are a few exceptions, especially when major milestones occur. In this chapter, you learn about gaining today's most up-to-date statistics, including current projections.

EXAMINING THE NUMBERS AND TRENDS

According to a May 2011 online collaboration (www.facebook.com/500kapps) by Chomp (an application search engine, located at www.chomp.com), 148Apps (a website at www.148apps.com that spotlights iOS applications), and Chillingo (an independent game publisher and division of Electronic Arts located at www.chillingo.com), the following was noted:

➤ In late May 2011, Apple approved its 500,000th app on all its current platforms (iPhone, iPod Touch, and iPad).

➤ As of September, 2011, the number of active apps available for download was roughly 500,000.

➤ There are roughly 86,000 unique developers.

➤ Of all apps, roughly 40 percent are free! There is a big push toward free and freemium (see Chapter 7).

➤ The average price of a paid app is $3.64, which seems on par from a plateau over the past couple of years, and reflects a sharp drop from an initial price of around $6 back in mid-2008.

➤ The average number of apps per developer is 4.6.

➤ The category distribution over time has stayed fairly constant from 2008 until today, with the big five categories accounting for 54 percent of all apps (Games at 16 percent, Books at 13 percent, Entertainment at 11 percent, Education at 7 percent, and Lifestyle at 7 percent). All other categories combined to account for roughly 46 percent.

Table 3-1(courtesy of `148apps.biz`) shows the most popular App Store categories, ranked by number of apps within the category. Of course, if you're reading this well past publication, these will undoubtedly have shifted and grown. But barring any major changes in the way the App Store functions, these should be representative of general rankings, give or take a few percentage points, for the foreseeable future. For the most up-to-date stats, it will always be best to check in with the source, in this case, `148apps.biz`.

TABLE 3-1: All Categories Ranked by Number of Apps within Category

CATEGORY	PERCENTAGE OF TOTAL APPS	ROUGH NUMBER OF APPS AVAILABLE
Games	16	76,000
Books	13	60,000
Entertainment	11	50,000
Education	9	42,000
Lifestyle	7	35,000
Utilities	6	27,000
Travel	5	26,000
Music	4	19,000
Business	4	18,000
Reference	4	17,000
Sports	3	15,000
News	3	13,000
Productivity	2.5	12,000
Healthcare & Fitness	2	11,000

CATEGORY	PERCENTAGE OF TOTAL APPS	ROUGH NUMBER OF APPS AVAILABLE
Photography	2	10,000
Finance	2	9,000
Navigation	2	9,000
Social Networking	2	9,000
Medical	2	9,000
Weather	0.5	2,000

Table 3-2 shows a breakdown of price.

TABLE 3-2: All Apps Broken Down by Price

PRICE	PERCENTAGE OF TOTAL APPS
Free	40
$0.99	28
$1.99	12
$2.99	6
$3.99	3
$4.99	3.5
$5.99	Less than 2
$6.99	Less than 1
$7.99	Less than 2
$8.99	Less than 1
$9.99	2
$10.99	Less than 0.5
$11.99	Less than 0.5
$12.99	Less than 0.5
$13.99	Less than 0.5
$14.99	Less than 0.5
$14.99 and above	2

The next several stats deal with revenue generated and expected, as well as those apps that have been most successful at Number 1.

➤ In 2010, 4.5 billion apps have sold to generate $6.8 billion in revenue (Gartner, Apple).

➤ Over the next two years, both the number of apps sold and revenue are expected to somewhat exponentially increase.

➤ Currently, based on time spent at Number 1 in the App Store, the top ten most popular apps of all time were all from the Games category.

➤ The top game, "Angry Birds," spent an amazing nine months (275 days) at Number 1. The next highest amount of time occupying the Number 1 slot was just 38 days, then 27 days, and even the Number 14 app of the year spent 20 days at Number 1.

These statistics show the one outlier, "Angry Birds," and then that the rest commonly last around 20 days for the most popular apps. In other words, positions at the top change quite frequently in the App Store. Despite this, it is typically possible to maintain or grow your general ranking with respect to competing apps in your niche over time, as Chapter 11 will demonstrate.

In the next section, "Making Decisions Based on Research," you'll find opinions on what these numbers and trends may mean for you, but first let's gobble up a few more statistics.

➤ According to AdMob (`metrics.admob.com`), in May 2010, there were roughly twice the number of iPhone users (67 percent) versus iPod Touch (31 percent), with iPad checking with only 2 percent of the users. That's likely shifted somewhat today, but the take-away here is that there are more iPhone users than iPod Touch users.

➤ However, iPod Touch users spend 20 percent more time with their apps than iPhone users — likely because it's a device similar to the iPad (where app use is more a primary feature, whereas iPhone users are split between calls and app use). All three have music capability, obviously.

➤ The average selling price of the top 300 apps for iPhone was $1.57, while for iPad it was $4.19 (according to "Insights into Apple's App EcoSystem: Comparing Mac, iPad and iPhone" at `www.distimo.com`).

➤ While the average price of a paid app was roughly $3.64 (according to the report cited earlier), the overall average (free *and* paid) was $2.26 (according to `www.148apps.biz`). For free and paid apps, the average *game* was just $1.05, and the *app* was $2.47 — which says something about the category.

MAKING DECISIONS BASED ON RESEARCH

If you're going to take the time and money to develop an app, you may as well make informed decisions to allow it the best chance to succeed. This section examines how to find key metrics that are available both in the App Store and via online resources, and then collecting and interpreting the data.

Although the statistics quoted earlier in this chapter provide a good overview, they are not anywhere close to being all-inclusive. Some meanings can be derived, however. So, before you get started with your research, here is a bit of analysis for the statistics presented earlier, as well as general things you can learn from them. Take these as rough guidelines, and feel free to be the exception to any of them:

➤ If you're doing a game, you will likely be charging the consumer less than any other type of app (free to $0.99 is the norm).

➤ iPad apps have a different price point, with users paying roughly 250 percent more per app than a paid iPhone app. Considering the ease with which a developer can port an app to iPad, it is usually worth the cost to deliver to both platforms.

➤ Price points of $3.99, $6.99, and $8.99 encompass a lower percentage of apps. So, if your app (after competitive research) can fit into one of these price points, it might help it stand out slightly easier. ("Archetype" was initially priced at $2.99.)

➤ Being in the top 100 to 200 apps gets an app on many more web lists, so aim for that.

➤ When doing competitive research on successful apps within your niche, be sure to note other apps by the same developer to see how that developer may have leveraged positioning, talent, or technology to build and market more apps.

➤ Because all apps have a 100-character keyword limit during submission, keyword density will be less in categories with fewer apps. (You learn more about keywords in the "Analyzing Successful Apps" section later in this chapter.)

➤ It may be easier to find a niche in categories other than Games. It may also be less costly to develop without a lot of art and special effects (mainly programming), and you may potentially realize more revenue from each app sold. It is logical to assume, then, that for the average developer, an app other than a game would be more feasible and possibly profitable to create.

> *Obviously, don't let that stop you if you have a great game idea, because the potential is always there for the next "Angry Birds."*

Opportunity Size: Is There a Hole in the Market?

Later in this chapter in the section, "Analyzing Successful Apps," you'll discover how to go about searching the App Store. Information about keywords and your notes on feature lists of other successful apps will help you to gauge whether there's an opening.

It's likely you already feel you know whether an opening exists. After all, you are interested in developing one of your ideas. However, don't make the mistake of assuming there's a hole in the market when there may not be. You'll want to use both Google (or insert your favorite search engine) and the iTunes App Store for this research.

So, how do you draw the conclusion that there is indeed room for your idea? Here is a list of some considerations:

➤ Is there a "successful" app (or more than one) in your niche already? If so, this might be a warning sign, but you'll need more information.

➤ Are you attempting to better existing features, or are you coming up with new ones? If you are evolving existing features, it becomes more risky, because you have fewer unique selling points.

➤ Is the category you're attempting to enter one of the most frequently downloaded? Table 3-1 should help answer that question. This just means more competition, but should not be a deterrent. It will only be a factor if most answers to other questions in this list are also "yes."

➤ Are competing apps being recently updated? If you can answer "no" (or, "not too much"), that's a positive sign that the other apps may have run their course.

➤ Can you be confident that you can do one or more features of a competing app (visual, performance, or functionality) better than the competitor can?

➤ If you are first to market with your app, are you willing to take pains to ensure that you are giving it all your effort so that it won't be so easy to emulate or better? This includes art, functionality, programming, and so on. If your app is remotely popular, people will take notice and fill the niche quickly with apps that may be better (that is, should you have a good idea, but lack in execution).

Whatever your answers to these questions, the one thing you'll want to concentrate on is flawlessly executing your core features, so that even if some of the presentation is lacking, the functionality more than makes up for it.

If you don't yet have a niche picked out, don't worry. You'll discover some pointers for how to find one next.

Choosing Your Niche

Let's say that you just want to get in on the iPhone App Store action and don't yet have a niche, or you've already begun one app and are ready to start your second. How do you go about finding a new niche?

Innovation generally begins with finding a need that's not being met, for whatever reason. When you use a lot of software, you'll inevitably come across those apps that seem to do the job you want, but are lacking in one or more key areas.

Therefore, finding a need usually comes about either naturally (by being suddenly inspired with an idea and wondering if it's been done), or by normal use of everyday products (and starting to develop an entrepreneur's analytical eye by asking, "Hey, wouldn't it be better if..." types of questions).

A need can also be proactively searched out. In fact, that's exactly what the Google Keyword Tool is all about (https://adwords.google.com/select/KeywordToolExternal). Taking a lesson from search engine optimization (SEO) research, finding a new niche can be as simple as discovering an unfulfilled sector — in this case, keywords about a certain product that don't have a lot of competition, but bring about a lot of searches. Then, should you be driven to, you are ready to capitalize on that need.

So, for apps, you can go about finding a need via several approaches, including the following:

➤ Use the method-driven research described later in this chapter to discover an unfulfilled need. (User reviews are a good place to begin, as well as category and search bar searches on keywords.)

➤ Discover a need by using apps within your field of expertise, or those revealed as potential candidates through other research.

➤ For any interesting niches or appealing apps, perform competitive research by combing user reviews and even critical reviews for missing elements.

➤ Analyze successful apps to find out what they have in common in a niche. (You will likely need these features.)

➤ Analyze unsuccessful apps within a niche you are interested in to find out what went wrong.

You can wrap up your search by answering these questions:

➤ Is this something that is ideal for mobile use touchscreens such as the iPhone/iPod/iPad?

➤ Is this something that users would be better suited using on another device such as the PC or Mac?

➤ Has this been done already on app stores for other devices, such as the Android market or the Mac App Store?

Perform Due Diligence Early

Once you have a planned niche, you're ready to start analyzing the competition. This step is crucial, and can not only save a lot of money and time, but make you money. Here is a rough list of benefits:

➤ You won't spend unnecessary time working on features that have been done more effectively in another app.

➤ You'll discover missed opportunities you can take advantage of, further branding your app as unique and innovative.

➤ You'll discover trends and/or technologies that have been used in ways you would not have thought of.

➤ You'll discover how other apps are promoting their brands via keywords, feature lists, and social media.

➤ You'll learn about the life cycle of an app in your niche, as well as the best ways to plan for and prolong it.

➤ You won't be "one-upped" by another app developer who had the same idea and was able to release earlier than you. There's always that chance, but that's why you keep your idea fairly hidden until other developers no longer have time to react.

Rough Planning Is Cheap

As you're putting together features for your app, begin early by building up mock-ups of its interface flow. You could use flowchart software such as Microsoft Visio, or online collaboration flowcharting such as that offered by Creately (www .Creately.com). This will allow you to make early tweaks when you start to narrow down your features.

Paper prototyping is dirt cheap as well, and a bit more visual. Glue, scissors, maybe some tape, and markers are all you need. Just remember not to be too attached (no pun intended) to your early mockups, and allow them to change and iterate with your research findings.

Aside from doing interface mockups, you might want to have an artist start to do some creative style mockups as well.

> *For "Archetype," the developers hadn't yet settled on a style for the weapons or character design (which were crucial to the overall atmosphere), and so the concept artist began almost before anyone else. The "story" and the art concept had a sort of symbiotic relationship.*

Development Is Expensive!

As you learned in Chapter 2, it costs quite a bit to develop an app properly, depending on scope. Make use of all the cheap tricks early, which include the following:

➤ Competitive research

➤ Paper prototyping

➤ Art style concept mockups

➤ Rough feature lists and concept documents (as discussed in more detail in Chapter 5)

➤ Online collaboration software for milestone planning (such as Basecamp offered by 37signals at www.basecapmhq.com)

Summary Decisions

There are some factors to be aware of as you're exploring and expanding features while researching the App Store. Let's take a look at some important ones.

Rough Budget versus Opportunity

When looking at the competition, you'll start to get an expert overview of your selected niche(s). During this time, try to do a little predicting about what type of outlook and opportunity is possible within your niche. Compare this with the budget you have in mind to determine just how much risk might be involved.

With more features comes more complexity, both with programming costs and with the possible cost of functionality, usability, as well as challenges with streamlining the interface. So, unless there's a definitive opportunity, be careful about adding too many features.

Is Profitability Possible? If Not, Stop, Re-Assess

Just as in web marketing with SEO keyword research, in the App Store, you'll find niches with relatively little competition, and others that are already somewhat saturated. Before even starting to look at the competition, learning to spot over-saturated niches will be a huge benefit to help you reassess whether your ideas have legs.

For example, are you entering a niche that includes a few bigger-budget apps with similar features and noticeable polish that you might have trouble competing with? If so, you might carefully consider your approach. In general, researching niche opportunity is the key before even researching the competition.

Pretend You're an Investor — Try to Poke Holes Aggressively

Sometimes it's difficult to look your million-dollar idea in the eye and be objective about it. Though it might hurt your ego a bit, ask others. Pitch it to friends and family to see what they say. The results could be surprising, and help shape how you proceed.

Scrutinize your earning potential as if you were an investor. Ask questions such as the following:

➤ What is the profit potential?

➤ What does the niche look like in terms of opportunity, and how saturated is it with competition?

➤ How strong is the competition?

➤ What is the competition charging, and how are they monetizing?

➤ What is your development budget?

➤ How experienced is your team?

ANALYZING SUCCESSFUL APPS

Before you start refining the usability and/or gameplay details of your app, it will be best to start by seeing what's out there. You should analyze how others have done it within your intended niche, as well as with apps outside of it, but that may share similar feature sets. This section demonstrates how to perform competitive research for your apps.

COMPARING TO "ANGRY BIRDS"

Considering the most popular mobile game thus far is a good place to start. As shown in the following figure, "Angry Birds" is a casual puzzle game where players sling shot birds at pigs that are perched on structures, trying to knock them over.

continues

continued

Released in December 2009, it's been downloaded more than 200 million times on all platforms (including special and theme editions), and has more than 12 million sold just on Apple's App Store.

Almost everyone these days wants to know how to achieve some of the same type of success that "Angry Birds" did (or better) with its record 275 days at Number 1 for the core title, and other lengthy reigns at Number 1 for special editions. When you start seeing the name of an app referenced in television sitcoms that are all about pop culture (such as *The Big Bang Theory*), or plush pets at major toy retailers, it's probably doing okay.

"Angry Birds" was one of the first games to be shown off in the new HTML 5 (http://chrome.angrybirds.com/), is possibly slated for an upcoming movie, has been ported to countless platforms (including consoles and now PCs), and has generally been a cultural phenomenon.

So, what exactly are the factors of its huge success? What can you take from this (if anything) and apply to apps in general? Conjecture and articles on reasons for its success are plentiful on the Internet. After having read many of the articles and playing the game, the following observations can be offered:

➤ **It's casual** — Although this is fairly obvious, of course, this does have a few poignant meanings. "Casual" means easy to learn, no long time commitment for game sessions, appealing usually to women as well as men, and it has a complexity that is delivered in small increments to the user. What this means from a general app standpoint is that if you have a utility app (say, a Twitter client), you want it to be as casual-friendly as possible, presenting a user interface that's simple and clear from the beginning in its core functionality, with hidden or uncovered complexity should users look for it. You'd want users to be able to quickly get in and get to the core functionality, then back out again.

➤ **It has humor** — Birds bounce, feathers ruffle, they make sounds, pigs squeal, glass and wood shatters, and the art style is "cartoony." If you're making a game, don't forget to add a sense of humor to lighten perceptions. If you're making a business app, attempt to make it easy to use and as engaging as possible.

➤ **It has goals and layers of sub-goals** — Each level is presented to the player as a clickable icon. When that's cleared, you unlock the next. That's goal 1. Goal 2 is the amount of stars you get on a level depending on performance. This is always shown, and encourages the player to get the maximum three stars for each level. Goal 3 is a high score. This is tied in with number of stars, but done in a unique way that rewards breaking more things, which is always random. This is all tied together in the meta-goal of clearing all the levels in one particular section. For a utility, give users reasons to come back to your app (for example, by stat-tracking certain features, or providing useful notifications to make them engaging to the user).

➤ **It has incredibly easy-to-learn and dynamic gameplay** — Flick the bird at the structure with pigs and see what happens. The reason that it's dynamic is because of the use of a physics engine where you never truly know what's going to happen, yet maintaining consistency, which allows you to reassess your trajectory after every attempt. Don't force the players/users to use help functionality to learn your app. The basic functionality should always be intuitive.

➤ **Session time is very short** — A level can be completed in less than 30 seconds. The casual player must be able to play for short durations at a time.

➤ **It introduces new challenges, just as you might be getting bored or too experienced, completely changing the core mechanic** — A general app might do this by providing users with core functionality that's immediately accessible and gratifying to use. Then, allow users to discover just through the main use other useful features. In the Twitter client idea, users may start to type, and then find they can easily now click the name of another user to automatically set up a "retweet." Intuitive discovery in this way can lead to very positive attachment.

➤ **It's cute** — Let's face it. The characters in this game were designed to appeal to both the female and male aesthetic senses — pseudo-angry, but round/fat innocent creatures, and comically cute pigs. That's perfect. No bullets, no blood, just animal versus animal, and stylistic poofs when they explode.

"Angry Birds" did one small thing and did it very well. It nailed its niche.

Let's start by creating a fictitious example — a new Twitter client. That niche happens to already be well saturated, but let's consider that you have new features that none of the other clients have, or perhaps a star programmer who can simply do it better. For whatever reason, you know there's a need, and you plan to fill it.

Although doing research for similar apps from your iPhone, iPad, or iPod Touch is certainly very feasible, don't forget you can easily start to browse from a home computer in iTunes. The first step of competitive research will go much quicker with a big screen and a mouse, with quick access to the Internet, reviews, and easy tabbed browsing.

The iTunes and iPad App Stores even have a couple of secret advantages. Whenever you search for a paid app, you can see that the bottom has the "customers also bought" window, which is where you really start to expand your search. And, at the top, the categories of your searched-for app are listed. This will clue you in to what categories are being targeted. Currently, this does not appear in the App Store on smaller devices such as iPod Touch.

In iTunes (or in the App Store on your device), start by entering the main keyword or words for your niche. In this case, simply enter **twitter**, as shown in Figure 3-1.

FIGURE 3-1: The App Store search bar is where many (or most) users will find your app via your keywords

APP STORE KEYWORDS

In 2009, Apple implemented the capability for developers to create 100 characters worth of keywords (including spaces) so that apps can be better searched for in the Store's search engine. When you're coming up with a keyword list for your app, there are a few rules to follow:

➤ After you enter keywords, they cannot be changed until you update your app.

➤ You are required to fill in keywords for an update.

Following are some steps to create both your keywords and app name so that they are more easily searched for:

1. Imagine yourself as the user, and consider all of the keywords you would normally use to look up your app.

2. Use the Google Keyword Tool (`https://adwords.google.com/select/KeywordToolExternal`) to search for the most common phrases related to your app, and the list you came up with.

3. Refine your search using the lists that come up in Google's Keyword Tool. (Normally this is used for Internet SEO, but it's also very useful for anywhere users can type in keywords or tags.)

4. Start typing your keywords into the App Store's search bar and see what comes up (if anything). Use this to refine your keywords even further.

5. Use keywords in your app title if possible, and again in your description, but as with any SEO, do not oversaturate, or you may get penalized or rejected.

As shown in Figure 3-2, when you type "twitter" into the App Store search bar, numerous entries come up as suggestions. Click one of these (usually they appear to come up in terms of popularity — which, for your niche at least, would be considered successful), and you'll be taken to a list of potential apps with that keyword or words.

Click any of the apps you see with a decent icon near the top (preferably paid, but okay if not). You'll want to download and install as many of these as you can as well.

Once inside the details for an app, there are three important factors when evaluating whether it's successful:

FIGURE 3-2: App Store search term suggestions

➤ Scroll down slightly and take a look at how many of five stars the current version of the app is rated at, and then also look at the overall rating. (However, it's not uncommon for a successful app to be rated at three to four stars out of five, merely because ratings alone are unreliable.)

➤ A bigger factor to consider is the number of ratings given. If it's in the thousands or more, this is a fairly popular app. If it's at 10,000 or more, it's an extremely popular app for its niche. Anything with more than 50,000 ratings is likely to be in the top 100 to 200 apps. The free app named "Twitter," for example, has had as many as 135,612 ratings and 14,000 reviews for all versions.

➤ You'll definitely want to read the user reviews when you delve into what makes this app successful. Just as with any reviews, there will be many people who don't really respond with constructive criticism, and there are always competitors who (either by themselves, or by paying others) rate a competing app just one star, along with a quick review, to get its value down. This is why you'll often see a disproportionate number of one-star ratings, rather than two, three, or four stars. However, it's here that you'll also find valuable information about what features users would like to see from legitimate customers.

There are four other quick and useful bits of information you can find on any app's page:

➤ You can find out how the developers have tailored the description, noting particular features and keywords you're interested in.

➤ You can note when the app was last updated, and specifically note whether the developer appears "done" with it (therefore, a positive for your app).

➤ As mentioned previously, take special note as to the category in which the app has been placed.

➤ With paid apps, on the iPad and iTunes versions of the App Store (which support bigger screens), right at the bottom you'll definitely want to go to the other apps people have purchased, and make the same comparisons.

If the app you've looked for is free, give it a try by installing it. If it is not free, determine whether there are features you are competing against or features you don't yet have, but may want, and determine whether it is worth the asking price. Fortunately, you're not dealing with retail console games at $50 a pop, and the most you'll likely spend doing this sort of research is around $100 — and that's being liberal. Note also that a great resource for seeing apps in action is Youtube .com. In most cases, you'll be able to find reviews or other footage, which can usually provide enough information for a quick assessment.

When you try an app, take special note of any interesting features and how they're implemented — both pros and cons. Noting deficiencies will give you a leg up when you develop your app. Always be asking the following questions:

➤ What combination of features and presentation is making this app successful?

➤ Is it partly a polished app icon?

➤ How easy is it to get into and out of the app's core features?

➤ What is the response time to your actions?

➤ What sorts of bells and whistles, or built-in social features, are included?

Fantastic (and perhaps even more useful) online tools are available for finding and analyzing top apps. One of the best might be found at Applyzer.com (Figure 3-3). This site features the top 1,000 stats for any app (you must register first), both iPhone/iPod and iPad stores, and currently provides free daily updates for an unlimited number of apps. For a small fee, you can opt in for hourly rankings as well, and register to chart your own apps.

Another web-based free(-mium) tool, equally as intriguing and useful in different ways, is called Appannie at www.appannie.com. As shown in Figure 3-4, one cool feature is a "Top 5 Matrix" that shows icons of all the top five paid, free, and grossing apps in all categories, all on one page, with links. Another is all the filters you can use to search for all apps, as well as ones of your choosing. The total package features a slick interface and good user feedback. Expect this one to rocket up to being at or near the top in ranking tools.

You can find more useful links for tools in Appendix B.

FIGURE 3-3: Applyzer is one of the best App Store ranking tools you can find

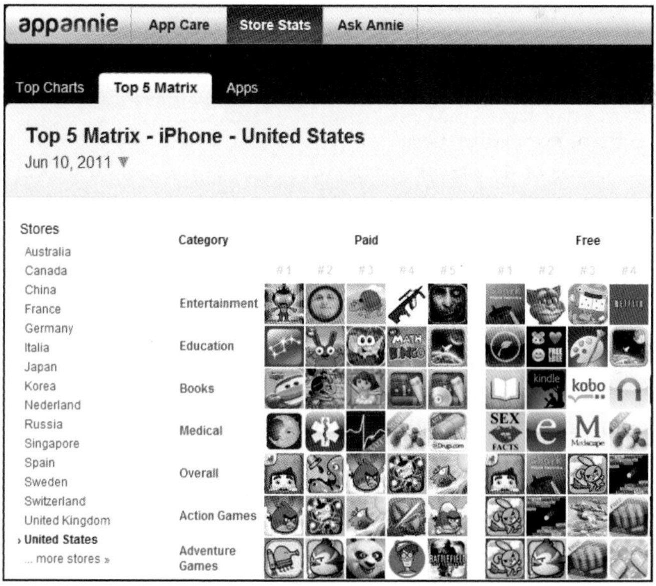

FIGURE 3-4: Appannie is feature-rich with incredible filter properties

Exploring Popular Features

As a rule, apps need to capture a distinctive or unique style (even if that is by being overly simplistic), or its chances of getting noticed are slim. A few still make it by, of course, but they're often forgettable. As far as visual style goes, "The Moron Test" shown in Figure 3-5 is one exception. It spent the second longest time at Number 1 on the charts (38 days). For the most part, the graphics are crude and mish-mashed together, the humor more so, but for that app, that combination worked. It also helped that it went viral because of its crass, in-your-face, no-apologies humor, essentially telling users that they are more stupid than they thought. A point must be scored for novelty.

FIGURE 3-5: "The Moron Test" spent 38 days at Number 1, the second longest of any app

It is very useful to note that "The Moron Test" did not compete in the highly popular Games category, but instead was positioned in the Entertainment category, which, in hindsight, was a brilliant move.

Another example, "Doodle Jump," was mentioned in Chapter 2. Its graphics are hand-drawn in an artsy-sketchy sort of way, ideal for a quick port to the iPhone and oft-duplicated later. But the art style really clicked with its ultra-simplistic controls (tilt and that's it!) and gameplay (go as high as you can). Casual gamers ate it up.

Now, consider once again "Angry Birds." Though, as shown in Figure 3-6, it has a cartoon style, it certainly has a level of polish most apps fail to achieve, from visual details (such as lingering smoke puffs as you slingshot your bird), to fine-tuned, physics-based gameplay, to every graphic element, sound effect, and thematic music samples fully supporting its brand of humor.

FIGURE 3-6: Cartoon art style from "Angry Birds," by Rovio

Exploring Visual Styles

If you're creating a game, one of the main considerations is the art style. Because of this, the following visual walkthrough of some of the most popular visual styles to hit the App Store may come in handy for you.

> *Note that the longer the App Store is around, users and players will naturally expect a progression of higher-quality visuals and functionality, simply based on the natural evolution of apps and saturation of niches, in addition to what's been expected in other mediums such as video or computer games. Back in the early days of the App Store, there weren't all the major companies there are now that are creating apps that cost hundreds of thousands of dollars to create. The bar has been raised. That said, if you can make something novel, it just may be that any style can work.*

As shown in Figure 3-7, "Pocket God" was one of the first App Store apps to feature highly polished and stylized vector-like graphics. Notice that there are no black stroke lines around many of the graphics, helping them have that illustrated render-like quality.

FIGURE 3-7: "Pocket God" spent 26 days at Number 1

As shown in Figure 3-8, "iFart Mobile" is a lot like "The Moron Test" in that it uses photo-realistic-like graphics, but is actually a bit more polished in that respect. Its use of grunge and textures is more professional Photoshop stuff than is found in the other app, and it integrates the default iPhone scroll mechanism beautifully to almost seem like it was made in the same style.

"Fieldrunners" was one of the first iPhone games to really wow people with graphics. As shown in Figure 3-9, its vibrant palette, highly stylized and detailed render-worthy cartoon graphics are still some of the very best seen on the device. What's even better is how fast the graphics are with absolutely zero slowdown. The programming team at Subatomic Studios is a group of miracle workers.

FIGURE 3-8: "iFart Mobile" spent 21 days at Number 1

FIGURE 3-9: "Fieldrunners" resides in the App Store Hall of Fame

Exploring Social Integration

When "Fieldrunners" was first released, it had almost no social features built in. However, it now supports Game Center, which is a third-party solution that many apps are now incorporating that allows players/users to connect with friends and earn achievements in the game, using one login across games.

Game Center (and another called Open Feint) is part of a huge push for social features in any app, along with the usual "post to Facebook" or Twitter functionality many apps now come with by default.

The reasoning is straightforward — the more social your app, the better chance it has to spread to more users, and, thus, sustain or even exponentially grow its popularity. If apps lack social integration, then once the initial hype or marketing push is over, over time, people start to forget (usually sooner than later), and the app has little chance of sustaining its momentum for a lengthy time. This was one problem developers had with "Archetype," even though they built in some social features.

> You'll find much more about social integration in Chapter 10.

Exploring the iPhone Hall of Fame

A good place to go for all-around browsing of the most successful apps of all time is the iPhone Hall of Fame from within the iTunes App Store (Figure 3-10). These aren't just games, but rather all apps that have resided at Number 1, or have been immensely popular for one reason or another. Many are paid, but some are free and worth perusing to get a feel for what's possible using the standard iPhone graphical user interface (GUI) within UIKit, in addition to custom-made graphics. Note also that any time you're looking at apps, pay special attention to how the all-important App Store icon is used.

FIGURE 3-10: A great place to call home for any app is the iPhone Hall of Fame

Avoiding Pesky Ego Traps

During your competitive analysis, it will be tempting to keep adding to your list the features others are including as if you also need to include them. Though it can bolster your ego to have an all-powerful app, you really need to focus your feature list. Absolutely compile a list of notes, but before deciding, you will want to trim the fat significantly, and save any extras for possible planned updates in the future. The alternative is spending a lot more time and money with an app that may do everything, but likely nothing exceptionally well.

Another ego trap is that of trying to "keep up with the Joneses." "Angry Birds" was astonishingly successful and, well, anything sitting in the top 100 is doing pretty well in that particular niche. Copycatting will only get you so far, and there are very few copycat success stories. This is not to say that because Twitter itself has an app that you don't make another one with better features and functional-ity and call it Twitterrific (already been done, as mentioned in Chapter 2). That would be doing it better.

STICKING TO CORE FEATURES

In the end, with "Archetype," the development team was able to keep the game focused on a core idea — providing multiplayer, team-based gameplay as smoothly as possible with minimal lag. The original competitive research pitted the team mainly against two apps: ngmoco's "Eliminate Pro" (a "freemium" game where paying real money can help you progress faster) and Gameloft's "N.O.V.A." (a sublime campaign-based shooter game a la the Halo series for Xbox consoles, only without that series' exquisite multiplayer). Both were highly polished shooters released less than a year prior to when "Archetype" would eventually be released.

"Eliminate Pro" was light on a story, but it did have features such as customization that the "Archetype" team really glommed onto, though they purposefully opted for a different business model. "N.O.V.A." had a light multiplayer mode, but was really focused on its story presentation and graphics. The niche was there, and, as it happens, remarkably still is.

What was tempting for the "Archetype" team (especially in the beginning) was adding other features that the game did not need. At the top of the feature list were more levels and customization. Second to that was a good story — the team even hashed one out early in development. However, because the goal was to make the app in a manageable amount of time without the budget, personnel, or clout of a development house like Gameloft, the team knew there had to be cuts, and that helped them focus on core features.

Story was something everyone believed in, and thus the "Archetype" team attempted a CGI intro when the opportunity arose. Although customization was also on the list, the team knew it felt more like an add-on than a requirement of the core game-play. Later in development, it was through gameplay testing and wanting to be main-stream that the team had to "feature creep" and, thus, designed and added a tutorial level with target dummies, calling it "Training," and providing some assessment and achievements to go along with it.

How many "Farmville" clones are there now on Facebook, as Flash games, as apps, and now on consoles? A zillion — and to make one yourself, you would have to compete with a saturated market. That would be doable if you have the right design and talent, but it would also be risky. "Angry Birds" has now spun off loads of copycats, "Doodle Jump" had its share, and so did "Pocket God." Any time you have a Number 1 app, chances are that people will take note, and then try to ride the wave. Perhaps it's feasible, but you will almost never achieve the same success as the first — the novelty will have worn off. A more reasonable chance for success would be to go for something innovative, or utilize your ego on one-upping some-thing that already exists, rather than to turn out a simple re-theme.

The bottom line here is not to be afraid to specialize and focus on core features within your niche, polishing them so that they stand out from the competition. In the end, you will save money, be able to deliver more apps, and likely have key unique selling points others don't.

Game Concepts: Old versus New

Generally, you'll have the potential for more success by being the first with a new innovation, or addressing a need that has yet to be met. That said, plenty of older game concepts have had a new lease on life.

One of the most recent examples is the new app by "Farmville" developer Zynga, and spending time at Number 1 on both the paid and free apps list. It's not surprising, given its absolute foothold on the social gaming scene with uber hits "Farmville," "Cityville," "Frontierville," "Café World," and so on, that this company would be able to market something to its millions of users and rocket it up to Number 1 on the iPhone. But it actually received good reviews as well.

The premise? Hangman. You try to figure out the word your opponent wrote by guessing one letter at a time. It's as old of a concept as it gets, kind of like Battleship, only with a little more skill and deduction involved, making it the better game overall. And, as is par with Zynga, the developers layered it with all sorts of social features like chat, playing simultaneous games with friends, Facebook connect, and push notifications. An old concept is now a social game that hadn't yet translated particularly well as a computer game. Now it has cute characters, appropriate social features, and simultaneous games to make it a novel, fun experience.

As for whether to take an old concept and make it new, or to seek out a brand new need, the important thing is to always find a need, and see if there's a niche for it, whichever order works. Old concepts can always be seen as new again as technology evolves to open up new ways of experiencing them.

TURNING THE OLD INTO NEW

Try this short exercise to help get you in the creative mindset of thinking up novel ways to make old concepts new. First, think of two or three old applications or game concepts, on any platform, that you remember as being kind of cool, novel, or fun back in the day.

With each concept, come up with at least two ways you could bring that app or game up-to-date with current iPhone/iPod/iPad technology and functionality. This could include controls (tilt, accelerometer, gyroscope), social networking or third-party lobby integration, push notifications, multiplayer, camera use, music integration, and so on.

Here's one spur of the moment, creatively challenging example. Having always been an early adopter of new technology (especially software), the author used to use the original Internet chat client ICQ on a PC. Because he was one of the first million users, this would have been around 1997-ish. The core features of ICQ were its notifications when you got new messages, file sharing (especially fun on a 28.8K-baud modem), and, of course, its instant chat and the logs it could keep.

continues

continued

In short, it was one of the first social apps. It encouraged multiple friends in your list. It notified you when they were online and off. You could add status messages and file share. (MP3 music sharing was common back then, though it took 15 to 20 minutes for one song.)

Because chatting is so prevalent in most everything we do (even more so now, in many cases, than e-mail in the working environment), new apps and services like Skype have risen to the forefront with video conferencing, screen sharing, drag-and-drop files, and so on.

The creatively challenging part is this. What could make ICQ or a similar chat client come back stronger than ever when almost any chat app has the same core features? A couple of things come to mind, and feel free to use them if you don't think they're rubbish and haven't yet been done. One is the idea of socially shared credit (that is, the more friends you have and share, the more credit you get). Skype already has paid credit, but this could be another source of promoting your app.

Another unique feature is that of chat achievements to unlock new features such as user icons, and so on—thus making it a game. Bring friends on, score points, and perhaps "level up." In other words, use the program, check it often, grow your contact list, and you earn special achievements that can be bragged about and shared on Facebook (for example, stars around your name, name on leader boards, new emoticons, and so on).

Traditional Brand Names Do Well; Traditional Concepts Do Not

As mentioned earlier, gameplay and user experience is evolving. What this means is that if you have an older concept, such as the prior example of Zynga's "Hanging with Friends" (Hangman), unless you update it to match with current standards and technology, it won't fly.

You can't bring "Asteroids" back by keeping the same gameplay and not adding anything new. A case in point is an Xbox 360 Live Arcade game named "Geometry Wars." It's basically "Asteroids," but has a few new twists to make it completely fresh:

➤ Its art style is completely vector in a futuristic and geometrically abstract look, completely filled with onscreen pyrotechnics.

➤ It introduced the capability to control the ship's cannon direction from the right joystick, and the movement from the left. Though that's not particularly novel, it allowed for responsive and intuitive gameplay.

➤ It introduced geometric "characters" that had consistent artificial intelligence (AI) "personalities," and would track you in various ways, unlike the random big and small rocks of the original.

In short, it was an old concept, with new tricks.

If you own or are able to pick up an older, somewhat known brand name, it should, however, be easier to market. A quick look at the top 200 will reveal several brand names and concepts you might already be familiar with — Scrabble, The Game of Life, Tetris, The Price is Right, Frogger, Battleship, The Sims, Risk, Yahtzee, and Trivial Pursuit, to name some.

For yet untapped brands that may hold potential, look to possibly licensing characters with some name recognition (for a reboot — those usually go over well), or even older well-known app names that may be able to be purchased. Generally, name recognition will help your app get a better head start if it is possible, but a concept will not. Old concepts always need to be improved to be up-to-date with current technology and trends.

New and Paid, Old and Free

Free apps get many more downloads than paid apps, but there is one big incentive for starting out paid and eventually going free. You have room to lower your price, provide promotions, and give a legitimate reason for some updates.

It doesn't have to be a mutually exclusive thing, though, because one of the more popular promotion strategies is releasing a free or lite version alongside your paid version, with an upgrade funnel built into the gameplay.

> *More on this is covered in Chapters 6 through 8.*

ANALYZING UNSUCCESSFUL APPS

You've now seen how to analyze and find successful apps, but what are the benefits of looking at the unsuccessful ones, and how do you go about finding them?

Let's begin by agreeing on a common definition of "unsuccessful" by examining what unsuccessful *isn't*. Just as a "successful" app does not mean it is a good app, an unsuccessful app does not mean it is a bad app. If you do a little digging, you can find many great apps with stellar reviews that, for one reason or another (related to promotion and marketing), didn't sell. On the flip side, you can find many successful apps and games with merely mediocre reviews.

In the game industry, a famous example of this was the PC-licensed title "Enter the Matrix" in 2003, which capitalized on the incredibly well-known movie, *The Matrix* (Figure 3-11). Many millions were spent on its marketing, and it did remarkably well in retail its first month, despite harsh critical and player reviews. Though it was solid in the short term and made the developers a lot of money before word of mouth could spread, times are different now.

FIGURE 3-11: "Enter the Matrix," a mediocre game at best by many measures, sold well largely because of initial marketing hype

A highly marketed retail game, even if it turns out mediocre or worse, may still be able to get away with the hype-to-sell approach simply because of the cost of entry. Look at the PC massively multiplayer online (MMO) "Star Wars: The Old Republic" and how much money has been spent promoting it over the past few years. Its 2010 and 2011 several-minute-long, purely cinematic trailers burned at least a few million to show it off, and, perhaps, by the time you read this, you'll know whether that tactic paid off.

On the other hand, apps have a more difficult time getting away with the hype-to-sell approach, though hype and promotion are still very important. A retail MMO in this sense has a lot in common with an app. *Retention* (that is, being able to lure users to stick around) still largely depends on either how good it is, or how much competition it has for its niche, just as MMOs do. One-off games without a subscription and new content might be able to recoup their initial expenses, but an MMO and iPhone apps need continued sales to flourish.

The App Store has a further risk factor as well. It not only has more competition because of the lower cost of entry and general ease of development, but also a far and away lower price point than any retail game. In the end, apps rely heavily on continued sales.

An unsuccessful app is, therefore, defined for purposes of this discussion as an app that didn't sell well (but not necessarily a bad app), or, even more importantly, an app that is no longer popular. Because it is much more difficult to find apps worth looking at but didn't sell well at all (since that includes most of them), you can learn much more from apps that are simply no longer as popular, but still on the radar. With this in mind, the benefit of analyzing these types of apps is twofold:

➤ You want to learn from their mistakes, be it in marketing (a best guess is okay) or implementation.

➤ And/or you want to learn why they are no longer popular (if they once were) — that is, how the market shifted.

To make the most efficient use of your time, there's an art to finding the unsuccessful apps you'd want to glean information from. The secret is in the user reviews, and using them as "links" for finding apps the users like better, hence guiding you from the "unsuccessful" category up to the "successful" app category.

If any such review seems suspicious or worth investigating, simply click their name link and you'll be taken to a list of their other reviews. This is a great way to weed out legitimate concerns.

Following is a definitive search technique to maximize info-gathering potential from unsuccessful apps as defined here:

1. Search by keyword to find a list of possible matches. (iTunes is your best bet here.)

2. Have a separate window open with a ranking website or two ready. `Appannie.com` or `Mobclix.com` (then under App Ranking) are a couple of good choices. These two sites allow you to see current rank, and, more importantly, `Mobclix` even allows you to search by keywords *and* rank, as well as showing a listing of reviews. (However, as of this writing, some of this info appears to be a couple of months out of date.) This can be useful to simultaneously search a site like `Mobclix` with the same keywords you use in iTunes, to see what comes up, and, more importantly, see a list of ranks for each search found. Try picking the ones anywhere from rank 100 through 1,000.

3. In iTunes, go into a few of the *first* pages of search results, because these are not necessarily those that are the top of the category — as you'll see when typing their names into your ranking search tool.

4. In the user reviews within iTunes (or your mobile App Store browser), take a look at these four things: number of ratings, whether or not it has at least a few reviews (skip it now if it doesn't), last date updated, and its current rating.

5. Simply check that the number or rating is fairly low (less than 1,000 should be good), *and* that it has at least a few reviews. Then quickly scan them, especially jotting down or copying names of other apps they like better, or concise features that are missing. If it does have just a few reviews, click the reviewer names for additional information on whether they may or may not be legitimate concerns.

6. If you are interested in going into further depth with the app (for example, its ranking history), type the app's name into a site like `Appannie.com` to get as much info as you can about it. Figure 3-12 shows `Appannie`'s excellent rank history tool at work with "The Moron Test."

Learning from Other People's Mistakes

You can learn just as much from an app that's *almost* at the top as you can from a Number 1 app, if not more. The core idea (or process) in this area is to start from one or more fairly lower ranking apps in your niche, then work your way up the ladder via reviews (user and journalist), as well as play-testing until you have a history of what makes apps in your niche relevant. This process will, therefore, make you an expert in your niche, and better prepared for guiding development when it begins.

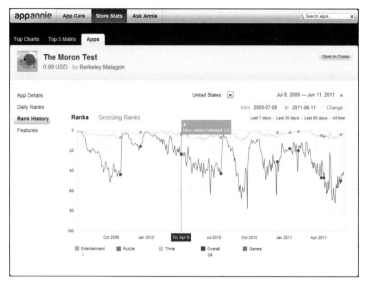

FIGURE 3-12: According to Appannie, "The Moron Test" holds steady over time, and it is interesting to note that it once was in the Puzzle and Games category

The real benefit to competitive app research is in figuring out what competing apps (both successful and unsuccessful) are missing or haven't done right, thus giving you a chance to provide it. As you come across new apps, play-test for faults or functionality, and always check user reviews for key missing features.

Journalist's reviews become more relevant for slightly more popular apps, because it's usually only the ones that are actively promoted that get reviewed in the first place. In general, journalist reviews are a good place to get the opinion of someone who looks at these for a living. After all, you will hopefully be getting positive marks by these same reviewers on your own app when it's released.

Learning from Other People's Complaints

To learn from the mistakes of other apps, it is helpful to look at the complaints. As mentioned previously, some complaints are invalid, or just not constructive, and you should avoid these. Complaints can be found mostly in user reviews within iTunes, but also look at the developer website forums (if they exist), in addition to doing a Google search for the name of the app, followed by "review." You'll likely bring up a large reading list for any marginally successful app.

Following is a short list of useful critical elements to look for in reviews:

➤ Wish list phrases such as "I wish it had <insert feature(s)>..." or "it would be better if..." or "it needs..."

➤ A list of cons, sometimes in the sidebar, at the end, or following a list of pros

➤ Summary sections of journalist reviews that usually get right to the point

As you start to see enough complaints or wish-list features, you'll get sort of a "cloud" effect, in that some will be seen more often. Take special note of these, and add to your list to possibly make a feature or to come back to during development, because maybe this particular feature is a particularly difficult/costly one to implement.

> *For example, after the release of "Archetype," the author compiled a huge sortable list of all feedback, exact phrasing used, and put each into categories. Far and away, the most wished-for feature was "needs more maps," but also a huge chunk fell into "needs a campaign" and also "needs more customization." For complaints, early on, developers got a lot of "friendly fire isn't working" or "melee axe is overpowered." If you were developing a competing app in this niche, depending on the intended focus, you'd want to differentiate it in key ways, and finding out what's missing from competitors via complaints would be a good place to look.*

MIXING AND MATCHING

You've now done a bit of competitive research, have a good idea of what the others are doing in your niche, and, if you followed the prior advice, likely built up a feature set for your app comprised of various missing features from other apps, as well as your planned innovations.

The next goal is to redefine your feature set to make your app appear truly unique.

Borrowing Style and Functionality from Mainstream Applications/Games (the Picasso Way)

There is nothing wrong with borrowing new features in successful apps. Picasso in fact, is well known to have borrowed styles from classical and contemporary artists, distilled down into his own geometrical style, and created a new work of art.

In this exact way, in fact, you should take highly lauded new features or styles from successful apps, and then apply your own sort of transformation on them to make them unique.

Let's consider "Doodle Jump," an example examined previously. Though it wasn't the first app to make use of that hand-drawn Napoleon Dynamite-esque "sketch" style of art, it certainly was the most successful to do so to that point. So, let's say you wanted to do a casual game and were inspired by the "Doodle Jump" art, not only because it more easily captures your imagination in the same way a book does more so than a movie, but also because it's simply easier to create. Fair enough, let's go with that style.

But let's also say you are intent on creating a productivity app and are wondering how in the world you can use the style from that game for a serious business app. Well, maybe that's exactly the thing that will make your app unique:

➤ A stock market ticker that's done in a cartoony way, making money more fun

➤ A chat client that doesn't look so "business-y" or "web 2.0-ish"

➤ A secure password safe-holder that's done in a cartoony way that makes it ironic that it can absolutely keep your data safe, but also perhaps emits the vibe of "hackers" who actually know *how* to keep data safe

Imagine the possibilities of this new art style applied to places that haven't yet adapted it.

In the same way, let's say you're creating a physics-based puzzle game and the obvious successful app to borrow something from is the Number 1-selling "Angry Birds," with its physics-based casual gameplay and cute creatures. Another good possibility is the indie runaway success "World of Goo." You don't want to appear too similar, so what do you do?

You distill what made "Angry Birds" successful with that approach — which is, in fact, how it applied the physics engine to an elegantly simple slingshot — and then mold it to fit your game. Perhaps you change from a side view to a top-down approach, and use a similar slingshot action that starts catapulting an object (or creature) forward in slow motion at a certain angle. And then, on the other side, you slingshot another object (maybe in real time). Your goal is to collide them and utilize the pinball mechanic to trigger reactions and see how well you scored. Done properly, that could actually work!

Pulling Out Successful Features for a Twist

To be unique, it will be important to selectively prune your feature list prior to development. If every competitor's app has feature A, B, C, D, and E, within your niche, consider firstly that you'll have unique selling features of your own other than those common elements to fall back on. Then, for a twist, consider which of those A-through-E features you can live without or modify (the Picasso way), and then either cut or mold them to better solidify your app as uniquely identifiable.

SUMMARY

If there's one thing you should take away from this chapter, it's the following walk-through for finding a niche, compiling a feature list for your app, and getting ready for development. At the end of this walkthrough, you should be ready to start.

1. Settle on a niche for your app, whether or not you have one already. If not, do the research.

2. Download and play/try all competing apps in your niche to help compile a feature list.

3. Analyze both successful and not-so-successful apps by data mining their reviews for missing features and other recommended apps.

4. As you both try any apps and data mine the reviews, note any do's and don'ts on a separate list, based off complaints and your own evaluation.

5. Compile a final feature list for your app so that your app stands out as unique.

6. Pare your feature list down to its essential functionality by removing unnecessary features.

7. *Prepare* to iterate on core features as other apps come out that you can evaluate for possible similarities/conflicts, and as you inevitably find new features that must be added based on the use of your own app.

In Chapter 4, you learn how to best prepare for developing the detailed functionality and iterating on your feature set by taking into account what customers expect. In other words, what you will have now is a great concept, and what you need when you start development is a good, *fairly* detailed design. After the next chapter, you'll be best prepared for starting your design document.

4

Knowing Your Customer

WHAT'S IN THIS CHAPTER?

➤ Developing an understanding of the root of App Store metrics

➤ Learning how traditional gaming genres have changed because of development on i-devices

➤ Understanding the different meanings of casual gaming

➤ Understanding why consistency in visual style is the key to nailing your presentation

➤ Learning what your customers will find and expect within all App Store categories

Many useful App Store statistics were discussed in Chapter 3, but examining that data comprises only one piece of the puzzle (albeit a large one). The other factor to be considered is why those stats exist, or determining the root of the problem.

Why, for example, are roughly 40 percent of all apps free? Why does the category distribution show productivity apps being half as popular from a development stand-point as that of a utility app? A simple answer to these questions is that the market dictates it. Though mostly true, that answer doesn't provide much insight into how you might be able to leverage this information to better position your app.

The real insight comes when you know what types of customers purchase which types of apps, and what their expectations are in your particular niche. For example, iPad customers are *generally* looking for something different than iPhone customers, who in turn are different from iPod Touch customers. Much of the same functional-ity exists for each of these devices, but your app must be targeted to specific cus-tomer needs in order to be more successful.

Knowing the expectations of your customer is, therefore, the topic of this chapter. Once you know what these are, it's only a matter of work and polish to figure out how to then exceed them to end up with at least one unique upsell point to your app so that it can't help but be noticed.

UNDERSTANDING APP STORE DEMOGRAPHICS

To understand what customers seek out in an app, let's look at some of the statistics from Chapter 3 in more detail, and how understanding the end-user expectations behind them may help in your niche.

Firstly, *more* than one out of three apps are free, and free plus 99-cent apps equate to roughly two-thirds of all apps, as shown in Figure 4-1. So, out of roughly 500,000 active apps, about 185,000 of them are free (according to 148apps.biz), and about 315,000 are free or just 99 cents. That's huge. More than likely, customers can find what they want in some form for free, or for minimal expense, even if it is just a lite version.

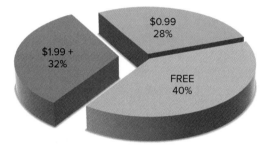

FIGURE 4-1: Two of every three apps are either free or just 99 cents

The expectation in a market like this is that unless your app has some standout features and functionality — usually accompanied by glowing user/critical reviews — it likely won't be able to compete at a higher premium level. Customers in this market are just used to getting more for less.

Secondly, let's look at price. In Chapter 3, you learned that the average price of apps (not including games) is roughly $2.63, and the overall average price is roughly $2.39. Then you have games, with a rough average price of just $1.05. This tells you without a doubt that customers have plenty of choices, and they are not willing to spend more on games without good reason, but are willing to justify shelling out more than twice that amount for other types of apps.

Let's not forget that apps for the iPad (which have an average selling price of roughly $4.19 compared with that of $1.57 for the iPhone) demand a much higher price point for its apps, and, because of the device's market, is able to do so. Part of this is the smaller market size, higher price point, and, thus, "exclusivity" that the iPad affords. It's the same reason Starbucks is able to charge more for a standard cup of its coffee than the local Tim Hortons (a Northeastern U.S. and Canadian coffee chain with great coffee for the price). The other part is why customers are buying iPads in the first place — for its combination of portability, plus a large vibrant screen, usability, and overall better functionality because of the larger touch screen.

Thirdly, looking at category popularity, there are roughly four distinct sections, laid out as shown in Figure 4-2. These statistics are utilizing the latest figures (as of this writing) from 148apps.biz. To be honest, it wasn't planned this way, but it just happens to be as easy as 1, 2, 3, and 4.

Ten percent of active apps (in the order of greatest to least) fall in the categories of Photography, Navigation, Finance, Social Networking, and Medical. Twenty percent fall in Music, Reference, Business, Sports, News, Productivity, and Healthcare & Fitness. Thirty percent fall in the four categories of Education, Lifestyle, Utilities, and Travel. And nearly 40 percent fall under the big three — Games, Books, and Entertainment. The Weather category has less than 0.5 percent of active apps, and was not listed because of it possibly seeming more relevant than intended. (Perhaps opportunities exist in that niche though!)

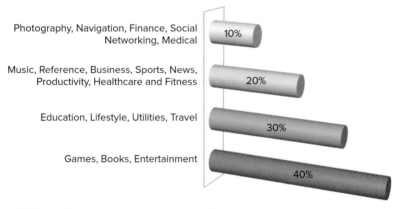

FIGURE 4-2: Category representation of total apps

All things being equal (and they're not), if you assume that the market dictates the current App Store atmosphere, then you can assume, in general, that category saturation is roughly equivalent to customer demand within any particular category. In other words, people prefer using their i-device apps for *leisure* (Games, Books, Entertainment) more often, as a rule, than for *productivity*.

Another way of looking at it might be that, for certain types of apps, people may have one or two loaded to suit their needs (Productivity — say, a list-maker app), and for others, look for a broad range (Games). Both ways are feasible and important.

Because the Games category takes up the largest percentage of active apps, if you happen to be creating one, it will be important to have an overview of what the customer expects from certain genres, hybrids, and of the overall experience found in any current game app.

Casual and Traditional Gaming Pillars

For the most part, games have finally made the segué from "geeky" and suitable only to a mostly male demographic to being an acceptable pastime for all types of people. This is thanks in part to a casual movement brought on mostly by catering to the masses for business reasons. More buyers equals more money. Nintendo has almost always relied on this formula with its main franchises and console philosophy, and almost all the most popular i-device apps as well as games in general ("The Sims," "Tetris") can be defined as "casual." Though "casual" has many definitions, it generally means "designed to appeal to as many people as possible."

If Nintendo were to open up a store back in the old days of gaming, (say the 1980s and 1990s), the number of categories would have been fewer than in today's App Store, hybrids would be rare ("Actraiser" — a unique hybrid of action and sim-like farming is still a cult favorite), and the term *casual* wouldn't really exist in the same way it does today. What Apple, the App Store, and iPhone have done is take casual gaming as defined here, and infused all traditional game categories with their KISS (keep it simple, stupid) design philosophy, as well as force new categories into existence that were never quite feasible before.

Let's look at considerations when choosing a category for your game, because traditional game categories have been modified somewhat by the nature of the App Store, today's newer definition of "casual," and the technology behind the devices themselves.

The App Store defines 19 common game categories, but with new ways of interacting (because of touch control, accelerometer, and gyroscope), many new genres and hybrids have actually been created than are shown, so it can be difficult to figure out where to place yours. For example, the popular game "Flight Control" is now considered a "line draw" game (draw a path using your finger), but there's no category for that, so they placed it in the Strategy subcategory. It does technically fit there, yet games in the Strategy subcategory have traditionally been more "hard-core."

This is the result of the effect of "casual" on traditional game categories — that how you used to perceive them no longer applies, because users have come to expect that all games within a category will be designed with care and the end user in mind.

HARD-CORE VERSUS CASUAL

If a casual game as defined here means to appeal to as broad a range of people as possible, what does "hard-core" mean? In gaming, it has traditionally meant a game that is highly targeted to gamers looking for a specific type of experience without sacrificing complexity (sometimes in controls or interface) or depth in gameplay. In other words, games that are involved enough to require players spending some time getting used to the system—games with a steeper learning curve—can typically be considered more hard-core. World War II strategy games, for example, are most definitely hard-core, but like anything, there's a range of "hard-core-ness" to be found.

That said, many gamers today now consider themselves "hard-core," and the term in that sense means a gamer that simply spends a lot of time with games, rather than the type of games they play. There are hard-core *games* and there are hardcore *gamers*. Both are used somewhat differently.

Likewise, a casual gamer is one whose game sessions tend to be sporadic and smaller than that of a hard-core gamer, who can spend hours at a time in front of the game.

With each app you submit, you will be able to choose from two categories — a *primary* (required) and *secondary* (optional). Many apps will be able to fit into several categories, so it's important to choose wisely, and not necessarily go with the most obvious choice.

For example, the very popular casual-friendly strategy board game "Settlers of Catan" that translated very well to the Xbox Live Arcade market and now is in the App Store (under the name "Catan," as shown in Figure 4-3) could have been chosen for Board games, Dice games (it uses two dice), Family games (this is how it is often seen in the board game community), and, of course, Strategy. As it happens, they chose Board and Strategy. As long as it is relevant to the category, it can be approved.

It is useful to note that the Games category is unique in that, because there are subcategories, you are actually featured in the App Store in at least three places: Games, primary category 1, and secondary category 2.

FIGURE 4-3: "Catan" has four viable categories, which shows that you should choose wisely when selecting your two submission categories

Looking at the game "Tetris" shown in Figure 4-4, it was placed in the more popular Action game subcategory — likely so that more people would be aware of it, because it's a very well-known brand — as well as the obvious Puzzle subcategory. It probably could have fit in the Arcade, Strategy, or Family game subcategories as well. If you were making a similar app, however, it probably wouldn't be recommended to place it in the Action subcategory, because a gamer looking for that type of experience likely wouldn't go there. But in the case of "Tetris," it worked.

A good example to illustrate this is the current free (with premium content) "puzzle" title that reached as high as Number 1 in the Arcade subcategory and Number 2 in the Puzzle subcategory. Its name is "Shape Shift" (shown in Figure 4-5), a self-described puzzle title with a twist on classic puzzle gameplay. Would this title have done well in the Action subcategory? Traditionally, that subcategory would not be where you might look for a title like this, though it still may have a chance to get approved based on its twitch gameplay. Unless you have a good reason not to do so, consider your categories carefully.

FIGURE 4-4: "Tetris" has at least five viable categories, but was placed differently than you might expect

Now that you're aware of potential considerations when choosing a game category, let's move on to what makes casual games on the iPhone unique.

iPhone Casual versus Traditional Casual

On the whole, app developers are now keen to the fact that, regardless of genre or complexity, in order to be most successful, their apps must be designed with the end user in mind. Traditional hard-core apps that are big in complexity and a beast to use would not have a market in the App Store. And, just because an app is made for a niche of sophisticated users, that doesn't mean that the experience must be anything but intuitive.

Traditionally, few games of yore would be classified as still casual in today's market. "Tetris" would be one, but "Super Mario Bros." would not be because of its rather tough gameplay (for the average gamer) and confusing nature.

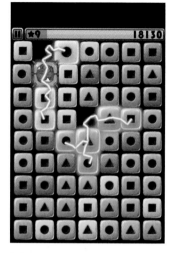

FIGURE 4-5: "Shape Shift," a top ranking free title with paid content, was placed in categories you might expect

"The Sims" (the biggest selling retail game of all time to this point) was virtually the definition of casual ten years ago, and continues to sell well in its third incarnation in the App Store. It's perhaps just a bit complex to maintain as strong a presence as it did on the PC, featuring quite a bit of micromanaging. A current successful spin-off trend is taking the customization features in "The Sims," and then creating an easier game out of it, tying it in with some monetization features like the capability to buy in-game currency to excel faster. One good example of this is "Smurfs' Village" for iPhone/iPad (Figure 4-6).

The invention of the iPhone has had a giant effect on all game genres in that it has brought (and continues to bring) all traditional gaming genres to a more casual level than ever before.

FIGURE 4-6: "Smurfs' Village" is a casual customization game that lets you create a world, share it, and play with very little stress

MEETING YOUR CUSTOMER'S EXPECTATIONS

Let's now take a higher-level view at what customers will expect to find in App Store categories, examples within each, as well as — in general — how feasible they are for the i-device with regard to both control features and "casualness."

The goal is to give you insight into current App Store expectations for each category, as well as ideas for what categories you might want to enter into with your new apps.

Visual and Graphical Expectations

Though visual styles were explored in Chapter 3 from an artistic standpoint, what in general do customers expect from the current App Store marketplace, in any category?

Even from the early days in the App Store, there have been some true stunners in terms of graphics and fluidity. Because these devices fully support three-dimensional (3D) capabilities and now all have relatively high-resolution graphics even on iPod touch (twice the pixels as before with 960×640 compared to 480×320 in the horizontal position), most all apps should be able to support this higher resolution, or what they dub "retina display" for clearer text and graphics. Apps may not only look inferior, but you cannot obviously list high-resolution as a selling point. In fact, many apps have already forgone support for legacy devices in favor of retina-only and iPad resolutions or greater.

As far as style goes, most anything is fair game and often found in the App Store, again with the caveat that presentation supports functionality or gameplay. (See the examples laid out in Chapter 3.)

What's not acceptable to customers is inconsistency. Don't make an app with a mix of styles or quality — keep it consistent. If you have a killer CGI intro but in-game graphics that look like an old Atari 2600 game, unless there's a great reason for it, don't do it.

In the same vein, don't make your character graphics and backgrounds stand out (especially with rough non-aliased edges), but at the same time have terrible animation. It's a disconnect that continues to resonate throughout the gaming industry, and is widely noted when it happens. Some big game companies get nailed for this very thing consistently and it hurts sales because of poor reviews.

With button and interface element styles, if you're using iPhone standard GUI elements, use them consistently in the same functional places, and also use your custom buttons and icons in other consistent places. This is common sense, but also gets missed.

Ensure that your app has consistent visual styles (whether consistently bad or good), and you'll have a better shot at being accepted with your audience.

It is recommended that you thoroughly analyze your competition in this regard so that you can exceed them, or differentiate accordingly.

Gameplay and Feature Set Expectations

To best illustrate gameplay and feature expectations, it will be beneficial to run down each App Store category and what can be found in the most popular apps, along with a few possible feature ideas for how you might enter that particular category when applicable. The goal is for this examination to be a brief, but useful, repository, feature comparison, and possible brainstorm tool for your current and future apps.

Categories are first presented in alphabetical order, followed by its current (as of this writing) percent of active apps in the App Store according to `148apps.biz`.

Books (About 13 Percent)

The top three and most of the top 20 paid apps currently are children's books, read by a professional narrator and with top-notch illustrated graphics, usually with a license (which often have style-guide graphics you can borrow or imitate) and no additional paid features. They come full out-of-the-box, and sometimes even include simple games like puzzles featuring the characters, as shown in Figure 4-7.

Tractor-tipping and driving backward are Mater's specialties, and the tow yard is his pride and joy.

FIGURE 4-7: *Lightning Was Here: My Puzzle Book* is more than just a book; it also has game activities

For free apps, a number of book-enhancement apps such as iBooks, Kindle, and Audible are sitting at the top. Other types of apps here are book "plazas," which are simply navigation hubs (featuring specific catalogs for example) for books you can buy through them.

The following are current popular features/functionality for this category:

➤ Books:

  ➤ Professional narration

  ➤ Finger-flip to turn page

  ➤ Other bonus activities

  ➤ Several modes (such as read-along manual, or auto-turn)

  ➤ Record voice or child's voice while reading

  ➤ Collectibles while reading

  ➤ Clickable fun events while reading

  ➤ Word games

  ➤ Blow into microphone to cause events

➤ Book Apps:

  ➤ Paid approach can be a repository for other books you can purchase from the vendor

  ➤ Wireless transfer

  ➤ Access to huge book collections

➤ Sample before you buy

➤ Deep search features

➤ Free book access

➤ Social network "what friends are reading" features via Facebook and Twitter

➤ Standard chapter navigation, bookmarking

➤ Book organizing

➤ Font and reading styles

➤ PDF support

➤ Print using AirPrint

The following are potential current or future ideas:

➤ Achievements

➤ Tie-in with school/possible curriculum

➤ Timers

Business (About 4 Percent)

Because this category contains hundreds of different types of apps, rather than providing a rundown of features, here are some common functions of Business apps:

➤ Scanners using a camera

➤ Standard document type open/edit (Word, Excel, PowerPoint, and so on)

➤ Scheduling and tie-in with web-scheduling accounts

➤ Contact lists/address books

➤ Recorders and dictation

➤ Job search apps

➤ Credit card terminals

➤ Mail apps

➤ Real estate searches

➤ Package delivery

➤ Task creators

➤ Calculators and converters

➤ Inventory apps

Education (About 9 Percent)

Again, app diversity is high in this category, so what follows is a list of common functions of Education apps. Early-education (such as pre-school) apps are prevalent throughout the top several hundred of this category.

The following are current popular apps/functionality for this category:

➤ Star charts/astronomy

➤ Pre-school activities:

- ➤ Math
- ➤ Sing-along
- ➤ Music
- ➤ Alphabet
- ➤ Art
- ➤ Cognitive puzzles
- ➤ Language/foreign language basics
- ➤ Foreign language lessons
- ➤ Art apps
- ➤ Brainteaser apps
- ➤ Vocabulary
- ➤ Most school/college subjects: anatomy, art, geography, math, chemistry
- ➤ Flashcard support for subjects

Entertainment (About 11 Percent)

Entertainment is like a catchall. It has games, utilities, and stuff you might find in Business. A large percentage of these apps (perhaps other than games or movie/TV viewing apps) could be considered one-off throwaways — that is, play them and forget them.

The following are current popular apps/functionality for this category:

- ➤ Casual games, or games requiring a small play session ("Pocket God," "Moron Test")
- ➤ Paint apps
- ➤ Novelty/gag apps (talking animals, fortunetelling)
- ➤ Photo special effects (aging, zombie, and so on)
- ➤ Movie/TV viewing apps (Netflix, Hulu, HBO)
- ➤ Fashion dress-up
- ➤ Customization apps ("Car Builder," "Gun Builder")
- ➤ Vision apps (night vision, flashlight)

Finance (About 2 Percent)

In this category, most apps congregate around the same general purpose — tracking personal finances, without a lot of leakage from other categories (as in the case of Entertainment). As shown in Figure 4-8, many of these apps feature excellent chart/graphing capabilities, so if you're planning something similar, that would

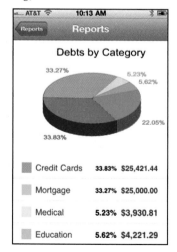

FIGURE 4-8: "Debt Free," like many finance apps, makes heavy use of charts and other visual aids

be a standard feature to include (not really an upsell point). The more visual the application is, the better.

The following are current popular apps/functionality for this category:

➤ Budget tracking

➤ Paying off debt

➤ Mobile banking (direct from banks and other lenders)

➤ Web-app finance tie-ins (Mint, Yahoo, and so on)

➤ Tracking bills

➤ Tracking expenses

➤ Portfolio/investment organizers and trackers

➤ Finance calculators (loans, tips, and so on)

➤ Credit card accepters

The following are potential current or future ideas:

➤ Dynamic charts/what-if scenarios

➤ New ways to visualize data in a more friendly manner, and utilizing iPhone gesture capabilities on these visualizations

Games (About 16 Percent)

For a game to succeed in the App Store, the gameplay must be distilled into something that is above all user-friendly. It must also be capable of smaller play sessions, even if it also features the capability for extended sessions, similar to what you might find in a role-playing or adventure game. These are mobile devices after all, and players are typically looking for something that can provide a quick fix, regardless of the app.

If you can infuse humor into your game, you have a greater chance at succeeding with the casual market. It doesn't have to be slapstick humor, but often entertainment, fun, and humor go together. Take your gameplay, but not your game, very seriously.

The following are current popular features/functionality for the overall Games category:

➤ Monetization and micro-transactions via paid upgrades on a "free" app

➤ Utilization of iPhone controls such as touch/gestures, tilt/accelerometer, and gyroscope

➤ Social integration with such things as Facebook connect for achievements, Twitter, competing with friends, sharing with friends/web, and rankings (local, global)

➤ Customization

➤ Use of 3D worlds even in traditional two-dimensional (2D) games

➤ Integration with third-party social apps like Game Center and OpenFeint to join friends and socialize achievements

Figure 4-9 shows an enlightening view of a market trend.

Let's now contrast Figure 4-9 with the top paid apps, as shown in Figure 4-10.

FIGURE 4-9: In this representation of the top 12 grossing apps, the dollar sign indicates it has "in-app purchases"

Courtesy `Appannie.com`

FIGURE 4-10: This representation of the top 12 paid apps shows an interesting turnaround when compared to Figure 4-9

Courtesy `Appannie.com`

What this says is that the true long-term money-makers are the apps trending in a grouping of in-app purchases and continuing revenue, rather than one-offs. You can have a game that's super popular, but it won't generally last as a top-grossing app ("Angry Birds" has in-app purchases) unless it has a continuing revenue stream. Just look at the massively popular multiplayer online computer games and the bandwagon that has created.

The foreseeable trend is going the way of Asia, even though it's taken Westerners a bit longer to reach it. "Free-to-play" (FTP) with micro transactions and in-game purchases, along with integrated social gameplay for most all games, is the next big wave, and it is starting to show up now.

For the Game category, let's delve a bit deeper into its multiple subcategories.

Action Games

Action games gauge a large part of performance on the dexterity of the player. As such, heavy use of realistic physics (3D where feasible) and iPhone controls (flicking, swiping, and so on) are big elements for action games.

The following are current popular features/functionality for this subcategory:

➤ Implementation of a physics engine (such as found in "Angry Birds" and "Pocket God").

➤ Heavy use of iPhone touch controls, including gesturing, flinging, tilting, and so on, as shown in Figure 4-11.

➤ Graphics tend to be pushed harder in the Action game subcategory because your game must either be uniquely styled visually with excellent responsive gameplay (such as "Doodle Jump"), or, if it is serious such as a first-person-shooter game, it must have better-than-average quality graphics to stand out.

Figure 4-12 shows a shooter released in 2011. Games in this subcategory also use more 3D levels for immersive gameplay.

➤ Competitive multiplayer (such as "Archetype," "Battlefield: Bad Company 2," and "Ultimate Mortal Kombat 3").

➤ Racing.

➤ Distance games (that is, games in which you try to get as far as you can).

FIGURE 4-11: "Fruit Ninja," ranked as a top app, makes good use of iPhone's gestures

FIGURE 4-12: "N.O.V.A . 2," a first-person-shooter, has first-rate graphics for today's i-device market

Adventure Games

Many Adventure games can be similar to Action games, but typically involve more of a story and character arc progression. A little less emphasis is placed on twitch-style dexterity gameplay, and using powers of the characters is a common theme.

There is also an extreme amount of cross-category infusion into the Adventure category, which is very similar to the Entertainment catchall. Games like "Fashion Story" (building up a boutique) and "Tap Zoo" (building a zoo) are more "sim-ish" than Adventure, and games such as "Eternal Legacy" are more suitable to RPG (role-playing game), traditionally speaking. But that's what you get when you are able to choose two categories.

Taking a deeper look at this subcategory, very few top games would fit into the traditional Adventure mold, and that is why other category cross-over is so prevalent here. It is almost like the subcategory isn't needed, and is very likely used as a secondary category for many games.

The following are current popular features/functionality for this subcategory:

➤ 3D action/adventure games with more of a story

➤ "Sim-like" games (with customization, or building worlds)

➤ Light action

➤ Arcade-like games with level progression

Arcade Games

Players coming here will typically expect light action, short gameplay sessions, level progression, or repeatable content where you try to better your score. Like Adventure games, a lot of cross-category games find their way here, though usually with the "action" or dexterity element in some form.

The following are current popular features/functionality for this subcategory:

➤ Fighting

➤ Light physics games (such as "Angry Birds")

➤ Distance games

➤ Sports/extreme

➤ Racing

➤ Fishing

Board Games

This subcategory features some of the most purely traditional games in electronic and iPhone format of any category. Looking at all the top games, there is very little cross-category trickle here, except for possibly Puzzle/Word games, which do show up at the top.

Another interesting fact is that there are very little in-app purchases in this subcategory, even at the top (see Figure 4-13). Perhaps that is a trend worth looking into.

	Paid		Free		Grossing	
1	Words With Friends	=	Words With Friends Free	=	Words With Friends	=
2	THE GAME OF LIFE Classic Edition	=	SCRABBLE Free	=	THE GAME OF LIFE Classic Edition	=
3	MONOPOLY	=	Sea Battles Lite	(new)	SCRABBLE	=
4	UNO™	=	Unblock Me FREE	▼1	MONOPOLY	=
5	RISK	=	Bubble Shooter Free	▼1	Carcassonne	=
6	SCRABBLE	=	$ Mr Giggle Lite	▼1	UNO™	=
7	The Heist	=	UNO™-FREE	▼1	RISK	=
8	$ Doodle God™	=	Tic Tac Toe Free	▼1	Phase 10	▲1
9	MONOPOLY Here & Now: The World Edition	▲1	ToobTrix Free	▲1	The Heist	▼1
10	BATTLESHIP	▼1	Snake Defense Free	▲11	$ Doodle God™	=

FIGURE 4-13: Looking at AppAnnie.com's ranking for any category is a good way to see which apps have in-app purchases (the dollar symbol)

The following are current popular features/functionality for this subcategory:

➤ Multiplayer competition

➤ Social integration

➤ Traditional board games

The following are potential current or future ideas:

➤ Board games with in-app purchases, including buy scenarios/boards/spaces

➤ Customizable board game bits

➤ Upgradable (rather than static) spaces

Card Games

This is another subcategory that has little cross-category infusion, except from Casino games, which is unsurprising, considering the subcategory name is specific to cards. It is interesting that most of the top-grossing apps (contrary to those in the Board game subcategory) do, in fact, include in-app purchases. Social competitive games like "Zynga Poker," "Texas Poker," and "Card Ace: Casino" have appeared at the top.

The following are current popular features/functionality for this subcategory:

➤ Social competitive integration.

➤ Game Center and OpenFeint plugins.

➤ High presentation value because you're dealing with cards. The big emphasis is on backgrounds, logos, and buttons.

➤ Less use of standard iPhone GUI graphics warranted here, because it's too easy to do this type of game using them.

Casino Games

Anything you can find in a Casino game (cards, slots, video slots, horse racing, and betting) can be found here. As shown in Figure 4-14, there is a lot of social integration, because playing with real people is way more fun than against artificial intelligence (AI). Top-grossing apps tend to have in-app purchases, whereas top paid apps do not.

FIGURE 4-14: "Texas Poker" is a top-ranked casino game where you play against others, using real pics

The following are current popular features/functionality for this subcategory:

➤ Social competitive integration

➤ In-game chat with other players

➤ Games simulate the casino experience

➤ A prevalence of in-app purchases (such as chips to play)

The following are potential current or future ideas:

➤ In-app purchases for customizing avatars.

➤ With not a lot of video slots near the top at this time, opportunities for capitalizing on this, especially since Casinos have mostly gone to these.

Dice Games

This subcategory looks much like the Board game subcategory with a lot of cross-over from that subcategory, as well as some with Casino (especially the game of craps). Not a lot of games with in-app purchases make up the top-grossing or paid apps here, also similar to Board games.

The following are current popular features/functionality for this subcategory:

➤ A lot of games with sub-par graphics here except for games with big budgets (such as top-ranking "Yahtzee Adventures" from Electronic Arts)

➤ Play with friends

➤ Local multiplayer, passing of the device

➤ Learning casino craps

➤ Poker dice

➤ Integration with third-party social solutions such as Game Center and OpenFeint

The following are potential current or future ideas:

➤ There are not a lot of unique newer games at the top of this subcategory, but rather some very well-known dice games. There is some room to capitalize on current popular dice game trends that aren't as familiar to breathe life into the subcategory.

➤ Borrow/license a current popular board game with dice and you could put it in this subcategory and have a chance at success.

Educational Games

This is a big subcategory, with a lot of toddler, pre-school, and grade school games dominating the ranks. The exceptions tend to be casual mental fitness games such as "Brain Trainer" by Luminosity, one of the few in-app purchase games that has seen time at the top (and which happens to be subscription-based). There is also some overlap with the Entertainment category, with quizzes, psychological evaluations, and casual-based food-maker games.

The following are current popular features/functionality for this subcategory:

➤ Enhance mental fitness

➤ Toddler's first learning games

➤ Pre-school, grade school

➤ Quizzes

➤ Puzzles

➤ Aquarium simulations

➤ Problem-solving, adventure

The following are potential current or future ideas:

➤ Graphics tend to be, with a few exceptions (that is, specifically for development houses with higher budgets), not as high quality as with some other categories. There is room for creating high-quality premium graphic quizzes/puzzles, perhaps subscription-based for younger players.

➤ You can combine the app with educational progress tracking, perhaps web-based.

➤ You can offer earning achievements to customize your online persona.

Family Games

This is another catchall subcategory with significant overlap from "sim-like" world-building games, game-show-type games, recreational games brought to digital format (such as table tennis, skee ball, and so on), and other customization games. Because of the prevalence of customization games, in-app purchases tend to be used often in this subcategory.

The following are current popular features/functionality for this subcategory:

➤ Invite friends to see creations

➤ In-app alternate currency that you purchase with real money to progress further (for example, "Smurfs' Village")

➤ In-app purchases to unlock more customization

Kids Games

Though the Kids subcategory shares some overlap with Educational, the kids games here tend to be more customization and light action/adventure games. These aren't meant just for toddlers and pre-schoolers, but the range appears to dip into the teenage range. Girl-targeted games are also prevalent here, such as "Pretty Pet Salon" (shown in Figure 4-15), a top-grossing, adult-style business simulation game themed down to appeal mostly to girls.

The following are current popular features/functionality for this subcategory:

➤ Achievements

➤ Customization

➤ Business running, adult lifestyle role-play

➤ Fashion

➤ Play with friends

FIGURE 4-15: "Pretty Pet Salon," a top app that targets the underutilized girls market

Music Games

The top paid and grossing apps in this category all have in-app purchases. There is some overlap with simulation/customization/fashion games here.

The following are current popular features/functionality for this subcategory:

➤ Mixing

➤ Rhythm (a la "Guitar Hero/Rock Band")

➤ Rock star trivia

➤ "Tap Rhythm to Dance" (avatar dancing)

➤ Name that tune

➤ In-app purchases for music, customization add-ons

➤ Fashion/style customization (somewhat surprisingly)

Puzzle Games

This is a fairly focused, but catchall, subcategory, bringing in suitable games from Word, Arcade, Adventure, Educational, Strategy, and Family games. The reason it's focused is that most short-session "arcade-y" type games could be considered puzzles. Many unique games in this subcategory are in the top rankings, and more cropping up all the time, unlike, for example, in the Card game subcategory. It appears this category has a higher acceptance rate for new styles of play.

The following are current popular features/functionality for this subcategory:

➤ Brainteasers

➤ Third-party social plug-ins, like Game Center and OpenFeint

➤ Stat tracking for high scores

➤ Unique applications for iPhone controls like tilt, swipe, and so on, within puzzles

➤ Word games

➤ Short level design

➤ Unique gameplay styles acceptable and preferred

➤ Physics heavily utilized (such as with "Angry Birds" and "Cut the Rope")

Racing Games

Racing games are somewhat tricky to make on the iPhone. They require precision controls first of all, as well as a great 3D engine and amazing art, because your big-budget competition will be stiff. Aside from this, they are mostly menu-driven affairs — which, to be honest, has always been sad. For example, where are the "SSX 3" (an extreme skiing game with innovative navigation) type games in which (when applied to racing) you step into your garage, fire up your engine, and seamlessly drive away to the next street race somewhere nearby? There's an opportunity here, even if it had to be scaled down to top-down view or doodles.

The following are current popular features/functionality for this subcategory:

➤ Physics

➤ Use of tilt, gyroscope, and accelerometer

➤ Creative race concepts (lawn mowing, falling through a tower, truck jumping, plane racing, and so on)

➤ 3D level design prevalent

➤ Sense of speed

➤ Unique vehicles and objects

➤ Different viewpoints utilized

Role Playing Games

If games are going to get you some in-app purchases, it's in this subcategory (see Figure 4-16) and in Simulation. The longer you play, the greater investment and commitment you have, so naturally the more chance you'll give a little as well. Games in this subcategory have some of the longest play session times. You'll find a lot of overlap from sim-like games here, and they can include the games with the most depth and complexity of all games (see Figure 4-17), requiring the steepest learning curve. As noted previously, this is tempered somewhat by the nature of most developers to take into account the i-device platform and "casual" them up.

	Paid		Free		Grossing	
1	Order & Chaos© Online	-	Top Girl	-	Top Girl	-
2	Baseball Superstars® II Pro	-	Crouching Panda Hidden Swine	▲ 183	Tap Pet Hotel	-
3	Eternal Legacy	-	Crime Inc. HD	▼ 1	Zombie Farm	-
4	Baseball Superstars® 2011 Pro	-	Tap Pet Hotel	-	Kingdoms at War	▲ 2
5	ZENONIA® 3	-	City Friends	▼ 2	iMobsters	▼ 1
6	Cartoon Wars-Gunner	-	Panda's Revenge	▼ 1	World War™	▼ 1
7	Cartoon Wars	▲ 1	Zombie Farm	▼ 1	Baseball Superstars® II Pro	-
8	Fantastic Knight	▼ 1	Baseball Superstars® 2011	▼ 1	Haypi kingdom	-
9	World Explorer - Made for MineCraft	-	Sushi Chain Life	▲ 6	Order & Chaos© Online	-
10	Drag Racer : Perfect Run	▲ 1	Racing Live™	-	City Friends	-

FIGURE 4-16: In-app purchases dominate the Role Playing subcategory at the top

The following are current popular features/functionality for this subcategory:

➤ Use of tutorials

➤ In-app purchase of alternate currency using real money for upgrades

➤ Prevalent alternate controls for movement, like on-screen joysticks

➤ Character progression

➤ Customization (in-game character, weapon, avatar)

➤ Combat heavy

➤ Simulation world building

Simulation Games

As shown in Figure 4-18, a look at the top 20 apps provides an insightful glimpse into how apps in this subcategory are making a lot of money. Again, it's through in-app purchases. The paid classification once again features significantly fewer in-app purchase games, and it's like that through the top 300 in this category. The trend is if you create a paid app, customers find it more difficult to justify the additional purchase of in-app merchandise and upgrades. There are a few exceptions, but as a business model, it is more risky.

As a subcategory, this is also one that does not see a lot of influx from other categories, save perhaps Sports and Role Playing, and instead trickles into secondary subcategories such as Strategy. Interestingly enough, "Smurfs' Village" opted to not enter this category, and it is a classic simulation world-building game.

The following are current popular features/functionality for this subcategory:

➤ World-building customization

➤ In-app purchases extremely prevalent for "free" games

➤ Full-feature sports game simulations

➤ Business-owning sims

➤ Social integration with Facebook friends, Game Center

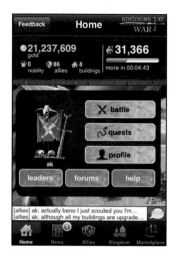

FIGURE 4-17: "Kingdoms at War" is a top-ranked and top-grossing app that features both depth of play and many in-app purchase options

FIGURE 4-18: The Simulation subcategory is completely dominated by apps with in-app purchases

Sports Games

There is some overlap with Racing and Arcade here, because those have sports or loosely recreational themes. Most games, however, are thematic to sports, from full-featured sims ("Tiger Woods PGA Tour" and "FIFA") to casual games ("Flick Golf Extreme").

The following are current popular features/functionality for this subcategory:

➤ Hard-core sports sims, as well as very casual short-session games

➤ In-game chat

➤ Statistics

➤ Leaderboards

➤ Regular use of iPhone controls and gestures

➤ Physics engine use

There is definitely room in this category for sports that have not been thought of yet, be it extreme or casual fun, and even humorous sports ("Beer Pong" comes to mind)

Strategy Games

The Strategy genre has traditionally been slightly more hard-core for PC and consoles, but not so in the App Store. Dominating the charts in this category are casual-friendly games such as "Plants vs. Zombies," tower-defense type games ("Fieldrunners" was a Number 1 game at one time), and simulation games.

The following are current popular features/functionality for this subcategory:

➤ Simulation/world building/business sim

➤ Tower-defense themed

➤ In-game chat

➤ Some puzzle games

➤ Chess

➤ Social integration, third-party apps such as Game Center and OpenFeint

Trivia Games

This is another subcategory with more focused games and little influx from other categories. Instead, based on the theme, it is more likely categories here trickle into appropriate subcategories such as Sports (for sports quizzes) or Family (for game show-type quizzes).

The following are current popular features/functionality for this subcategory:

➤ Many popular game shows placed here ("Price is Right," "Deal or No Deal," "Jeopardy," "Wheel of Fortune," and so on)

➤ A tendency to have rather below-average graphics, even in the top apps, when a game is not licensed

➤ In-app purchases equating to access to more content/trivia

➤ Local multiplayer, pass the device

➤ Play against friends and compete online

➤ Career modes

➤ High scores/leaderboards

➤ Third-party social integration with Game Center and OpenFeint

➤ No repeat questions

➤ Mental fitness games

Word Games

There is some crossover here from the Family and Board Game subcategories, but again, most apps you find here are tightly focused. Apps that tend to do best are ones in which you play with friends or online directly with others.

The following are current popular features/functionality for this subcategory:

➤ Multiple simultaneous games

➤ Easy/instant matching with opponents

➤ Push notifications when it's your turn

➤ In-game chat

➤ Shake features to scramble

➤ Progress tracking

➤ Multiple word games in one

➤ Social integration

➤ Word search, crossword, anagram

➤ Many unique word games here, open to new invention

Healthcare and Fitness (About 2 Percent)

Top apps in this category include unique ways to visualize your fitness, with neat charts and graphs, as well as stylized buttons. When you get past a certain amount of features, there doesn't seem to be a lot of variety in this category, so the apps fighting at the top tend to be graphically superior. There also tends to be an equal amount of specifically targeted apps (such as for calorie counting), as well as full-featured regimen apps that might include built-in calorie counting.

The following are current popular features/functionality for this category:

➤ Weight loss apps/trackers/goal setting

➤ Exercise apps

➤ Integration with maps/GPS

➤ Calorie counters

➤ Nutrition databases

➤ Workout regimes (such as running, weight training, stretching, and abs/specific body targets)

➤ Charting progress/workout history

➤ Healthy recipe indexes

➤ Medical symptoms

➤ In-app video demonstrations

Lifestyle (About 8 Percent)

This is a catchall category that generally applies to everything you can do around your house, or locally in your area — cooking/ordering food, shopping, driving, searching the Internet, journaling, and so on. It's also a fairly popular category, at 8 percent of the total apps. Customers coming here are expecting tips and small helper apps on getting everyday things done, as well as shopping helpers.

The following are current popular features/functionality for this category:

➤ Shopping

➤ Coupon finders

➤ Cooking/recipes

➤ Popular menus

➤ Store catalogues

➤ Daily journals

➤ Wallpapers for iPhone

➤ Local driving-destination finders

Medical (About 2 Percent)

In-app purchases are popular here for the top-ranked, top-grossing apps, as well as fairly expensive and mostly subscription-based or module-based. Most apps in this category do not have in-app purchases.

The following are current popular features/functionality for this category:

➤ Subscription-based access to updated medical resources

➤ Refilling prescriptions/prescription trackers

➤ Drug reference guides

➤ Pill identification

➤ Herbal and alternative therapy

➤ Sound/sleep enhancers

➤ Sex facts/tips

➤ Medical quizzes for students/nurses

➤ Educational guides to anatomy and other body systems (for example with 3D models and rotation)

➤ Symptom guides

➤ Specific disease guides and information

Music (About 4 Percent)

Streaming and radio apps dominate the top of the charts, as do a few mixing and DJ apps. In-app purchases are typically add-on packs such as new songs, making the streaming/radio app ad-free, and sometimes pro musician add-ons for upward of $99.

The following are current popular features/functionality for this category:

➤ Streaming music apps (Pandora, Rhapsody)

➤ Radio apps (AM/FM)

➤ Mixing/DJ

➤ Musician tools ("Guitar Tabs Pro," "Virtuoso Piano")

➤ Drums

➤ Single instrument simulations ("Ocarina," "PocketGuitar")

➤ Equalizers

➤ Music identifiers

➤ Voice transformers/modulators

➤ Karaoke

➤ Ringtone makers

➤ Social music sharing ("Shazam")

➤ Watch music videos

➤ Recorders

Navigation (About 2 Percent)

Overlap categories would be Utilities, Productivity, and Lifestyle, though this category appears pretty focused on maps and getting to where you want to go.

The following are current popular features/functionality for this category:

➤ Voice GPS navigation apps (major brands tend to be fairly expensive):

    ➤ Live traffic flow

    ➤ Local search

    ➤ Magnetic compass

    ➤ Phone from search

    ➤ Save waypoints

    ➤ Share location with friends/family

    ➤ Integration with Google Maps for world navigation

    ➤ Voice navigation

➤ Geocaching

➤ People trackers

➤ Directions and maps to specific areas (New York City subway, for example)

➤ Marine and sea charts (such as for tides, currents, and wind forecasts)

➤ Astronomy

➤ Specific city maps and points of interest

➤ Traffic reporters

➤ GPS-based stats (speed, distance traveled, altitude)

➤ In-app purchases for more accurate GPS tracking

News (About 3 Percent)

This is a fairly straightforward category, with little overlap from other categories and few in-app purchases.

The following are current popular features/functionality for this category:

➤ Police scanners (worldwide and local)

➤ Major newspapers

➤ Web news sites (such as Reddit)

➤ News radio

➤ Specific local newscasts

➤ Game/technology news

➤ RSS readers

➤ New app news and current reviews

➤ Music news

➤ Newspaper collections

➤ Favorite podcast updates

➤ Some social integration or post news to Facebook/Twitter

➤ E-mail links to friends

➤ Built-in web browsers

➤ Dynamic updates

Photography (About 2 Percent)

Most apps here involve editing and sharing of some sort, with some Entertainment category apps thrown in as well (such as comparing photos). In-app purchases mostly have to do with additional filters/tools to enjoy in your editing app.

The following are current popular features/functionality for this category:

➤ Photo editing:

    ➤ Special effects/filters/add-on effects

    ➤ Panorama stitching

➤ Upload new images to Facebook, Flickr, e-mail

➤ Movie editing:

    ➤ Add soundtrack

    ➤ Record audio

➤ Gesture to control (swipe, pinch, and so on)

➤ Filter overlay effects

Productivity (About 3 Percent)

This is another grab bag from a variety of potential categories, especially Utilities, Lifestyle, and Education.

The following are current popular features/functionality for this category:

➤ To-do lists

➤ Schedulers/calendars/reminders

➤ Chat clients

➤ Office apps (documents, spreadsheets, presentations)

➤ Copy/paste apps

➤ Download managers

➤ Note-taking, including audio recorders

➤ Scanners (using the Camera), along with the sharing, e-mailing, and faxing of scans

➤ File sharing

➤ Translation

➤ Lists (shopping, organizing)

➤ Push notifications for most apps

➤ Calculators

➤ Sync to home computer

➤ Flashlight

Reference (About 4 Percent)

Reference is another targeted category, with few apps that have in-app purchases near the top. As you get lower down the rankings, specific guides for most anything popular in pop culture (games, news, stars, and so on) begin to appear. This is another category where efforts are put more into functionality than in visual presentation.

The following are current popular features/functionality for this category:

➤ Search tools (including web search, phone search, and Wikipedia search)

➤ Dictionaries (including voice pronunciation, shaking for random words, word of the day, and sharing new words with friends)

➤ Bible apps with search

➤ Translators

➤ Vocabulary builders

➤ Geography

➤ Cooking reference

➤ Quotes (which can be shared via Facebook, Twitter, e-mail, and so on)

➤ Encyclopedias (more specific than general, unless for web-based search, such as "Guns")

➤ Language learning

Social Networking (About 2 Percent)

Nearly the entire top 20 current grossing apps are made up of those that support in-app purchases. What's also noticeable is that many of the names of apps are attempting to capitalize on clever, abstract naming. Some examples are "ooVoo," "Piictu," "Skout," "WeeMee," "Grindr," "Omegle," "Tapatalk," "Facely," "Fring," "Tumblr," and "Viber." These are all examples within the top 20, and it doesn't stop as you go down in the ranks.

The following are current popular features/functionality for this category:

➤ Apps by the current top web social sites (Facebook, Twitter, Skype, and so on)

➤ Apps to support Facebook/Twitter

➤ Chat/group chat

➤ Avatar creators with sharing and in-app purchases

➤ Forum software

➤ Text messaging/Short Message Service (SMS)/Multimedia Messaging Service (MMS)

➤ Dating software (including geo-targeting to locate nearby people, and profiles)

➤ Professional online portfolio sites (LinkedIn)

➤ Video calls

➤ Free calling

➤ People locators

Sports (About 3 Percent)

You might think this category has sports games, but not in the traditional sense. Instead, you will find fantasy league analyzers (but not leagues themselves) and the occasional hunting game. There are a great many sports news apps, specific sports tips and guides (golf), and some sports supporting apps thrown in (such as "Pitch Speed Test" and GPS golf course helpers). Most apps here do not currently include in-app purchases.

The following are current popular features/functionality for this category:

➤ Radio sportscasts

➤ Scoreboards

➤ GPS golf apps (including range finders, specific courses for download, score-cards, game analysis, stat tracking, and satellite data)

➤ Major sports event calendars

➤ Sports news videos and highlights

➤ Sport training (for example, golf)

➤ Golf analysis using built-in camera

Travel (About 6 Percent)

The bulk of apps at the top of the Travel category are review and ratings apps, as well as travel search engines. There are very few apps with in-app purchases in this category. As you go farther down in the rankings, you'll get to specific destination guides and maps. There is some crossover from the Lifestyle and Navigation categories here.

The following are current popular features/functionality for this category:

➤ Travel meta-search engines such as KAYAK (congregating data from several sources)

➤ Opinion/review/rating apps (such as Yelp, Urbanspoon, TripAdvisor) and GPS locators

➤ Popular destination travel guides

➤ Flight trackers (for such things as checking the flight status of most flights and finding alternate flights)

➤ Tour guides and travel planners like TripIt

➤ Major airline-specific apps

➤ Gas price apps

➤ Specific city metro system apps

➤ Language translators

Utilities (About 6 Percent)

The Utilities category is like the Entertainment version of the Productivity category, with a lot of influx from Productivity, and some of Lifestyle as well. It's a complete grab bag here of novelty apps, some productivity, and some purely for small pockets of practicality in your life (for example, "Dog Whistle"). Very few in-app purchases are seen within this category.

The following are current popular features/functionality for this category:

➤ Bundles of apps full of different functionality (for example, "AppZilla," as shown in Figure 4-19)

➤ Camera zoom apps (may be outdated with new iPhone technology)

➤ Alarm clocks

➤ Scanners

➤ Barcode scanners

➤ Photo editors

➤ Web search engines (such as Craigslist)

➤ Password security apps

➤ Download managers

FIGURE 4-19: "AppZilla" is a bundle of 100 different apps with completely different features

Weather (Less than 1 Percent)

This category represents the fewest number of active apps, perhaps because it could be seen as being similar to Utilities. As you'll see from the following description, there is not a lot of trickle here from other categories, and it's all about the weather. There are a few apps with in-app purchases in the Radar subcategory and alerts.

The following are current popular features/functionality for this category:

➤ Tide tables

➤ Severe weather notifications/alerts

➤ Tie-in apps for popular weather news sources (such as The Weather Channel)

➤ Weather radar in different map styles

➤ Extended forecasts

➤ Global weather

➤ Weather radio

Competitive Feedback Research

In Chapter 3, you learned the importance of competitive research and how looking at customer feedback in reviews helped to define a feature list. This can be one of the most valuable types research, namely because you can download and use it yourself, and, thus, should be able to "compare notes" with reviewers! Even better, you can more easily sift through reviews that aren't legitimate without needing to click their name's link (as mentioned in Chapter 3).

SUMMARY

In this chapter, you learned about customer expectations when interpreting App Store metrics. You were also provided with a guide for what customers can currently find within all App Store categories, and might expect to find with your app. With this information, you can now more aptly define and position your app.

The preparatory work is done, and you're now ready to begin the development process in earnest. Chapter 5 examines how you can effectively maintain scope throughout development, while self-correcting issues that arise by splitting the process into many manageable chunks. It discusses how not to get ahead of yourself on any one thing, such as programming certain details before it's clear whether they really ought to be in the app at all. You'll learn about techniques you can apply to help you and your team stay on course and on budget throughout the process.

Plotting the Stages of Development

Development of a new app can be a daunting task, particularly for the uninitiated. At its root is typically fear — of failure, of success, of cost overruns, of the unknown. As correctly spelled out in many motivational books, the only way to master fear is to take action — in this case, by putting aside any misgivings and getting to work. Mistakes are inevitable during application development, but to best mitigate them, you should rely on a fairly systematic process of iteration and agile development throughout. Such a process is spelled out in this chapter, with suggested reading noted in the (unlikely) chance that you are left wanting more information.

Before diving into the details of this chapter, you should be aware of the creative process. Working with new platforms such as multitouch iOS devices has a very "Wild West" sort of feel to it — exciting, new, and lawless. With relatively very little history behind touch devices, opportunities for new user interface (UI) design and ways to interact still abound. Unlike desktop or even web applications, there are few "rules," and even those can be bent or broken. But just as the potential for innovation and/or success is monumental, the risk of failure (or, perhaps worse, a brief swim in mediocrity) also looms quite large in the App Store market.

So, on one hand, to offer the best chance at success, new apps must innovate on at least one level. And, on the other hand, innovation is no good without a process of delivery. If you've ever wondered how you can manage to innovate while adhering to processes, you're not alone; entire books are devoted to the conundrum.

Therefore, this chapter examines techniques designed to enhance app innovation by directing your thinking to the right places before even a single dialog box is created. While multitouch design is relatively new, creating software, fortunately, is not. Learning from the mistakes and failures of competitors, as well as a smart approach to innovation, will help bring to the masses new experiences *worth sharing* through your new iOS app.

> For more information on adhering to processes while being innovative see The Creative Habit: Learn It and Use It for Life *by Twyla Tharp (New York: Simon & Shuster, 2005),* The Design of Everyday Things *by Donald A. Norman (New York: Basic Books, 2002), and* The Design of Design: Essays from a Computer Scientist *by Frederick P. Brooks, Jr. (Boston: Addison-Wesley, 2010).*

Let's start by examining some tips for laying a foundation to properly build a solid team through leadership, information about team roles, and why you should start with a written vision for your app.

LEADERSHIP AND YOUR TEAM

Let's accept as a rule that the best chance at app success rests with the people on your team. Therefore, for any size team, it's vitally important that competent leadership be demonstrated from the top down. Of course, not everyone was born a charismatic and natural leader. But, based on this author's experience, it is something that can be learned, practiced, and honed to at least semi-competency.

The following traits from those in a leadership position will be appreciated by the rest of your team, thus ensuring a smoother development process:

➤ **Leave your ego at the door** — The best leaders are those who make others feel valued. Lead by example, rather than expecting others to automatically follow because of your title or past achievements.

➤ **Empower others** — Allow others a sense of control and ownership over their parts, and they'll achieve much better results than when you hand-hold them. This also allows you more time to manage the project.

➤ **Be positive and enthusiastic** — Show that you're excited about the project and it will rub off on others.

➤ **Accept criticism** — Be willing to find the truth in any criticism, and how to politely ignore that which won't result in being productive.

➤ **Be honest** — If you're wrong, admit it and get back on track. If you don't know, find out or ask. Just don't pretend.

➤ **Make decisions** — Being indecisive is counter-productive to the team in that you're being relied upon for action. Learn to make decisions early so that you can maximize the time for action. Also, practice providing your team with some insight into your decision-making process so that they know you're not blindly making those decisions.

➤ **Be reliable** — Following through with your commitments and making decisions objectively (and without allowing emotion to tug you one way or another) demonstrates integrity. People respect and follow integrity.

Obviously, it takes much more than a few guidelines to become an efficient leader. However, these should provide a helpful framework or reminder for the mindset needed to complete an app.

Assumptions about Your Role

Because you've chosen to delve into this particular book, the advice presented here assumes that you want to become a factor in (or you already are a factor in) at least some of the major decision-making processes throughout development of your app. These will most typically include some or all of the following:

➤ Design and/or direction of a design document (sometimes referred to as a *functional spec* or *specification*)

➤ Creating/managing production schedules

➤ Assessing/planning milestones

➤ Directly hiring or managing in-house or external producer(s), designer(s), coder(s), audio engineer(s), and/or artist(s)

➤ Finding/evaluating new tools for efficiency

➤ Making frequent high-level decisions about adding/cutting features

➤ Managing the bug-tracking process

➤ Making marketing strategy decisions

The many (often simultaneous) processes shown here need at least a few people to manage in full. But the one role that manages most of these the best is the Producer. In the game industry, the Producer is typically responsible for planning, scheduling, hiring, assessing risk, managing teams, being aware of and mitigating development issues, facilitating getting things done, and making decisions on issues that crop up (with consensus being the goal).

Your Starting Lineup

Rather than go into too much in-depth examination of each role on a development team (other development books do that), and instead focusing on the business aspect, let's concentrate on team composition, the individuals you'll need to get things done, and what they'll do for you.

Producer

As mentioned previously, a Producer is the facilitator of action and the mitigator against risk. You'll have a team member performing this role to begin with and throughout development, even if someone on the team doesn't have this specific title. For very small teams, sometimes it's the lead programmer, one or both managing partners, or sometimes even the president of the company! It's the person wearing the Producer's hat who initially works with the Designer in fleshing out a game or app idea, and then facilitates getting it actually made throughout all development stages.

Designer(s)

At the beginning of a project, a Designer is the team member tasked with coming up with a detailed concept, and then (when the concept is approved) creating a functional design document or design plan. When work starts, the Designer will shift focus to testing early prototypes and iterating on the design to iron out flaws or tweak/cut existing features. Notice that adding new features was not included in that description — that's what's known as "feature creep," and is usually bad for development schedules and the bottom line. You'll learn more about the design process soon.

For many small studios that are producing one or two apps, hiring a freelance designer makes more sense than having a full-time designer, even if that person helps out for the duration of the title. Because of complexity, a designer would more commonly help out throughout development of a game or full-featured application (for user experience tweaking) than for a simple app.

Programmer(s)

As perhaps one of your largest variables during development, it is crucial that you hire a Programmer, or put together a team with experience in your genre of app, and ask for references and demos. If it is a three-dimensional (3D) app, you'll want people who have proof that they have done that before. For example, many outsourcing "we can do it all" teams claim to have experience with interactive games, but actually outsource the work again to those with questionable track records.

Programmers will be responsible for early prototypes using placeholder art/sounds as necessary, and then for delivering normal milestone builds that can be tested frequently and iterated upon.

Artist(s)

Most apps need art, even if (or, rather, especially if) it's just for the App Store Icon. As you saw in Chapter 3, your art style is critical. Whether polished or unrefined, it will define your app, and should consistently match the theme and functionality you are trying to convey. If your app is a simple utility, it may be easy enough to get away with art mostly from the standard iPhone GUI library. However, in all likelihood, you'll need a bit here or there regardless of app type (for loading screens, icons, and so on), and even more so for games. For smaller studios, art is almost always outsourced.

> *If you're creating a game, it's likely that one artist will not be enough. You may need a 3D artist capable of rendering 3D characters/meshes, or a user interface artist good at graphic design and UI layouts. Another artist might have an extensive portfolio of icons, so you might outsource your app icon using their services.*

Audio Engineer(s)

Although it may not be a problem for some simple apps, with most projects, a few sounds in key places can go a long way toward making your app feel fleshed out. The job of an Audio Engineer is almost always outsourced. Your Audio Engineer(s) will be responsible for music and/or required sound effects (commonly referred to as "sfx") throughout your game or app. If you have talent within your studio, you can do this fairly cheaply using royalty-free libraries (with links provided in Appendix B). For games especially, it cannot be stressed enough how music and sound can influence not only the feel, but the responsiveness of your app.

Quality Assurance

Unless you're a major game application developer (and you may be), chances are you'll need a few people — rather than a full-time test house (those can be expensive) — helping to find bugs and entering them into a database for the Producer or Quality Assurance (QA) lead to assign to programmers. With smaller applications, this can be done in house. But for more complex apps, you'll definitely want to outsource QA. Of course, you will have to add in the cost of providing the test devices to these users, and be sure to keep legacy iOS devices kicking around just for this purpose!

Speaking of QA, there are now new innovations for testing applications. One such example is an actual integrated web and iOS app named TestFlight (https://testflightapp.com/). It automatically loads a provisioning profile onto test devices, and can make installing new builds seamless, wireless, and amazingly quick. It even has e-mail notifications when a new build is uploaded. This is a highly recommended approach!

> *While working on "Archetype" (a first-person multiplayer shooter for the iPhone), the team included a couple of guys who were pulled in-house full time to help the external developers with QA. It's quicker that way when they have direct access to the programming team, and communication is fast. However, everyone on the team tested and provided feedback when they could.*

Localization

Localization is the process of translating every word in your app to one or more languages using localization translators. The extra revenue you get from making your app available in multiple languages can be worth it if you can keep costs and implementation down using just one or two people managing the process, rather than adding another communication channel (such as at a full-service QA company). This translation is almost always outsourced.

> *For "Archetype," the team used Elance quite successfully for its 12 languages.*

Marketing

Prior to launch, you should have a marketing plan, and then budget accordingly so that, when released, as much "hype" and buzz as possible surrounds your app. How to do this is explained in the section "Coordinating Marketing," later in this chapter. The better your app does initially, the easier it is to stay afloat, or even sail to success.

Parting Note about Roles

Whichever the role, for better production output and creativity, it's important that each individual on the team be autonomously empowered to take ownership of his or her particular task(s). With outsourced teams becoming more the norm, that communication should be effective and filtered through the right channels. You learn more about efficient methods of communication in the section, "Coordinating Outsourcing and Effective Communication," later in this chapter.

With a good overview of the general functions each role provides for developing (and shipping!) a software product under your belt — in this case, for iOS devices — you'll have an easier time throughout development if you begin with the following advice that can help direct effective decision making.

A Controlling Idea to Kick Things Off

At the beginning of development, it is important for everyone to be on the same page as far as the overall direction of the project (which can prevent questions and problems down the line). Those who are in charge should come up with and agree upon what's called a *controlling idea* — which is a one-sentence, concise *vision* of the ideal of the app or game. Here's an example for an app:

> MyAppName *simplifies social networking by allowing users to use Facebook and Twitter's core functionality with minimum fuss and maximum efficiency.*

The controlling idea *is a bit similar to a* business positioning statement *(but more directed at software development and features). Its objective is to capture the essence of what you want it to accomplish, to do, to be. It can also be known as a* vision statement, *but the term "controlling" infers less of an "I'd like to..." or "I have this pie in the sky vision" feel, and more of a committed "We're going to..." feel.*

Beginning a project with a controlling idea is a technique the author learned while at Fisher-Price during a Masterclass seminar led by Pixar Story Artist Matthew Luhn. It drives the entire creative cycle of each of Pixar's amazing cinematic successes. What he conveyed was that for each project, the teams at Pixar buy into the controlling idea so that whenever an issue of "should we add this?" or "does this fit?" or even "in general, should we *do* this?" comes up, the team refers back to the controlling idea and typically finds the answer.

That's a powerful thing. While providing focus and direction throughout development, one simple sentence can prevent many of the creative conundrums that are so common.

So, what constitutes a good controlling idea? For the idea itself, you'll want to include simple, specific ways to subjectively look at the concept. In the previous example, several subjectively measurable terms were used. For example, the phrase "simplifies social networking" was used to imply that social networking can be complex and could be more manageable. How? That's how you get your features! It could mean other things, too, but those would (and should) be part of a more robust initial features list.

Let's keep going. Another subjective term used was "core functionality." So, what exactly is that? That's what you want team members (in particular, the Designer) to reflect on, extract, and then highlight when creating features. It is specific enough to mean something definite for each team member. For example, Facebook's core functionality could be reading updates about friends. Or, it could be posting to your own wall. But, objectively, you might all see "playing flash games" as not a part of Facebook's core functionality, because that can be done on most any platform.

The phrase "minimum fuss" may mean "with fewer clicks" to some, or "accomplished in a fast manner" to others. Both interpretations are correct. Finally, "maximum efficiency" may mean accomplishing more with less, in whatever manner that can be done (maybe fewer menu layers and more icons on a single screen, for example).

The reason to be subjective rather than objective is that each person will have his or her own ideas as to how far each of these terms goes. But on the whole, each person should have his or her own intuitive "clue" about what is needed when a particular issue arises. On the whole, this can lead to better innovation.

This is not to say that each team member should take what he or she wants from the controlling idea and run with it in his or her own way. Rather, the overriding theme is to use the controlling idea when considering whether features stay or go.

> The controlling idea's *essence and strength is in laying boundaries and setting goals.*

Designers can use the controlling idea to help with assigning features. Artists can use it as a general direction for creating simplistic, efficient icons. Audio engineers can use it for not getting too dramatic with special effects — simplicity and efficiency are key. Programmers can use it to maximize menu-driven responsiveness.

Just to round out this discussion, consider what actually makes a *bad* controlling idea. Following is an example:

> MyAppName *will achieve #1 in sales through excellence in its genre and the dedication of its team.*

Ouch! That was even hard to put a period on. It's a lofty enough goal, but for providing boundaries, direction, or answering any sort of creative questions or issues that arise, it is just plain generic and unhelpful.

In Chapter 9, there are further tips on how to create what they call a definition statement, so when you're ready for this step, be sure to reference that as well in the "Value-Added Benefits" section.

By now you should have a concrete handle on how to create a controlling idea. It is time to discuss the overall method you'll use for development and get agile.

CONCEPT THROUGH RELEASE

As you would imagine, there are many inefficient ways to complete the development of a software title. The most common early methodology (and the one used most often until perhaps very recently) stemmed from a 1970s paper by Winston Royce named the "waterfall method." As shown in Figure 5-1, this process chops up development into several distinct stages that occur one after another:

➤ Concept and planning

➤ Design

➤ Code and assets

➤ Test

➤ Release

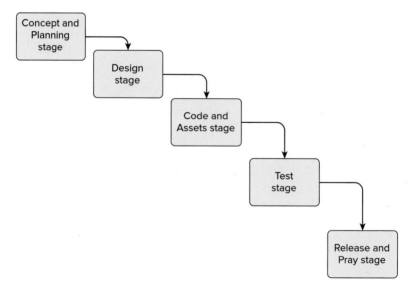

FIGURE 5-1: The "waterfall" development method

> For more information on Royce's description of the waterfall
> development model, see "Managing the Development of a
> Large Software System" (a paper from the Proceedings of IEEE
> WESCON, August 1970).

Development that follows the waterfall method attempts to lay down a solid (but rigid) foundation early so that risks are mitigated. However, the most common problem with waterfall development is that lots of time and money are spent and accumulated throughout the early stages. By the end of development, the product may not look exactly how you envisioned, yet was locked into its design at the outset.

Although this may still be a feasible method for some projects, for complex projects, it's simply not the best way to achieve success and user approval. Unless you are an absolute genius at design and planning, there are systems that you're going to want to iterate on and change as a result of actual testing — systems that even the best designers cannot possibly foresee.

Maximizing Your App through Agile Development

Thankfully, there is one methodology that has been used more and more frequently over the past ten years, with quite a bit of success. The *agile software development method* is often paired with what are called "Scrum" project management techniques. These aren't just slick terms, but instead represent proven processes for what's called *lightweight software development*. In other words, these are processes of development that can be adaptable to change more quickly than by using traditional methods such as with waterfall development.

> For an absolute gem and much more in-depth look into agile and
> Scrum development for use with any app or game team, see Agile
> Software Development with Scrum *by Clinton Keith (Boston:
> Addison-Wesley, 2010). You can also brush up on several methodologies with* Balancing Agility and Discipline: A Guide for the
> Perplexed *by Bary Boehm and Richard Turner (Boston: Addison-
> Wesley, 2003).*

What kinds of changes are we talking about? These include valuable user feedback, market shifts, financial changes, new technology, perhaps a CEO with a kid who likes red balloons, or anything that can cause the software to "need to be changed."

The fundamentals of lightweight software development were fleshed out in the mid 1990s. In 2001, a group of developers met to discuss lightweight methods, and the outcome was a new process they referred to as an "Agile Manifesto" (available for your viewing pleasure at www.agilemanifesto.org).

It reads exactly as follows:

> *We are uncovering better ways of developing software by doing it and helping others do it.*
>
> *Through this work we have come to value:*
>
> *Individuals and interactions over processes and tools*
>
> *Working software over comprehensive documentation*
>
> *Customer collaboration over contract negotiation*
>
> *Responding to change over following a plan*
>
> *That is, while there is value in the items on the right, we value the items on the left more.*

The essence of agile development is to deliver higher-quality software faster and with more end-user acceptance (because of constantly adapting to feedback) than can be achieved by using traditional methods.

The group also created 12 principles to back up this manifesto. The principles revolve around a team-centric approach to quick software turnarounds and high adaptability, with iteration based on feedback from others, as well as meta-feedback from the team itself.

Table 5-1 provides a brief look at how the 12 agile development principles can help with developing an app. Once you understand the principles, you'll begin to understand how this method can help solve traditional problems.

TABLE 5-1: The 12 Principles of Agile Development

PRINCIPLE	COMMENTS
(1) Our highest priority is to satisfy the customer through early and continuous delivery of valuable software.	"Early" and "continuous" are the key words here. Think of your app launching early to satisfy a growing niche, in addition to frequent updates to maintain the community.
(2) Welcome changing requirements, even late in development. Agile processes harness change for the customer's competitive advantage.	Whether the market shifts or competitors beat you to new innovation you thought you'd come out with first, it's to your advantage to be able to change your direction — even late in development. This is simply not possible with traditional methods.
(3) Deliver working software frequently, from a couple of weeks to a couple of months, with a preference to the shorter timescale.	The process of agile development is to have shorter blocks of complete software cycles — planning, design, code, test, release. This allows ample feedback and iteration possibilities while adapting to any changing requirements. For apps, about two weeks per iteration cycle is a good standard to aim for. This includes design of any new features, implementation, and testing.

PRINCIPLE	COMMENTS
(4) Business people and developers must work together daily throughout the project.	Communication from business needs to the development team typically is filtered through the Producer, but should occur frequently.
(5) Build projects around motivated individuals. Give them the environment and support they need, and trust them to get the job done.	For smaller teams especially, this is crucial because everyone's role is amplified. With outsourcing so popular in app development, this can be somewhat difficult to do. But effective and frequent communication and feedback can help mitigate support issues, and motivate even remote teams.
(6) The most efficient and effective method of conveying information to and within a development team is face-to-face conversation.	One word for those not able to communicate in a true face-to-face fashion (which is becoming most common nowadays): Skype (www.skype.com). Nothing beats the immediacy and resolution of an instant chat or face-to-face. E-mail is actually becoming more ineffective as a communication device when compared to instant messaging (IM) or conferencing software simply because of IM's lack of a delay in the resolution of issues. There are many other capable conferencing solutions as well, including GotoMeeting (www.gotomeeting.com).
(7) Working software is the primary measure of progress.	Agile development pushes working software over separate contained system milestones. This is simply because you get to see how it all interacts as a whole, and analyze it as a complete entity (often raw and unfinished, but as complete as can be). The alternative is making assumptions about how feature X will interact with feature Y once implemented, and that's highly unpredictable.
(8) Agile processes promote sustainable development. The sponsors, developers, and users should be able to maintain a constant pace indefinitely.	Because of consistent feedback loops and flexibility to change requirements, in addition to continuously building on a complete whole rather than plugging in many systems at once (and hoping for the best), these smaller increments in software production produce fewer large errors capable of derailing the project and/or team.
(9) Continuous attention to technical excellence and good design enhances agility.	Adhering to excellence and good design early reduces mistakes, and therefore, more resources remain open to change direction or iterate when the time comes.

continues

TABLE 5-1 *(continued)*

PRINCIPLE	COMMENTS
(10) The more your team focuses on technical excellence and good design, the less mistakes are made and therefore the more resources remain open to change direction when the time comes.	By keeping things simple (and thus maximizing the amount of perhaps unneeded waste that is able to be trimmed from your software), you keep cost and complexity low, allow for maximum agility when changes are needed, maximize speed to market with simpler coding, have less testing for complex systems, and keep resources open for future iteration.
(11) The best architectures, requirements, and designs emerge from self-organizing teams.	When a team works together as an organic, integrated whole to devise and plow through the implementation of new systems rather than as a group of separated specialists, the working result of any iteration of a project becomes intrinsically stronger. It is capable of mitigating and making less chaotic the unpredictable (but inevitable) shocks that occur during development. It sounds a little glossy-eyed, but it's true, and no different really than much of the newer research about evolution on a nano-scale, such as getting a bunch of bacteria in a Petri dish to "work out" a problem organically through many generations of rapid evolution, rather than have a programmer or current computer solve the same process. As you may guess, it's much, much faster when figured out organically.
(12) At regular intervals, the team reflects on how to become more effective, then tunes and adjusts its behavior accordingly.	On any given software project, a number of tasks get relegated to the "backlog" and eventually prioritized. In order to evolve, the team should make a priority of self-monitoring the way things are being done, and be flexible enough to adjust to more efficient methods if possible. The team should also take notice when tasks that used to be important are now just waste.

With that brief look into the merits of Agile development, it is time to start delving into the actual process of developing an app. In the next section, you won't find as much detail on each stage as you might in some books focused solely on software development. But you will come away with a good idea how each stage pertains specifically to iOS application development, in addition to a Case Study on the development timeline of "Archetype."

Planning — Envisioning Your Vision

Rolling out an app occurs in six main stages:

➤ Concept

> ➤ Pre-Production
> ➤ Production
> ➤ Testing
> ➤ Launch
> ➤ Post Release (which encompasses all the others)

The Post Release stage is where you bring out new features and customer feedback fixes (hopefully not too many bug fixes) in paid or unpaid updates.

Depending on the size of your iOS software, you can expect the entire process to take anywhere from 3 or 4 weeks (for a *very* simple utility app) to quite possibly more than 12 months or more (for a fully realized 3D game). This is true regardless of the size of your design and programming staff. In other words, software development takes a certain amount of time to be created, even with "more" of everything — more libraries, more designers, and so on.

In his book *The Mythical Man-Month: Essays on Software Engineering, Second Edition* (Boston: Addison-Wesley, 1995), legendary IBM manager Fred Brooks wrote, "Nine women can't make a baby in a month." Brooks is famous among programmers for Brooks' Law, which states, "Adding manpower to a late software project [only] makes it later."

CASE STUDY: DEVELOPMENT TIMELINE FOR "ARCHETYPE"

"Archetype" was initially going to be a six-month app. It had a fairly focused concept; the team knew they wanted a 3D purely multiplayer-only team-based first-person shooter. They wanted this type of action to be playable over Wi-Fi and 3G, which hadn't been attempted yet. However, the team had a rather large problem. This was the most ambitious app they had yet attempted, and, at that point, they had no experience doing 3D on the iPhone. Not only that, they had no developer.

So, they started simply and dove in headfirst:

> ➤ Once they had a concept, they formulated a controlling idea/vision for the game.
>
> ➤ They found an up-and-coming developer with previous game development experience who was somewhat flexible on cost in exchange for recognition and getting his own feet wet. The developer managed 3D engine programming as well as art and level design asset development (and eventually testing as well).
>
> ➤ They utilized an existing sound studio for music/sound effects.
>
> ➤ They did a lot of work producing and designing an interface, combat elements, level features, and gameplay themselves.

continues

continued

➤ They made a really good deal for their computer generated (CG) intro FMV (short for Full Motion Video, a term carried over from the CD-ROM days), which turned out even better than expected — and, in fact, upped the polish expectations.

➤ Finally, they created an excellent playable and testable/tunable "prototype" within five months with most critical features implemented, just not fleshed out.

By this time, the team had a solid foundation, but not enough content. The interface art and level designs (which were good starters) really needed to be significantly polished.

The team made the mistake of having several "completion deadlines" around this point, not quite knowing when it was they wanted to finalize and release what they had. They thought they just had to get it out to beat any unforeseen competition.

But they didn't release.

It started to become clear that they had something special, and that releasing it early or unpolished would only hurt their chances with sloppy implementation. With this in mind, they added a couple of months of padding to where they were, used the agile method to re-evaluate features and priorities, and got to work on critical issues, testing, and fixing.

For a few months, they were in a state of "yeah, this is shaping up pretty good, but...." As their deadlines approached those "buts" became a new shifting of priorities. They shifted focus entirely to polish, player value features (many previously backlogged), and longevity issues, such as the following:

➤ They needed more polish on their tutorial and playable training mode.

➤ They needed to build in social features to promote the game.

➤ They needed to test and tweak character progression and in-game medals.

➤ The interface wasn't quite there in terms of performance and consistency.

➤ They needed final balancing for combat and multiplayer level design.

➤ They needed auto-matchmaking tweaks so that the experience was seamless and stupidly easy.

At this time, there were always bugs and fixing, with lots of small localization issues. The team wanted to have all localization done for a near simultaneous launch, and there was one more thing they decided to do that made the final difference in the finished product.

Because they had the Portuguese localization finished up, they decided to submit and release in that market, test the waters, get initial feedback in a less substantiated market, then iterate one last time for the U.S. and rest-of-the-world push.

By the time they released, the team had its marketing strike ready to hit, and really got some few-day-early positive buzz going. (The buzz certainly could have been negative, but this new-fangled 5v5 hadn't been done yet, and people were really hopeful and anxious to see whether it worked as advertised.) So, when the team launched the product, they launched "big" — as big as the rather limited marketing budget would allow.

In its second week, "Archetype" became the App Store Game of the Week, which generated instant sales. It became IGN's Mobile Game of the Month for July, and later that year, earned a spot in Apple's App Store Hall of Fame. There were even a couple of days when it surpassed the perpetual "Angry Birds" as the top grossing paid app — though that was short-lived and bound to happen. "Archetype" is at best a somewhat niche game with fringes of casual-inspired hard-core gameplay, while "Angry Birds" is casual all the way.

Here is the initial controlling idea for "Archetype" (known then as "FPS"), which the author wrote then tweaked via team feedback 11 months, 3 weeks before official launch:

"'FPS' is an iPhone-optimized team-based first-person shooter initially featuring multiplayer deathmatch gameplay only and the ability for the player to have a freedom of play style via weapon design, pickups, and strategic positioning."

Further, the team had an idea about the story that it wanted locked down, so they threw this in as well:

"'FPS' is set in a future sci-fi dystopian Earth where genetically augmented/evolved humans and technologically enhanced humans battle for survival."

One year later, the end result matched really well with the initial idea.

One unfortunate reality is that your app will likely take longer and cost more than you expect. No matter how well you lay those plans, or how awesome your rock star programmers and designers are, your app will run into unforeseen difficulties. Take a preventative deep breath and get it out now. Some nasty bug will rear its ugly little green head, or a missing feature will jump out and smack you in the face during testing. *Expect problems* and work through them with the meekness of a battering ram.

Steve Jobs is right: "Real artists ship" and the rest are phonies. Don't let development delays kill your dreams. You're simply building character by beating down every last problem that gets in your way. Software development *can* often be a long, hard slog, but the rewards are intoxicating.

Scheduling

There are three truisms in this world:

➤ People will always die.

➤ Taxes will be too high.

➤ Software development will run late.

The best schedules will almost always slip because people typically have trouble meeting deadlines. Not on purpose, mind you. It's a fundamental flaw in the human psyche that makes us rarely on time, and it's one that you must prepare for. But that doesn't mean you have to accept it.

There are many methodologies for scheduling software projects, and many are more in-depth than can be covered in this book. But the basics for new developers/publishers to get through an app are provided here (along with a little more for those who wish to really streamline the process).

If you have a set amount of time to deliver your app ("I must ship this in four months," for example), one method is what former Microsoft manager (and now a program management guru) Scott Berkun calls the "rule of thirds." That is, divide your allotted time into three phases:

➤ Planning/design

➤ UI/art and coding

➤ Testing

Devoting the final chunk to testing may seem superfluous, but it isn't. You only get one chance to make an impression on the App Store, and no amount of updates can rescue an app's initial tattered reputation.

If you haven't decided on a set timeframe to deliver your app, or you prefer other options, which method used ultimately isn't the most important factor. What matters is having the flexibility to tweak your schedule as you go. The more you learn about the intricacies of your project, the more accurate (note the word "more") your schedule can be. Keep in mind the "twice the time/cost" warning though, and prepare fallback plans in case schedule and cost overages begin affecting your app.

Simple Scheduling Formula

There's a bit of uncertainty with any schedule. To help with this, program managers have for quite some time used a simple formula to estimate the time it takes for any project or task. What this does is provide weights to three different outcomes to produce a reasonable expected duration, while accounting for uncertainty. The original project management formula is this:

Expected Time (with built-in uncertainty) =
(Best Case Time + Worst Case Time + 4*Most Likely Time) / 6

This can be summarized as follows:

$$E_T = (B_T + W_T + 4M_T) / 6$$

This works, but you may want to use the modified one Dan Irish recommends in his book, *The Game Producer's Handbook* (Upper Saddle River, NJ: Prentice Hall, 2005), because game development in general has a bit more uncertainty.

Here is a simple tweak that gives more weight to the Worst Case Time (and, therefore, skews the expected time in that direction):

Expected Time (with built-in uncertainty) =
(Best Case Time + 3*Worst Case Time + 2*Most Likely Time) / 6

This can be summarized as follows:

$$E_T = (B_T + 3W_T + 2M_T) / 6$$

As an example task, let's imagine you need to hook up Facebook Connect with your app as stated in the design doc. You ask your programmers for a best case (which they say will be 1 week or 5 days), worst case (3 weeks or 15 days), and most likely case (2 weeks or 10 days). Plugging this in to the equation, you get the following:

$$E_T = (5 + 3(15) + 2(10)) / 6 \ldots \text{or} \ldots E_T = 70 / 6$$

Therefore, the Expected Time equals 11.67 days, so you round up to 12. If you extrapolate this over the course of a project, the end result can be dramatically different than if you simply go by most-likely scenarios and also appropriately account for risk, as well as can be expected at least.

Critical Path

App development will be segmented into a series of measurable deliverables called *milestones*, which most of you have likely heard of or used on past projects. These are how you're going to evaluate your progress and third-party deliverables, as well as base your payment schedule. It's very important that you balance your project cash flow with money you'll pay out for milestones, in addition to keeping to the critical path early in order to keep risks low.

In project management, the *critical path* is the route of sequential activities from where you are now to the end of the project that takes the longest time to do. In other words, what activity must get done before another in order for the project to continue, then what must be done after that, and so on, until the end, where their total time to complete would be longer than the time of any other activities to complete.

At the start of a project, the critical path determines the total duration of the project. If you want to shorten the development cycle, you will need to run more activities in parallel, which is called *fast tracking*. The only other way to shorten development time (without cutting features) is what's called *crashing* the critical path, or putting more resources on any activity.

In app development, the critical path might be to prototype a UI shell, then add a series of features that are dependent on one another. For example, in order for the app to be a success, you need feature C. But for feature C to be implemented, you first need feature B, which is dependent on feature A. The time it takes to do A to B to C is the critical path.

There will likely be other paths with different tasks that are dependent on one another that do not take as long overall to complete. Although important, these would not be on the main critical path. Figure 5-2 shows two different paths, the left one being the critical path (taking eight weeks), while the other one is projected to be seven weeks.

It will be up to the project manager (again, typically the Producer) to continually manage the critical path and update/revise it as milestones are completed. In app and game development, things change constantly, so don't expect the critical path to remain static throughout, or that another one won't replace it. And remember that, within each milestone, there will be critical paths to completing it, just as there is an overall critical path to completing the app. Focus most of your energy on getting these out of the way, and you'll be much less likely to overrun on time.

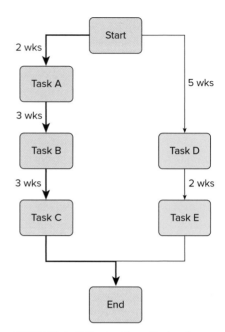

FIGURE 5-2: Following the critical path

Calculating Risk

At the start of development, it's a good idea to lay out potential risks in the planning stage. Likewise, when creating a schedule and prioritizing tasks for the next iteration or milestone, it's important that your team be on top of factors that could slow down or stall development. This can be done rather elegantly with a simple risk analysis matrix, which is designed to point out your highest risk factors so you can plan to take action.

Table 5-2 shows a worksheet that demonstrates what some of the factors were for "Archetype" at project kick-off. Column 1 lists the potential risk, column 2 the probability of the risk occurring, column 3 the potential impact if it occurred, and column 4 multiplies columns 2 and 3 together to get an overall rating

TABLE 5-2: Risk Analysis

POTENTIAL RISK	PROBABILITY FACTOR	IMPACT FACTOR	P X I (PI) RATING
No experience in iPhone 3D	90 percent	70 percent	63 percent
Game budget vs. Cost	90 percent	90 percent	81 percent
Wi-Fi or 3G multiplayer tech feasibility	60 percent	90 percent	54 percent
No developer relationship yet for this type of project	90 percent	50 percent	45 percent

These were a few for illustration purposes, but, of course, there were many more. So, what do you do with the numbers? You assign those with the highest overall rating to be your next immediate action items. It's your call as to what the cutoffs are for unacceptable risk versus acceptable risk. But anything over 80 percent is definitely unacceptable, and at about 33 percent you generally have a safer risk situation. In-between items should be examined and likely acted upon to reduce risk.

Once again, in the essential resource for producers, *The Game Producer's Handbook*, Dan Irish lists some fantastic tips to reduce risk, as paraphrased here with additions:

> ➤ Don't start production without a mostly complete design. By doing this, you'll save a lot of time by not figuring things out (and wasting time and money) as you go along.

> ➤ Eliminate the unknowns early by figuring out what it is you don't know, then do the research to know what to expect over the course of the project.

> ➤ Have a backup plan in case something goes wrong. This would be especially true for highest risk factors.

> ➤ Prototype first if possible. Don't get too far into your app only to have various pieces come together, and find out it just doesn't work.

> ➤ Put the best talent on highest risks first, thus significantly reducing (or eliminating) these risk factors and paving the way to smoother future development.

> ➤ Use third-party tools or other solutions for anything that your team lacks the expertise to do.

> ➤ Eliminate and cut features early and often. (These are his exact words, but absolutely true — if it can be simplified, do so.)

Reducing Feature Creep

Feature creep (that is, adding in features that weren't planned for) is typically detrimental to the product schedule and cost. Thus, it can be extremely risky if not controlled.

> *Though developers kept pretty close to the original design, "Archetype" had its share of feature creep moments. The development team had to come to terms with a realistic deadline, and accept that these new features they wanted to add could be implemented in future updates.*

Feature creep is common on projects with a lot of flexibility, or with very ambitious designers, coders, and even execs. To reduce it, maintain and prioritize a feature request or "I'd like to have" list. When prioritizing, keep in mind cost and risk in terms of implementing, the feature's value to the end user, and its relevance to the controlling idea or vision of the app.

Coordinating Outsourcing and Effective Communication

Outsourcing is almost always required for a small to medium-sized developer, and can include everything from complete coding, art asset development, through QA and marketing. Have a Producer on hand or someone who handles those responsibilities and comes up with separate milestone schedules for each source of outsourcing.

Because it's important that everyone on your team communicates effectively and together to solve, be informed, and ideate on issues, there are a few tips for effectively making these things happen:

➤ Use some sort of online project management software. A great example is Basecamp, available at www.basecamp.com. The one used for "Archetype" was GoPlan, available at www.goplanapp.com. Several other full-featured project management and online collaboration software solutions are available, but those are two that are recommended, with the leg up in support and functionality going to Basecamp. In each case, they'll offer full collaboration and notifications for new issues, milestone tracking, planning, issue tracking, and file management.

> It's important to note that full software development companies will likely use their own versioning software and methods of check-in or asset management. But these online solutions are good for coordinating the entire team.

➤ Have an instant chat and group video conference solution. As of this writing, the best is Skype (available at www.skype.com), though other reasonably easy-to-use methods exist for just instant messaging (such as Gmail chat). Skype offers invaluable face-to-face video conference meetings and/or free calls to anywhere in the world (user to user).

➤ Use Google Documents available from docs.google.com (or other cloud-based document solution) for any documents that you need your outsourcers to see, but you're unsure whether they have the exact version of Excel or Word that you do (and this includes most people). It's just better to be sure than to waste time in most cases with the back-and-forth versions. Plus, new versions are always updated, and you can set people to just "view" your documents, which is handy. Note that anyone viewing in private (safe from the public) must also have a Gmail account. But they're free to sign up for, and Gmail makes it easy and fast. Plus, it's the best free e-mail out there.

➤ Be specific and detailed with requests, and use clarifying questions a lot, especially when a heated or controversial issue arises. Some (or many) of your outsourcers may be from other countries. Therefore, it's not uncommon for a portion of communication to be naturally lost in translation. Those in some countries in particular (not that this is a bad thing) can tend to be very literal with meaning, so avoid using colloquial slang or language that is open to interpretation.

➤ Being specific also saves time, thus saving money. A misunderstood request to a translator can mean them having to do the work again, and, being in different time zones, that can produce a bottleneck in the workflow.

Localization

Unless you are absolutely sure you're not going to ever translate your game into another language (and even then…), you should plan for *localization* (translating your software into other languages) wherever there is text in your app.

Many languages aren't as concise as English in terms of size, and there are a couple you'll want to watch out for. For example, French and Russian have a tendency on the whole to be more lengthy. In general, though, it will be up to you or the Producer in charge of localization to direct the translator to stick within the interface or window boundaries as much as possible. In some cases, it's just not possible if your text area is too small.

> *As mentioned previously, the "Archetype" team found all translators effectively on Elance. The author was also in charge of managing and paying them, as well as implementing all the text into the game using Xcode and various methods of Excel and Google spreadsheets.*

Over the course of the app, text and phrasing can (and will) change, so it's important that you begin the localization process as early as possible. This should be when the writing is mostly locked down if, indeed, you are planning to localize and release in multiple markets simultaneously. For most projects, this means starting the process during the last one-third of production so that, when implemented during the testing stage, localization bugs — most of which are a) text too long instances, b) text missing, or c) context not correct — are reported, in addition to the normal ones.

CASE STUDY: AN IPHONE GAME IN 12 LANGUAGES

Many large development houses/publishers use outsourced full-feature localization services with their own software and techniques. To save (likely lots of) money, the "Archetype" team managed it all in house using Elance-hired translators. The target languages were English, Dutch, French, German, Italian, Japanese, Korean, Mandarin Chinese, Portuguese, Russian, Spanish, and Swedish.

The process went like this. From an Elance account, 12 new projects were started, each with a good direction in their summary, namely that they should be technology and/or game savvy, have access to and be able to use Excel, and be able to produce quick turnarounds. For an iPhone app, you not only need translated text for the set UI elements and app content, but you need your marketing press releases, as well as frequent iPhone updates and fix lists, also translated. Therefore, these translators must be "on call" — which posed the occasional problem, but it was manageable.

continues

continued

The translators were managed from the Elance "workroom," and for each assignment, they were given an Excel spreadsheet to fill in that could then be exported fairly easily into the type of text that the programmers needed for the game. For additional help, the programmers created a script that was run whenever additions were made in each language. The script checked consistency with the English source file, and let the team know when errors in space or formatting occurred.

It was vitally important (and they got much better over time) that the translators kept as close to the source language length as possible, while, of course, keeping to context and grammar to reduce the amount of revision. To aid with that, context notes were added in another column anywhere there might be ambiguity. This was especially the case with anything related to marketing.

Turnarounds were generally within a day or two for each language. As often happens when using outsourced on-call talent, if occasionally there was a lack of communication or turnaround, it was necessary in a few cases to start a new project and have a backup translator. All of them were willing to work as needed by project, and to simply keep adding new "milestones" with separate payments onto the initial project, which kept Elance maintenance at a minimum.

What also helped was a copy/paste method of communication using the first message or instruction to a translator as a "template," then copying and pasting that for every new translator, but using their name. Of course, you'd have to address individual issues or questions as needed, but this helped speed up communication.

Another big motivator was to give an occasional milestone bonus to each translator after a period of extended effort. Often, they work for relatively very small wages and not full time on the project, so this was much appreciated.

> To save memory the text elements for "Archetype" were rendered via Apple's built-in fonts, rather than images. This also saved on localization time, because it meant inputting text, rather than having to create new design elements.

When laying out new graphic user interfaces (GUIs) or writing dialogue, it's important that localization be considered. Here are some tips:

➤ Use more iconography that doesn't need translation — checkmarks, close icons, and even some small words like "OK" work for most languages these days. That said, all iconography must be intuitive and consistent.

➤ For "cells" with headings, titles, or short phrases without the use of scroll bars — that is, static boxes of text — keep in mind the space and font size. As a rule, allow for roughly one-and-a-half times the size of English text when you can.

➤ Standard Arabic numbers work in most all languages, so space considerations for these rarely need to be considered.

➤ Many phrases and colloquialisms in English don't translate well to other languages. So, keep these to a minimum, or be prepared to let your translators know that they can be creative when coming up with an appropriate colloquialism in their native language. This most often occurs when it's time for marketing.

➤ Include context notes whenever you can so that you reduce the amount of questions translators have.

Production and Stages of Development

So far, this chapter has discussed elements of production such as how to be agile, plan, schedule, and reduce risk. *Production* is the process of officially starting to create code or assets for the design. If you can, it's often a very good idea to have your programmers throw a prototype together first using art asset placeholders whenever possible. With this, you find the fun and/or prove out the concepts first, then commit to going full-scale with production, and iterate on that throughout.

As mentioned, with agile development, each of these stages is meant to be rolled into a single iteration. At the very beginning, however, it begins with a controlling idea or vision for the app. Next, you'll want to develop a concept document.

Concept

As mentioned, the concept is defined in a brief document (typically one to three pages — the fewer the better to fully present it) with some visual aids in the form of a screen grab, mockup or two, and a concise bullet point list of primary features according to the vision of the app. Who's this for? It should be discussed and passed around to everyone who makes decisions on the app's design: Producer, executive management, lead designers/coders, and so on, for feedback and feasibility. Expect this to be iterated on somewhat as it goes around the table a few times in the process of ironing out its main features.

Scott Berkun recommends creating a *marketing requirements document* (MRD), in addition to the concept document, except that he uses the term "vision document." The content of the MRD can be included in the vision document, but may contain sensitive data that shouldn't be circulated. The MRD is a summary of your market research. What opportunities do you see in the App Store that aren't being exploited? Are there competitors in your chosen genre or subgenre of app? If so, what areas are they ignoring? What assumptions (either by end users or software developers) can be overturned or re-imagined?

> *For a more in-depth discussion of each of the MRD and a concept (or vision) document, along with extremely useful anecdotes and exercises, see* Making Ideas Happen: Mastering Project Management *by Scott Berkun (Sebastopol, CA: O'Reilly, 2008). Berkun's book cannot be recommended enough — it's a must-have for anyone involved in creating software. Avoid confusing Belkun's book with* Making Ideas Happen *by Scott Belsky (New York: Penguin, 2010), which is useful, but not nearly as in-depth.*

The MRD should also serve as the foundation for beginning the discussion on features — both to be added and avoided. Remember that analyzing the market for your app means fleshing out what it is and isn't; where you are specifically not going is often just as important as where you aim to succeed.

As with the concept document, remember you are not trying to impress or convince anyone with the MRD. Providing clear, concise (but easy-to-understand) answers is more important than buzz words and marketing-speak. As you write these documents (or direct them to be written), imagine the horror of a feature gone wrong because your lead programmer misunderstood portions of your controlling idea, or made wrong assumptions based on marketing answers.

You should roll your concept document into the beginning of the main functional spec or design document — the less to keep track of, the better.

> *Arguably, the term* functional spec *isn't used as much in game development as design document—for one reason. Very generally, when using the term* functional specification, *you are speaking of a very detailed document (all "i's" dotted and "t's" crossed), whereas the term* design document *could mean a detailed functional document in the same vein, but just as well might mean more a detailed design plan without some of the absolute fine details.*

The rule of thumb is, if it's a game (or app), it can just be a design document, and it's up to the team to decide how much detail goes in. Sometimes, the less detail the better, because design of a complex project is highly iterative. If you're implementing agile development, it's more important that you build in the fun and/or usability, rather than knowing that the exact ammo capacity of your shotgun cartridge is 4 or 12, or that you can filter 250 messages at a time instead of 500. These things change quickly with real user testing. For that example, it's good enough to know that shotguns use up shotgun shells, or that the messages can be filtered. The exact number can be set by the designer/programmers.

Once concept/MRD is completed, you will need to proceed to the Pre-production stage, also known as Design. If you're building a prototype, it's often a good idea to do both simultaneously.

Pre-Production (Design)

This is where the handwringing really begins — the hair-pulling, gut-wrenching process of solving problems, one after the other, until you're happy with the results. The designer Paul Rand (famous for creating the iconic IBM logo, Steve Jobs' NeXT cube, and plenty of others) once said, "Design is everything!" And he's right.

The good news is that your spec is not written in stone. It remains a fluid document, with open issues and incomplete information, until you've solved each particular problem or resolved each issue. Some will tell you a spec is never truly finished, even right through the end of final bug testing. But as long as you continue updating the spec throughout development, your app will benefit from the efficiency.

Expect this process to take anywhere from two to four weeks for a rather simple app, or more with some iteration for a very complex app or game. One writer should author the document throughout. A consistent voice is important and design-by-committee (other than including them in brainstorming or team discussion) is typically never a good foundation point for a document. The design doc will likely be from about 20 or so pages, up to more than 100 for complex apps/games with many assets. At this stage, you needn't worry about it being too fleshed out in terms of exact details. (Those will come with play and user testing, but no one wants to read a spec as big as the local phone book, so diagram and use visual aids as much as possible.)

> *This bears repeating. Steer your designers to use mockups, charts, tables, and any other visual aids and/or flowcharts as much as possible. Walls of text are difficult and boring to read.*

There is one caution about too little information. Past experience as a designer has proven that programmers, if given too little information, must guess at exactly how many tasks are supposed to work. It's usually not necessary that you spell out every last detail such as timing (which can be tweaked), especially if it's commonly seen in similar designs. But don't take for granted that the end result will be what you originally envisioned if you don't take the time to clearly (but concisely) state some of the key logic and flow.

Pre-production (Design) is also where you'll be setting up your production systems and plans, such as asset management, version sourcing, team communication resources, assembling your team, and getting contracts ready.

Production

Make milestones, lock down core features while iterating on peripheral features to reduce waste (core features should have been found and locked down by now in Pre-production), and utilize agile development whenever you can for each iteration.

For each milestone, ensure that you have a concept, planning, production, and testing phase (even if it's just the owners) before moving onto the next.

Testing and Post-Production

In general, you're happy with your app and its functionality, but it needs much polish, be it in art, execution, optimization, interface, controls, gameplay tweaking, timing, and so on.

Testing and Post-production is the stage where you'll work on ensuring that the entire experience lives up (and hopefully goes beyond) the original vision, and is what a user would expect from a competitive app in the same genre. Namely, this is your final testing and tweaking push to iron out all issues before release.

An app or game generally goes through two main test stages prior to launch: alpha and beta. The later the stage, the less tweaking is done to core gameplay elements, and the more stability and usability are required.

Alpha

Once all the major issues have been worked out in the Production stage, it's time to jump into the trenches. An *alpha* app will have most features complete, perhaps a few peripheral features incomplete, and may be using some placeholder art, but the core functionality will be in place. Some major show-stoppers may be present (for now).

Alpha-stage apps are sometimes demonstrated to the press, but that should be discouraged. You may be eager to show your awesome new app to the world, but showing too soon may yield inaccurate expectations among your potential users (either positive or negative). Users and the press will also begin the release countdown, too, and interest may wane well before your final release date nears. Unless you absolutely must, save demos for late beta or (preferably) release candidate stage.

Beta

In *beta*, all major features detailed in the design spec are in and working to a degree. Many problems still exist, but major pipelines are in place, and functioning properly. Entire app testing begins in earnest as the last peripheral features are added and tweaked, and all art is in.

You may find yourself updating the spec document throughout beta as your app's remaining feature sets are coded, tested, iterated, and finalized. In late beta, the app is some significant percentage complete (hopefully 80 percent or more); some issues remain, and the focus in testing is wiping out crash, major gameplay, and other instability bugs first and foremost. Testing has been ongoing (and tested on every generation iOS device you can get your hands on — right?). The entire team should be using the app on a daily basis. In fact, if by late beta you don't want to ever see your app again, you're in good shape.

Release Candidate/Launch

Often, multiple release candidates are issued as new bugs crop up and are beaten back to where they came from. Your app is almost ready to submit to Apple — huzzah! But resist the very strong urge to toss any remaining bug reports out the nearest window. It may be tempting, but you will regret not hanging on for those last few weeks when the negative reviews come pouring in. The App Store is so crowded that apps with even minor annoyances are often set aside without a second thought. Your app should be the one that performs flawlessly.

If you're near your budget (or worse, over it) and you have no choice, release your app and consider noting specific fixes being worked on in the description. Don't — repeat *don't* — promise features or fixes you aren't working on. It just sets you up for failure if you can't deliver. Plenty of developers over-promise in the App Store, and nothing enrages iOS users more.

It goes without saying that *the* cardinal sin for apps are crashes. If your app crashes, and you absolutely, positively don't have to submit, *don't*! Nothing says "amateur" like a crashing app. Users don't care if they really should have rebooted their device or closed out all those extra Mobile Safari Web pages first. It doesn't matter; they will not hesitate to leave bad one-star reviews for apps that crash. *Never release apps that crash under any circumstances.* It is the death knell for any iOS app, period.

How do you know what bugs to ignore? Cutting features shouldn't be an issue at this stage. If it is, you're confused as to what stage your project is in. Bugs should be prioritized on a scale from "major" to "minor," and anything at the bottom of the "minor" list is a candidate to be fixed after release. Use your common sense to decide. Ask yourself, if you only had (insert price of your app here) to spend this month and you bought this app, would you be upset if this bug happened? Be honest with yourself here. Otherwise, seek help from friends and family.

Finally, note that Apple's review process is merely a series of checks on your app. They don't do bug testing of any kind. If you find bugs that need to be fixed after submission, you can request they suspend the review. But you'll have to resubmit and restart the process once the bug(s) are stomped.

> *Apple has begun publishing a list — mainly full of "not to dos" — that will get your app rejected. Be sure to sign up for notification of updates.*

Post Release

Prior even to Production finishing, you should start making plans to expand or update your app, because updates (especially free if you can) tell your community that you are invested in the life of the app along with them, through thick and thin. Think of this as following through with your wedding vows, because that's pretty much how the consumers see it when they fork out the difficult $0.99. Well, to be honest — at $0.99, it's more like a budding relationship, hoping it might go somewhere. When you go for anything $1.99 and up, suddenly it's like marriage, and divorces can be ugly — especially on the App Store review page.

Seriously, though, you should start working on your first updates after your submission, and have the first ready very soon after you launch. Your post-release plan should be developed sometime during production (if there is one) with minor content updates regularly occurring throughout the afterlife of release. These can be holiday-related (as in themes), graphic upgrades, compatibility with new devices (iPad, retina display), new languages added, and so on. Users want to see that you care, and they will hang around and continue to spread the word if you do.

Coordinating Marketing

It's tough to predict when your app will be rejected or (hopefully) approved, but a good rule of thumb is two weeks from submission. The review rosters surge during certain times of the year — particularly October through December in anticipation of the Christmas holiday.

> *In fact, so many new iOS devices are activated during the holidays that the App Store has taken to shutting down during the week of Christmas to halt the flood of review requests.*

One tool you can utilize for marketing planning is to set the release date far enough into the future that your app will almost certainly be approved. It's still risky, because anything can happen, but if you happen to be developing in safer genres (for example, games or uncontroversial books), it's a good way to lock in advertising. Almost all reputable websites will work with you to change your ad schedules if needed. (It's a common practice; ad schedules change all the time.) If they don't, look elsewhere in the future.

One caveat though is to be sure to finish all your marketing plans, get your promotional videos and websites done, and anything else you need to finalize all before you submit your app. The last thing you need is to be frantically rushing crucial marketing material because your app was approved well before you expected.

Q&A WITH DANE BAKER, VILLAIN CEO AND HEAD HONCHO (IN CHARGE OF THE UNIVERSE, AND SO ON, AND SO ON)

Dane Baker was kind enough to provide his insight and wisdom for these Marketing "do's and don'ts."

When to Release

Do — Release when Apple is releasing a new iPhone. There are always tons of new early adopters who are eager to snap up new apps, even ones that are "old" for the rest of us. The same goes for new carriers getting the iPhone for the first time (like Verizon did in the U.S. in February 2011).

> *In addition, you'll be able to capitalize on new features or technologies that are coming out with the new device. For example, when the gyroscope feature was launched, it was ideal to be pushing an app that supported this feature. Market this aspect, but be aware that gimmicky apps abound, so ensure yours is not.*

Do — Release around major holidays, especially Thanksgiving and Christmas. iOS device sales skyrocket during gift-giving seasons, and you should tailor releases or updates to fit.

> *Note that, in the exact week of Christmas, the App Store shuts down, so by holidays, in essence that week is excluded.*

Don't — Delay your app for significant time periods to release at a certain time. Release early and build your audience. "Angry Birds" wasn't a hit overnight, and chances are your app won't be, either.

Don't — Release too early! The number one killer of apps is bugs, particularly crash bugs. With more than 300,000 other choices, users will give up on your app in a New York Minute if you don't absolutely ooze quality and stability.

Making a Big Splash

Do — Build truly unique *and* useful apps. The cheapest and best marketing pitch is your product itself. You will either succeed on a $0 marketing budget, or spend a ton, depending on how unique and useful your app is.

Do — Carefully build rapport with site editors. This is a delicate dance that must be done cautiously. Aim to be useful to them, not a pain in the neck. Suggest story ideas unrelated to your app, help with research, or making connections.

Don't — Be annoying. Press releases, sending mass spam e-mails constantly — all of these are ways to virtually guarantee editors and writers will ignore you. Be creative, appropriate, and professional. Don't be obnoxious.

Don't — Bother with press releases. Imagine that you're the editor of an iPhone site. Now, imagine what your inbox looks like on a Monday morning. Don't waste your time.

Don't — Spend too much on advertising. If you're a paid app, it's a tall order to get enough downloads to make ads (even "cheap" Google text ads or mobile banners) break even. Consider no ads at all, and be creative instead. Above all, stay away from print, TV, or radio advertising; it's hard enough to convince users actually sitting at their computer!

Maintaining the Hype

Do — Release often. Updates may not increase sales, but they will ensure sales remain constant.

Do — Give people new things worth talking about. If it's not really interesting, why would anyone care? The App Store is brutal; come prepared.

Do — Leverage your existing audience to the fullest extent. Give them free stuff. Give them stuff they want to gift to friends. Give them a reason to keep coming back.

Don't — Release "too" often. Too many updates mean too many trips to the App Store update page just for your app. Every week or so is about right.

SUMMARY

This chapter should have helped as you build a team around an agile development process (when able). This chapter also provided you with production tips that can help get your app ready sooner, be more in line with your vision and customers' ultimate satisfaction, and be ready for issues that — with traditional methods — would have had the potential to derail a project.

In Chapter 6, you'll become familiar with many of the guidelines that can help as you move through development, from how to price your app, to ways in which you can implement metaphors to enhance your brand.

6

Guidelines and Expectations for Developing Your App

WHAT'S IN THIS CHAPTER?

➤ Understanding pricing considerations and business models

➤ Learning how to create an app in the half-second window you have for engaging your user

➤ Understanding why it is important to use physical metaphors whenever possible

➤ Learning how to ideate and implement physical metaphors

The App Store, of course, has an immense range of business models and app prices. But when looking for patterns, three of them emerge.

As you saw in Chapter 3, 99-cent apps make up roughly 25 to 30 percent of the current available apps. This is a natural evolution of the App Store in that that's as low as you can go without going free: no more room to undercut your competition and remain paid. In fact, games (which are consistently in the top one or two categories) are averaging slightly above the 99-cent price, whereas the average price of an app in all categories is well over $2. Free apps make up roughly another 40 percent (and this looks to be climbing because of apps with in-app purchases). The remaining roughly one-third of the App Store is divided up with various "premium" app prices of $4.99 and upward.

Beginning with this chapter, the next three chapters take a look at these patterns in app pricing (free, freemium, and paid), the reasons behind pricing models, and how to develop your app to stay ahead of your competition in that price range. In addition, this particular chapter also houses many general principles and examples you will want to consider when creating an app in any price range, because many apps did not start out at their current price.

POTENTIAL RISK AND REWARD

As you'll see in Chapter 8, one of the several reasons to create an app that's a bit more expensive (such as at $1.99 and above) is that you can count on successive price-reduction updates or promotions to lift a potentially sagging sales curve. If you start with your app at 99 cents, for example, there's nowhere to go but free.

Well, there used to be nowhere to go. Back before in-app purchases became available, creating a free app had some definite points against it — among them, how to properly upsell your associated premium app, or how best to utilize in-app advertising. Now that all apps can use this functionality, it's becoming a dominating factor in app design. Free apps not only are downloaded more often, but now have the potential to earn big revenue through in-app purchases in addition to the tried and sometimes true ad payouts.

In summary, creating a free app presents much less risk *if* you're planning on using in-app purchases, or have another version you want people to buy, because it will likely get viewed more often. Why, then, would you want a low priced, 99-cent app? Should you charge more? Let's take a look at the considerations you'll need to work out before deciding on a price point, whether 99 cents or more.

Paid Apps Are Seen as WYSIWYG

There's an expectation from customers that if they pay for an app, little to no additional payment will be requested post purchase. What you see is what you get (WYSIWYG). The value should be built into the app price, and the higher that price, the stronger the mentality. Though customers are beginning to find in-app purchases as more of a standard offering, and are less inclined to complain, the basic assumption going into a paid app is still that it should present more overall value than a free app.

What Incentives Can You Provide When Sales Dwindle?

Updates beyond bug fixing (though also important) are a great way to keep your app visible. Will your app be able to provide feature or content updates post release? If not, you may want to consider alternatives to 99-cent pricing to keep potential incentives in place, unless you're sure of a maintainable position in your niche (whether game or app). Having said that, because games are not selling features per se, but rather entertainment, it is important to make the distinction that when an app is based on a feature set (say, Twitter), it is more likely to become outdone or outdated, and at a quicker pace.

Are You Planning on In-App Purchases?

Do your plans include in-app purchases for downloadable content such as new levels, modes, items, or functionality (for example, the removal of ads for a price)? If so, be sure there's a lot of value present at 99 cents before asking users to pay for more. The balance of value vs. paid in-app purchases in paid apps will be discussed in Chapter 8.

Can You Go Free?

With significantly more downloads for free apps than paid apps, if you're considering the 99-cents price point, it's worth considering whether you can support going free.

For free apps, and before in-app purchases, creating a "lite" restricted version for users to try with an upsell to the paid version (that unlocks certain functionality) is an early and still highly-recommended strategy. The newer alternative is making it free and fully functional, and then using in-app purchases, add the option to buy ("unlock") new content or features (such as levels or modes).

Like Winning the Lottery

You never really know whether your app is going to take off. After all, many great apps (for one reason or another) simply don't. If you have one that's not as popular as it could be, usually it can be attributed to one or more items from the following list, sometimes in combination:

➤ You have insufficient marketing. Did you target the right channels? For example, did you spend on print over online, or pay for a single banner ad for a popular related site, and so on?

➤ You have ill-timed marketing. This could cover everything from your release date to when you launch targeted campaigns.

➤ Your app keywords are not appropriately bringing traffic.

➤ Your submitted category is not the best-suited to your app.

➤ Your niche is already saturated with other more popular and/or similarly featured apps.

The eventual goal is to make it into the Top 100, which is considered by many to be the point at which your app can self-sustain its sales primarily because of visibility and the number of downloads (even though number of downloads per app are top-heavy even within the top 100).

Another in-iTunes occurrence is the possibility of making it onto the incredibly small list of "App of the Week" titles. If you manage either of these distinctions, it can feel like winning the lottery.

> *With "Archetype," the developers did not submit for "App of the Week," nor did they know it was selected. The exact process Apple has for selection is unfortunately secret, so there is no definitive formula.*

Following are some general (though important) guidelines for not only having a hit, but making it into the "App of the Week" (which gets your app prominently featured at the top of the App Store in a large rotating banner):

➤ **Create a good app** — Yes, this is completely obvious. However, if you are in the market mostly to capitalize on a niche that hasn't been saturated yet, without exactly the care or polish that Apple takes seriously, you may make it into the Top 100, but will have no chance of making "App of the Week." Carve out a definitive niche, keep it bug free, and respond to feedback.

➤ **Get good press** — If most of your reviews are positive, those at Apple who are often gamers and do take note of popular i-device blogs and review sites will notice. They'll see the buzz, and your app may have a better chance. It's what the developers of "Archetype" did, and it did work for them.

➤ **Be an underdog** — Sometimes the big companies with hyped releases get snubbed for the "App of the Week." More often, apps from new developers will appear out of nowhere to be prominently featured. This is good news for most of us. After all, if the Average Joe and indie developers of the world can't dream of hitting it big in the App Store, then it wouldn't be nearly as popular as it has been. It's the same psychological process that goes on with the lottery.

➤ **Carve out a niche of your own** — Be different from your competitors in tangible ways. This goes back to competitive research, but ensure that your app has unique selling points that make it indispensible in terms of fun and/ or value. Clones of other games usually need not apply here.

So, creating a hit app can sometimes feel like winning a lottery, but unlike the lottery, revenue can be unpredictable.

Revenue Like a Rollercoaster

Whether or not your app hits it big, the App Store market will continue to fluctuate. Just as in any business, you'll see periods of growth and decline (hopefully much more of the former). As you keep an eye on sales and competitors, you'll have to adapt accordingly to changing conditions, perhaps with price decreases to offset a competitor's launch. If you were to graph the expected revenue of your average paid app (not including ad revenue), it would look something like a rollercoaster, as shown in Figure 6-1.

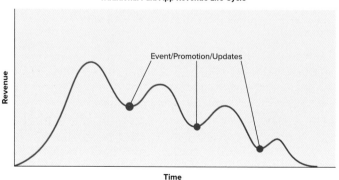

FIGURE 6-1: When revenue is tied to sales only, it can look like a rollercoaster over the app's life cycle

These days, however, with in-app purchases, there is the potential to even out the ride, and continue to earn revenue because it no longer depends only on app sales. Once you can get a steady stream of users and utilize in-app purchases with regular updates, you'll be earning revenue even in periods of slow app sales/downloads.

Figure 6-2 shows the sales curve from before, along with the new in-app purchase revenue curve. This type of in-app purchase curve might best apply to a free app with in-app purchases and regular updates. As you can see, even when sales or downloads dwindle, you can still earn revenue through updates that might include more in-app purchases.

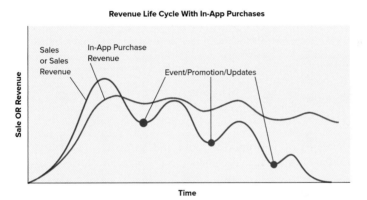

FIGURE 6-2: With in-app purchases, you have a chance at more steady revenue, even after sales decline

APP STORE BUSINESS MODELS

Now that you've gone through some basic considerations, let's take a more specific look at most of the business models currently in the App Store. Chapter 7 examines the differences of creating free and "freemium" apps (those where you are limited in content without in-app purchases), and Chapter 8 explores paid and premium apps (those that are above the $4.99 price point).

Free Apps

Free apps are not the same as free-to-play — or "freemium" — apps. The free-to-play models have a significant content restriction that requires an investment of real money to unlock, and are discussed in detail in Chapter 7.

Free apps fall into two categories: apps that have all their content available, and lite versions (which, in most cases, are content- or time-restricted versions of paid apps).

Free and Lite App Revenue Models

Free apps that are not lite versions are almost always ad-driven, as are the occasional lite versions of paid apps. Sometimes the only difference between the free and paid version is the removal of ads, which can be quite an incentive for some users, depending on how intrusive they are versus how addictive or practical the app is.

Many third-party ad networks exist such as AdMob and JumpTap (see Appendix B for a good list). However, a reliable source that doesn't take you out of your app for ads was released in 2010 — none other than Apple's own iAd (http://developer.apple.com/iad/). Ads delivered via iAd are typically heavy on animation and user engagement, and some users report better payouts than for some other networks. Of course, like most anything, it varies. This is discussed in detail in Chapter 7.

The other type of free app is the lite version of paid apps, which can also be supported by ads, as well as attempting to upsell their paid version. The model here — aside from ads, which depending on factors discussed next chapter, may or may not pay as much as you want — is the same as providing a demo for any console or PC games. The hope is that users will find it compelling enough to purchase the paid version. Conversion rates vary wildly, of course, so there are many strategies to accomplish this.

In Figure 6-3, "Fruit Ninja HD Lite" for the iPad had a main menu with some modes that did not look any different from the "classic" mode. When tapping (or, in this case, swishing) through the mode icon (see the section "Using Physical Metaphors to Delight Your Audience" later in this chapter), you were taken to this "landing page."

FIGURE 6-3: Lite apps have content that is available only if you buy their paid versions

Note the Buy Now button on the bottom of the screen, which takes you to the App Store's buy page shown in Figure 6-4 for the full paid version. In this case, the app is $2.99, which, for the iPad, is relatively cheap for a full-price game.

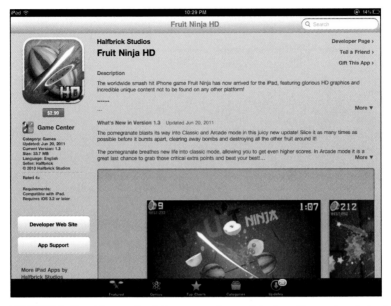

FIGURE 6-4: Your lite app should have many in-app links from lite versions to land you here, right on your app's paid App Store page

Freemium Revenue Model

For a number of years, the freemium (or microtransaction) model of pricing has been the base revenue model for games in Asia, and has most recently been gaining incredible momentum in North America as well — so much so, in fact, that it's completely trending the App Store toward in-app purchases. As a matter of fact, go into any Target or Walmart (or similar store) and you'll be able to find a wall somewhere with dozens of colorful prepaid cards supporting all sorts of subscription plans or other monetization for both free-to-play and trial-based games.

Now, technically, a number of related terms concerning the word freemium include *downloadable content* (DLC) and *microtransactions*, and not all definitions are the same. These are discussed in Chapter 7. For now, the model is that you release a title that is free to play, but either completely restrict certain features from being accessible until the user pays, or severely limit the user's capability to excel (such as a game like "Smurfs' Village" by Capcom Mobile).

Most of these titles are not ad-supported, and instead rely on the revenue from steady in-app purchases from users, whether subscription-based, paid DLC, or via microtransactions. The microtransaction model has been generating more revenue than any other methods of late.

Paid App Revenue Models and Price Expectations

Paid apps range from $0.99 to $999.99, and anything at or above $4.99 (for iPhone) or about $9.99 for iPad is believed to be a premium app. That definition changes, and should be treated as only a guideline. Believe it or not, more than 20 apps are currently in the App Store listed at $999.99. Whether many of these are truly priced to sell or are joke apps is uncertain, but none is anywhere near the Top 100 apps in terms of gross revenue.

Paid apps are typically content complete, though an increasing number are using paid DLC or additional subscription options (such as in navigation software, or any that provide access to libraries of assets). Revenue earned via paid apps is typically not ad supported (because customers would think this was over the line), and is mostly all direct sales based, except, of course, for paid DLC purchases.

Because pricing can vary quite a bit, what follows is an overview of the various pricing models and expectations (to be explained in further detail in Chapter 8).

$0.99 to $2.99 Apps

Though the average price of apps may be declining because of free apps with in-app purchases becoming more popular, some are saying that paid apps have reached a bottom plateau and are starting to edge up a bit in price — finally being confident enough that the consumer is willing to pay for a good, novel app. Although, a couple of years ago, a $2.99 iPhone app might have been in a higher price category, it can now almost be considered an impulse buy, just as the $1.99 and $0.99 apps are.

Most gaming or entertainment apps fall into this price category. Anything that's business-oriented, practical, or educational may fetch a more premium price. The revenue model is typically pure sales here. Developers often provide free content updates with these types of apps, providing new features and fixes at no cost.

As mentioned, however, the alternative is to have your app at this price, and, in addition, offer paid DLC that was not part of the base experience. If you do this, beware that the base app should already offer significant value, and the DLC is not seen as something that should be included for free.

$3.99 to $4.99 Apps

For iPhone apps (and iPad games), this price range is now considered premium territory. If you have a $4.99 app, it should offer something that other apps in your niche fail to provide, whether exquisite graphics or a unique feature that may take competitors a bit of time to emulate. Games that are offered at this price point must provide an excessive amount of polish, detail, and, if at all possible, multiplayer gameplay. All games in this category should offer free lite versions, so that more users will give it a try. There are simply too many games to try if you're not already an established brand.

The revenue here is typically via sales, and, generally, any app that is in premium territory is not expected to also have DLC or additional microtransactions (at least, not yet).

For the iPad, a $3.99 or $4.99 app is not uncommon. Therefore, the premium range for an iPad general app would be roughly $6.99 and up. However, games have slightly different expectations on the iPad — because it is bigger, and, therefore, has more room to maneuver. So, if you're pricing your app in this range, it should still be incredibly polished, and feature something unique to help it stand out, or else you can expect sales to wither.

$5.99 to $9.99 Apps

According to 148apps.biz, the vast percentage of apps in this category are not games. This makes sense, because games at lesser price points already pretty much offer as much entertainment value as you can on the device.

Apps in this price range are usually either from premium development studios (which are typically able to create value and extensive polish faster and for less cost), or offer something you can't get with an app in a cheaper price range.

Figure 6-5 shows one of the more expensive games in the App Store, priced at $9.99 for both iPhone and iPad. It's adapted from one of the most popular board games in recent years, "Carcassonne." Since its release, it has consistently been mentioned as an example of polish and excellent interface design, taking full advantage of touch features with an elegant and infinite play board, and satisfying user feedback for most actions.

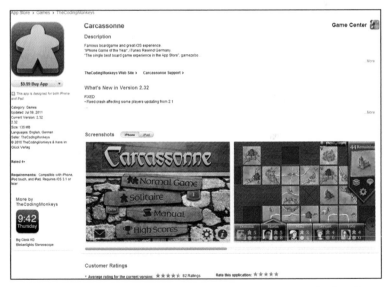

FIGURE 6-5: Carcassonne is one of the most expensive games in the App Store, but can back up its price with polish and gameplay

Revenue for apps in this price range is, again, mostly sales-based, with almost no room for ads. But at least on the iPad, because of its bigger screen and keyboard, a moderate number of productivity apps at this price are offering either subscriptions or additional DLC packs.

$10.99 and More Apps

Generally, apps in this price range are targeted to very specific types of needs in a particular niche (such as business, navigation, education, or other niche that may require mostly proprietary data or functionality). Rarely will you see a game charge anything more than $9.99.

Apps in this price range hope to capture a certain niche market, and revenue is typically very spiky, but can be profitable because development often uses proprietary knowledge and can, therefore, rely less on the need for advanced graphics, art, or animation (which can be costly). That being said, programming costs can also vary, depending on complexity of the app.

Figure 6-6 shows an example of an app that charges the max possible, $999.99. In this case, "BarMax" justifies the price by claiming proprietary knowledge, and explicitly targets lawyers preparing for the bar exam.

FIGURE 6-6: If you create an expensive app, note that proprietary information and projected value are key marketing strategies

Now that you have an overview of App Store business models, let's ensure that you have an engaging app. The remainder of the chapter focuses on guidelines for what to do and not do, as well as an important exercise for ensuring maximum user engagement.

CREATING FOR A MULTITASKING WORLD

Because people are drawn in a million different directions per day, more and more they're turning to their smartphone as a solution for organization as well as entertainment. Everything from calls and conferences, notifications, schedules, reports, directions, references, and, of course, leisure for those few minutes of relief can all be achieved from the smartphone or, while at work, your computer.

Paper and pen are mostly a thing of the past. Because instant communication, knowledge, and gratification have so penetrated our daily lives, people are learning to spend only moments on one thing at a time, and constantly shifting focus. This short amount of attention is likely the small window you'll have for capturing their interest and holding them there. You learn more about this opportunity later in this chapter in the section, "The Half-Second Window." For now, let's take a glimpse into what is happening in the brain when you are multitasking, and the effects of multitasking on your ability to focus so that you can better take advantage of the small time you're allotted.

Understanding the Effects of Multitasking on the Brain

According to research published on the Proceedings of the National Academy of Sciences (PNAS) in 2009 about cognitive control in media multitaskers, participants who (after a series of questions) were pegged "heavy multitaskers" had more trouble focusing and shutting out irrelevant information, in addition to being less efficient at task-switching in general.

Many other studies have concluded the same thing. Multitasking is actually counter-productive to efficiency, and heavy multitaskers (such as those you might find using an i-device) are actually very prone to new distractions, limiting the time and focus they have for your app.

Seeing the Phone as the Ultimate Multitasking Tool

The iPhone (or any such device) is the ultimate tool for accomplishing multiple tasks in one session. It's portable, has instant notifications, can (now) efficiently multitask and switch to different programs, can accept and make calls, can chat, update and be social, can provide directions or light your way, keep lists and reminders, can keep you entertained, and has a near infinite other possible uses as well.

The take-home message from this section is that iPhone users are heavy multi-taskers, and any app that requires effort to concentrate is thus likely to not be received as well. So, the need to keep the app itself simple and focused is, there-fore, critically important, at least at the beginning. Some targeted niches (such as specific educational or utility apps) will, of course, need to break the rules some-what. But for these, it's likely that your niche knows what it's getting into before even trying it out. That said, keeping it as simple as possible in the beginning will go a long way toward engaging your user.

Let's now take a look at how to best take advantage of the limited time you have for user engagement.

THE HALF-SECOND WINDOW

The sheer number of apps available for the iPhone or other i-device means that users will only give your app a minimum trial at best before making a judgment. Because users are able to quickly jump from one task to another on the iPhone or other i-device, the time you have for first engaging the user is incredibly minute — but significant.

To avoid any faux-pas that might cause the user to exit your app, let's take a brief look into how users will interact with your app in the short "half-second window," and then how to make your initial interactions more engaging.

Understanding Typical User Tendencies with Touch Screens

Touch screen users currently know how to swipe, tap, pinch, and (only because it's been bundled with iPhones and relatives) tilt and shake. If your app is going to require any user input other than these actions, be aware that it might present a barrier to your customer's engagement with the app.

Without getting into the math, Fitt's Law states that the time to rapidly move to a target is a function of the distance to the target, as well as its size. In other words, ensure that frequent actions by the user are easier to accomplish.

How would you go about doing this? Combining Fitt's Law, with what is known about user tendencies, it is possible to formulate the following dos and don'ts:

➤ **Do** — create large buttons for common actions, while keeping smaller buttons (if needed) for actions that aren't performed much.

➤ **Do** — make all actions that are performed the most require the least amount of steps to complete. (In other words, if the user is always going back to the main menu, put a Home icon along the top and keep it there.)

➤ **Don't** — make any icons so small that a user's fingers have difficulty hitting the target. There's nothing more frustrating than having a commonly pressed button in the upper corner, where hitting it even when you concentrate results in a 40 percent success rate.

➤ **Don't** — make unnecessary or gimmicky controls just because you're on a touch screen. If a simple tap works, don't require the user to perform a complicated gesture just because it seems more fun.

➤ **Don't** — use tilt or gyroscopic controls unless needed, because these methods tend to be less precise.

➤ **Do** — experiment with alternative controls such as tilt and gyro just to see if they are needed or could be a potential selling point. Experiment with these controls in games. If either of these methods is implemented, you should absolutely implement alternative control methods for your users if possible.

> *Not having gyro controls was a frequent early complaint for "Archetype," remedied in an update not long after release.*

➤ **Do** — remember that programmers can make the "tappable" areas of buttons even larger than the button so that larger fingers can hit seemingly smaller targets. However, it's better to make these areas as consistent as possible with the button.

Building Initial Interactions That Meet the "Half-Second Window"

Because the time to engage your users is incredibly short, it's important to understand how to grab them in the initial moments of using your app. You may want to see how your initial interactions match up with the following list of brief guidelines. This is by no means an extensive list, so you may also come up with other unique ways of doing so in the important initial moments.

➤ Make it absolutely apparent what users should do as soon as they're on the main menu or in your app. If it's selecting a mode from a list, animate the most common mode, or make the button bigger. A world-building freemium game, for example, might instantly have a welcome pop-up message that exhibits enthusiasm.

➤ If possible, have some animation on the main screen. This increases interest and conveys polish.

➤ Do not go into a lengthy tutorial or display a wall of text before playing. Many users will not read this, and will assume that, if your app is worth playing/using, they'll be able to figure it out without reading. At most, try to have one help/control screen prior to launch. Sometimes this can even be beneficial.

➤ Have some of your best art appear on the intro screen or in the first level. Don't save it for later levels, because this is your chance to impress the user. For example, if you are creating a utility app, have an interesting welcome pop-up message that very briefly instructs users where to click next, with an animated arrow on the interface if needed.

➤ Keep your initial main menu as simple as possible. Don't present a lot of options; the fewer the better.

➤ Have a physical metaphor (which can simply be an illustration) that users can identify with when they first get into the app. See the section, "Depicting the Physical World," later in this chapter for details on how to accomplish this.

HOW THE IPHONE'S LIMITED MEMORY CAN AFFECT INITIAL ENGAGEMENT

In the initial puzzle game the author designed for the iPhone, "Matchlings," he and his team ran up against a potential big problem in that whenever users first downloaded the app, on first launch, it would suffer from animation stuttering and framerate problems. Interestingly enough, on reboot, the problems would go away. This may have been a problem only with earlier iPhones and iPod Touch's, but at the time, it was an absolute mystery.

The team eventually found that it had to do with memory limitations, and corrected the problem prior to release. But imagine the first impression users would get if a puzzle game with heavy animation had framerate stuttering and problems responding to touch.

Developers should be aware that RAM in an i-device is still fairly limited these days (compared to, say, a PC), and that your app's performance can suffer, especially if you have other apps open or taking up memory. Ensure that your app has been tested for performance on a fresh install versus after a reboot.

DEPICTING THE PHYSICAL WORLD

Many successful apps and games have already been mentioned in this book with some of their core features analyzed. When it comes down to examining just why they've been a hit, however, usually there are many theories, ranging from right place and right time, to marketing, entertainment value, addictive gameplay, amazing graphics, and so on. Yet, one of the most fascinating and least-discussed elements (even in game or app reviews — which means that it's typically taken for granted) also happens to be a critical component to user interaction and interface design: metaphors.

If you know how to build this one component into your game or app, you'll get more identification, engagement, and often retention as a result. Let's take a deeper look at one of the key components that makes any game or app *mysteriously* more engaging and intuitive without users necessarily taking notice. The term "mysterious" is used because of the element's being taken for granted in good apps as that special ingredient that just makes it click with users.

Using Physical Metaphors to Delight Your Audience

Even in the earliest computer interfaces, as a means to get a grip on the mental model of binary data, designers and engineers came up with the term *files* for individual collections of bits with a certain purpose, *folders* for storing collections of files, *windows* for collections of folders, *trash* for deleting these, and other such metaphors rooted in the physical world. The core purpose of using metaphors is to relate something new and unknown to that which is already known, and thus familiar. In other words, it's easier to learn something new when you relate it to something you already know.

This powerful mechanism has been in place for decades as an effective user interface technique, but is seldom (or only briefly) discussed in books about game or app design. Its potential to grab and engage users is why you should be taking advantage whenever you can in your own apps.

Let's look at some examples, and then learn how to integrate them into your apps where appropriate.

In the popular "Fruit Ninja" app, your finger is the sword swinging away at the fruit. In "Cut the Rope," your finger is the scissors. In "Angry Birds," your finger pulls back the metaphorical slingshot to launch birds into towers. And in "Pocket God," well, your finger is the higher being where it can literally hold, swing, and throw innocent villagers around.

When *tweeting* using Twitter, you become the metaphorical bird using short, staccato sound-phrases to update your latest happenings. When looking at Twitter's iconic bird and interface, it all comes together to make sense more quickly, and its new paradigm is easier to digest.

> *You can see from this Twitter example that metaphors can and should extend to the brand when possible, to the name and/or logo, as a way of communicating the message or idea of the brand.*

Consider Facebook's *wall*, where, when you post something, other users can stop by and take a look. This makes perfect sense, and is completely understood by the average user.

For the very successful app iBooks (mainly because it was developed by Apple, and has its backing and marketing), Apple ensured the user interface made sense metaphorically.

Shopping carts or baskets from Amazon and other online retailers help users store items for future purchase while they continue to browse. So, you might ask why not continue with the metaphor and use aisles? The answer is that the store metaphor can be taken only so far before it begins to be ineffective for current applications. After all, the Internet is much better at sorting and finding items than it is at being a physical store.

Certainly an Internet or in-game store may *someday* use the aisles metaphor — when it makes sense to do so. For example, consider adapting the iPod's Cover Flow feature to the aisle metaphor where swiping left and right might whisk you across the aisles, each being a different category of products. Then, when it was tapped or clicked, you might be swooshed forward, perhaps even to another view, where you're actually facing the side of the aisle, with categories narrowed even further, while keeping with the physical store metaphor. At the very least, it would be more interesting than clicking from a vertical menu, if it was responsive enough!

The lists in the following sections should help you understand what types of metaphors have been used in apps and games, so as to more easily create your own.

Physical Metaphors Used in App/Web/Program Design

Following are some physical metaphors used in the design of apps, web pages, and programs:

- ➤ Tabs for categories (from physical folder tabs)
- ➤ A magnifying glass to indicate searching
- ➤ A mailbox to indicate e-mail
- ➤ Using a plus sign (+) to signify adding (or, by convention, adding a "new item")
- ➤ Using a green checkmark to indicate accept or confirm, while a red checkmark equals cancel, close, or stop (taking cues from both traffic lights and teacher's marks)
- ➤ Shopping carts and baskets as a means to hold items to order
- ➤ The eraser in paint programs
- ➤ Using a whiteboard for writing
- ➤ Sticky notes
- ➤ Home button (usually meaning go back to the "main menu" or otherwise starting point to the program)

Physical Metaphors Used in Game Design

Following are some physical metaphors used in game design:

- ➤ Using a backpack for a player's inventory

- Stores to buy things
- Journals to keep track of quests
- Books to tell a story or use as your spell inventory
- Hearts to indicate life
- Using the color red to indicate life (blood), such as in health bars
- Potion bottles/flasks for health pickups (medicine)
- Maps that look like real maps
- Using metaphor-based icons to be easily recognizable with less need for instruction, such as the following:
    - A sword to indicate an attack
    - A shield to indicate defense
    - A backpack to indicate inventory
    - Gears/wrench to indicate options/tools
    - A trophy to indicate achievements/rewards
    - A sound to indicate a speaker
- On touch devices, your user uses a finger to do the following:
    - Tap a drum or piano, or strum a guitar
    - Pull the slingshot
    - Swipe the sword
    - Throw objects
    - Serve as a writing instrument

WHY TOUCH DEVICES ARE PERFECTLY SUITED FOR PHYSICAL METAPHORS

Prior to touch (and motion) devices, users, of course, could only interact with the screen using the standard keyboard, mouse, or, in the case of gaming, a joystick with buttons. Though these devices continue to be effective for fast input, they're not exactly intuitive, because any button can be mapped to any sort of action, and, thus, the user would need some instruction before knowing what might happen. Ever try playing a recent sports game on one of the current consoles with 12 buttons, each assigned to a different action, and sometimes arbitrarily placed? There would be no way to know what each does without sufficient training, trial and error, or committing to memory.

An early adaptation to a more physical metaphor approach to mouse-driven interfaces was the use of context-sensitive cursors. When you put your cursor over an interactive object or area, the cursor changes its look, depending on what you're hovering over. The Internet continues to do this when you hover over links, turning into a hand (a symbol for interaction), which, perhaps, could further be improved if it was depicted by a chain link, as some web-design programs or blogging tools have done.

In games, early context sensitivity was used in point-and-click adventures of the late 1980s and early 1990s. Prior to this, you had to hunt and peck to find or interact with an item on screen. Once context sensitivity was implemented, adventures started phasing into what hard-core gamers used to call "easy mode," and actually changed the cursor into a hand when, say, over an object that you could interact with. It was easier, of course, but less challenging, which meant puzzle makers had to adapt by stepping up their game in terms of complexity, instead of keeping the challenge by hiding single pixels.

With context sensitivity, the metaphor became the pointer. For example, your pointer is the hand that manipulates the object or interface element, or the sword that activates combat. It works as a means to understand, but it still is a step removed from what touch devices are capable of, with your body as the metaphor — not the button.

With touch devices (and the same goes with motion devices such as the Wii), your finger/body can finally be the object interacting with the screen, thus making physical metaphors that much more intuitive and, thus, important to implement. Want to pour liquid? Tilt. Need to erase? Just wipe away. Of course, there's not an action for *everything*, but it's a great start for the use of one-to-one physical metaphors in user interaction.

In the future, you'll likely see built-in sensors (small gloves perhaps?) that can recognize three-dimensional (3D) spatial positioning in relation to the device (the Microsoft Kinect is already headed there in a basic way), and then will begin a wave of new interaction, even more accurately being able to simulate physical metaphors with user interaction.

Designer/Branding Exercise: Creating Metaphors for Your App

Whether you are developing a game or other app, coming up with a list of how you can better communicate this new system to users is important. Though the following exercise can be done at any time, generally you'll want to start somewhere near the beginning of the design phase because user scenarios can help flesh out the design.

Therefore, this is best done using (or in communication with) a designer. Regardless of where you are in the development timeline, don't skip this step, because even if you're near release, there might be a key ingredient that would attract the user even more than you may otherwise — especially with respect to branding.

Step 1: Brainstorm Metaphors around Your Concept

Take your concept and brainstorm a list of all metaphors related to it. Have your feature list handy, because there may be new metaphors you could come up with that are specific to certain features. Don't worry about whether they're good or bad yet. The point is to eventually see where your users might be able to be helped, and be able to speed through the act of understanding.

As an example, let's say that you have an inventory app that manages your collections (books, movies, DVDs, audio, and so on). Part of your list might look something like the following, again some good and some that may not be applicable or feasible:

➤ File cabinet/folders

➤ Cubbies/mailroom

➤ Bookshelves

➤ Rolodex

➤ Glass cases

➤ Candy bins

➤ Concept of thumbing through

➤ Sifter (for sorting) — an example that probably won't work, but included here in case it spurs ideas

➤ Coin sorter

➤ Warehouse (because it has inventory)

➤ Boxes

➤ Crates

➤ Delivery truck

➤ Computers

➤ Theater complex (for a movie collection)

➤ iPod Cover Flow (which is virtual, but also a convention that many users are already used to)

➤ Jukebox

➤ Notepad paper

➤ Shopping checklist

Step 2: Create User Scenarios

Create a list of possible main user scenarios, which are simple text descriptions of performing main tasks in your app. It's best if you don't get too detailed, because this will leave open opportunities to see where you could simplify the process and add metaphors as needed. If an aspect of the scenario isn't designed yet, just use your best guess, and include what users might be thinking about as you are going through the process. Keep in mind that these are just projections, and that users may experience the app in different ways.

Let's use the inventory app as an example.

Arthur has an extensive DVD/Blu-ray and music collection, and somehow found your inventory app (likely because of his seeing your fabulous App Store icon that perfectly depicted an inventory and conveyed fun/easy as well).

He enters the app and finds that it is refreshingly simple to start a new collection, or to go through a predefined list of category icons (without names). He sees the

DVD icon, taps it, and enters his name for the category. He is then taken to an empty area where he can start adding items.

After adding a couple of items, he decides to start another few categories to get them set up. There's no sense in going too overboard yet, and he would like to see if this app suits him for overall use before committing too much.

Arthur idly wonders how long it will take to add all his titles by hand, whether it's really going to be worth it, and wonders if it would be possible to tie in to a movie database that it could just take a few letters and offer up suggestions in a small list to choose from, similar to smart searches in search engines.

Step 3: Identify Opportunities for Metaphors

Go over the user scenario one sentence at a time, and see where you might be able to add any of the metaphors you came up with in your list. Highlight or underline phrases that stand out as potential targets for using a metaphor.

An easy mnemonic to remember what might be suitable to use as a metaphor is, "AAck!!" — with the "AA" being *actions* and *assets*. Whenever the user performs an action, it becomes a potential target, as well as any assets that are required for doing so, or getting them from one place to another.

Note that the goal isn't to inject your app with metaphors whenever possible, but to use them where appropriate to help the user become engaged and quickly familiar with it.

In the user scenario devised thus far, notice that not too many design specifics were given. The phrase "finds it refreshingly simple to start a new collection" could have been specific and said Arthur was presented with a big plus sign to add the first category. But, instead, it stayed general, and mentioned the simplistic process. For example, maybe the plus symbol isn't the best metaphor to add here after all. In any case, the phrase "finds it refreshingly simple to start a new collection" should be highlighted/underlined as a potential metaphor target.

With that, let's go through a couple of others. The first mention of the App Store icon states that it depicts inventory plus "fun/easy," all in one. This description is completely arbitrary, of course — it was purposely added to be an *opportunity* for a metaphor. But the key with this particular phrase will be to remember to use a metaphor (if appropriate) for the App Store icon as part of your brand/message.

Next, let's take the phrase "is then taken to an empty area where he can start adding items." How might this area be presented? This would be a good opportunity to assign a few metaphors, so highlight it.

Another phrase worth noting is "he decides to start another few categories and get them set up." How would he perform this action? A metaphor might be used here.

Step 4: Assign and Group Metaphors to User Actions

For each highlighted action from the user scenario, assign metaphors from your list, along with any new ones that come up while doing so. Don't spend too much time coming up with new ones yet until you've gone through your list once and exhausted it.

The now-highlighted phrase "finds it refreshingly simple to start a new collection" is a metaphor magnet. The obvious and conventional method here would be the plus symbol somewhere on screen, which wasn't on your inventory metaphor list, but could have been. Are there others from the list? How about the following:

➤ Delivery trucks

➤ File cabinets

➤ Cubbies/mailroom

➤ Crates

After you've gone through your highlights once and added items to the list, come back to this and briefly brainstorm other possibilities just to be sure.

Assuming you could be doing this on a computer (optional but optimal), another phrase that might be in your document would be "is then taken to an empty area where he can start adding items." This introduces more possibilities, such as the following:

➤ Bookshelves

➤ Glass cases

➤ Candy bins

Step 5: Trim List

Go through the list and jot down notes about how these might fit in with the user scenario. Remove any metaphors that you don't think will work for the following reasons:

➤ It's a mismatch in that it doesn't work with other metaphors or the overall metaphor (for example, using a farming metaphor with an office metaphor).

➤ It doesn't work with the brand.

➤ It's not viable per available resources (including time).

After trimming the list, what you should be left with are viable metaphors that you can keep or rule out again by repeating this step using the preceding criteria.

In this example user scenario, with the phrase "finds it refreshingly simple to start a new collection," the list was delivery trucks, file cabinets, cubbies/mailroom, and crates. For each, you might have some additional considerations.

For example, with delivery trucks, perhaps once you click the plus sign, an animated truck pulls up with no "brand logo" on its side. So, the keyboard appears for you to type a category name. Then, when you enter a category name, it appears on the trailer's side. Tapping on it speeds it away to its destination, transitioning you to the next screen. This type of animation may seem too complicated and resource-heavy, plus the metaphor might not fit with the flavor of the app or all categories, so it's in jeopardy of being removed.

An empty crate might be feasible here as an asset with a plus symbol on it. Perhaps the background is inside a warehouse (a nice one to be sure, or maybe you can upgrade it with points you earn from filling out categories), with your first empty crate on the ground, and a plus symbol on it.

Cubbies like you might find in a mailroom sounds like it might work interface-wise, but here you have a mismatch. Some of the items within the categories are not likely to fit inside a cubby hole. File cabinets may also work — after all, these are lists — but it's not very exciting.

In the end, the best idea seems to be the warehouse/crates metaphor. But, depending on budget and resources, you probably will opt for the conventional plus symbol and some sort of regular (but polished) interface. But then, you never know. After all, each category may actually be using a new metaphor such as a bookshelf for its category, and that might better solve the mismatch of a bookshelf somehow being in a crate.

You should by now have a good grasp of how to implement metaphors into your app, either for user actions, assets that are there when being taken to or arriving in different sections of your app, or its overall brand (think Twitter). Next, let's look at something that has been only technologically possible fairly recently for mobile/portable devices, which is the use of physics.

Utilizing Physical Forces: Gravity, Weather, Objects

If you're planning on having any action in your app (most often in games or entertainment apps), consider using a basic physics engine to support realism and allow for emergent gameplay.

Emergent gameplay means effects that come about over the course of playing that weren't necessarily designed. Emergent gameplay is most often seen in two types of games: games that use a physics engine of some sort, and games that feature advanced artificial intelligence (AI).

Take "Angry Birds," for example. It uses a physics engine to determine how all the blocks will fall against one another in a big heap. Gravity, mass, and momentum are usually taken into account, and almost always, you'll never be able to reproduce the exact same destruction as the time before.

With games that use complex AI, sometimes it's difficult to predict how one system will react with another, which then may trigger a response that wasn't intended. Usually, what you'll get are funny things or bugs. But sometimes, if you have all the right fences in place to keep those from happening, truly emergent gameplay can occur and act as a marketable bullet point for the game.

You can also use weather dynamics to help or hinder gameplay. Think of wind for sailing, rain/snow for visibility or hindering of movement, ice for sliding, or even sun for melting. Whenever you can use weather, it has the potential to enhance the sense of immersion and connection with the game. Keep in mind that realism does not equal fun, and that too much simulation is often a detriment to gameplay, rather than an enhancer — after all, people use games to escape the real world. In other words, use this only where it might enhance the connection to the real world, yet also add fun.

Finally, think about utilizing properties of objects when applicable, such as mass and momentum, or texture and friction, to possibly enhance the connection with real-world objects.

The Importance of Sound in Physical Metaphors

Every action the user takes in your app should have appropriate feedback, and anything you can do to reinforce physical metaphors is going that extra mile toward engaging the user with your new system. As previously mentioned in Chapter 2, since tactile feedback is lacking for current iDevices (buttons, vibrations, and so on), sound becomes even more important as a method of feedback.

Aside from feedback, an often-overlooked element in game or app design is the importance of sound on immersion. Consider "Fruit Ninja" as an example. When you swish that knife, if you had the sound turned off, you wouldn't get that exciting swish sound with visceral pulping of the fruit against the background.

Sound is unique in that the user's attention can be on the game or app itself (just like in a movie), and you can hear thematic sound in the background that you take in subconsciously to enhance the effect of the story. In the same way, utilizing sound to enhance your physical metaphors will strengthen the user's bond with them.

SUMMARY

In this chapter, you learned about key features of most of the main business models being in the App Store, including the one that currently has the most momentum: freemium. In addition, you learned how important it is to engage a user within the limited window in their multitasking lives, and incentivize them to keep them returning (retention). Finally, you learned techniques for how to utilize metaphors in order to better support your game's theme and your overall brand.

Chapter 7 covers key app vocabulary, and delves into the process of creating both free and freemium apps, including ad support, lite versions, and much more.

7
Creating Free and Freemium Apps

WHAT'S IN THIS CHAPTER?

➤ Learning App Store revenue terminology

➤ Understanding the business reasons behind choosing a particular type of revenue model

➤ Further considering risks and rewards of particular revenue models

➤ Learning what ingredients to bake into a free, lite, and freemium app to maximize its potential for success

In the next two chapters, you learn how to build the various types of apps from a business perspective. This chapter looks at free and "freemium" apps, which, for most developers, will be the quickest path to the most revenue. Even if you decide on a particular revenue model and price for your app, you should thoroughly read this chapter and Chapter 8 because a portion of the content can apply to both free and paid apps.

Let's start by breaking down the App Store into two categories: anything free and anything paid. This chapter deals with anything free, which can be split up into three subcategories: purely free, "lite," and "freemium."

Chapter 8 deals with the paid apps, which includes non-premium apps (lower cost, and sometimes used as a synonym for "paid" in general), and premium apps (higher cost subset of paid apps with particular expectations). Any time metrics are used to discuss "paid" apps, they're generally referring to the entire gamut of paid apps (including premium).

With this understanding, let's take a look at some of the popular terms that are being thrown around as viable business strategies, or components of them.

APP REVENUE TERMINOLOGY

Just as when any new catchphrase or term begins to spread, some of the terms used in this book regarding the sale of apps may mean different things to different people. For example, what's the difference between a microtransaction and DLC? Or, what does a "Long Tail strategy" mean?

This same phenomenon applied when "Web 2.0" meant a great many things (and still does) to many people when it first appeared. To some, it simply meant anything that was Ajax-coded (that is, neat tricks you could put into websites without a reload). To others, it meant a new way of looking at website design as a simpler, more intuitive user experience (which is what it eventually morphed into).

Terms usually go from meaning specific things to more general definitions. To illuminate this room of indefinite floating terminology in the hopes of providing a better understanding for each term, consider the following short glossary, which, to facilitate easier understanding, is not in alphabetical order.

Microtransaction

A *microtransaction* is a small purchase in terms of its effect on the game using real money. In most cases, microtransactions are by themselves not critical to your success or enjoyment of the app. But, as a whole, they can offer a few to nearly unlimited ways to customize, enhance, or accelerate your experience. Cost is also irrelevant because it ranges from low to very high.

One example of a microtransaction-based game is "Smurfs' Village" (shown in Figure 7-1), where buying the largest pack of smurfberries (its premium virtual currency) costs about $100, and can be used up by voracious players in a hurry.

In the video game industry, Bethesda infamously released a set of horse armor for its great role-playing game, "Oblivion," and called it paid DLC (which is discussed next). In this case, though, it was a virtual good meant mostly for appearance, and it was more substantial in that it was released alone (and not with a slew of other downloadable items for the game). Contrast this with some games such as "Farmville" on Facebook (and also on iPhone, but much less played) where there's a zillion premium customization options (which would, in this case, be considered microtransactions). In this case, a distinction is that you don't use real money to purchase any individual microtransaction, but instead "microtransact" the virtual currency.

Downloadable Content (DLC)

Downloadable content (DLC) is featured widely in games as extra, downloadable add-on packs such as levels, bundles of content, or new modes. This is usually distinguished from a microtransaction in that DLC is a one-time, standalone download that may not be built into the app (and, thus, must be downloaded separately). It is also usually downloaded as a supplement to the core program, and, thus, is not unlocked. Finally, DLC typically adds a piece of slightly more substantial content to the experience than would microtransactions, which are usually lumped with one another in groups.

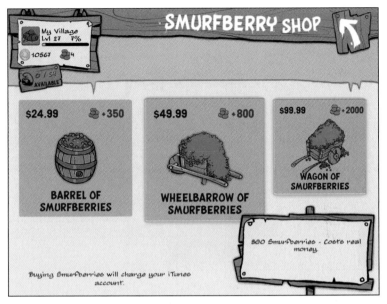

FIGURE 7-1: As a microtransaction example, in "Smurfs' Village," the cost per microtransaction can be low or very high, which is an example where it's not the size (of the download) that counts

For example, a microtransaction-based system would include large selections of virtual goods that can be bought individually (which, in this case, is almost never classified as DLC). Microtransactions can also include virtual currency that could actually run out (and, thus, be available continuously as an option). Another important distinction is that microtransactions are usually built into the app/game and are, thus, just waiting to be bought or unlocked.

As an example, consider a translation app that offers translation in a few major languages, but then offers Portuguese, Mandarin, and so on as paid DLC options for those who would use them. Most users would probably need only one or two. If you're the developer, you're not going to offer all these packs bundled into the initial download or for free, of course, and, therefore, you offer them as paid DLC, each with its own separate download.

Another example would be a GPS app (such as the one shown in Figure 7-2) that offers paid DLC packs of different voices for the navigator.

In essence, the core difference between DLC and microtransactions is that, with DLC, the content is not already a part of the app, and must be downloaded separately. Hence, it can *add* to the experience, but is not already a part of the core experience.

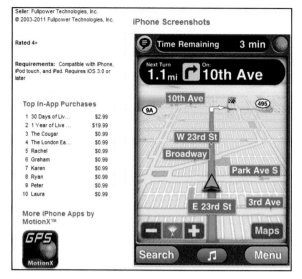

FIGURE 7-2: In this GPS app by MotionX, DLC is indistinguishable from microtransactions

Free App

A purely *free app* is just that. There are no strings attached for the user, if you don't count the likelihood of being upsold or cross-sold other items, or having the occasional ad interrupt your experience. If a free app offers microtransactions or DLC to enhance or extend the experience, then, for all intents and purposes, it is called "freemium."

Freemium App

Freemium is a combination of "free" and "premium." Although the model is not, the term is relatively new, and is synonymous with "free-to-play" when referring to games. This app will always be free to try or download, but users can opt in with real money for premium content, features, or other items, whether via subscription, microtransaction, or, for the purposes of this book, DLC.

So, could DLC be considered freemium when caged within a free app?

Some app developers with separate, paid DLC refer to their apps as freemium when, in fact, traditionally this would not be the case. Until now, freemium has meant that you have content that must be unlocked via payment or microtransaction, not an optional download.

However, these developers may eventually get their way, because there really is no term yet for a free app that offers separate DLC, and freemium should work just as well for those — as in the generic *free app that offers additional paid options.* Therefore, this book will also adopt the term "freemium" to include free apps with separate paid DLC options.

In-App Purchase

An in-app purchase is anything users can purchase while staying within the app, usually after entering their Apple passwords. This can be anything from a micro-transaction, to unlocking new features (or removing unwanted features such as ads), to purchasing a subscription to DLC. Note that in-app purchases can be turned off in any i-device's settings, but to the developer's benefit, users will still be allowed to see and attempt to purchase, before getting a notification that the setting is turned off.

Free-to-Play App (F2P)

Mostly used when referring to games, a *free-to-play* (*F2P*) app is synonymous with "freemium." The "free" part means that only *some* of it is free. Otherwise, it would just be simply "free" and not free-to-play (that is, a marketing creation).

Lite App

A *lite app* is a restricted version of a paid app (either in terms of content, or in some other way) that, once bought, removes any such restrictions. Lite versions often include cleverly placed screens and other links to a paid and unrestricted version of the same app. Traditionally, tapping one of these links would take you to the App Store. In that case, this would not be a microtransaction or in-app purchase, but a direct download of the paid version.

However, apps are migrating to a new method — that of actually building this in as an in-app purchase. A current game that was rated Number 1 for the iPad, in fact, does this — "Mahjong Towers Touch HD," shown Figure 7-3.

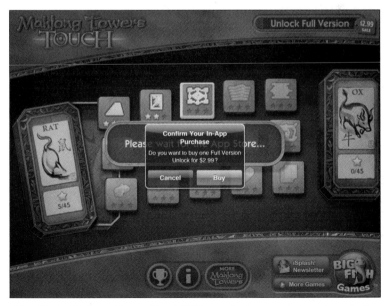

FIGURE 7-3: "Mahjong Towers Touch HD" uses the in-app purchase for unlocking the full version

Long Tail Strategy

The term "Long Tail" gained popularity in a 2004 *Wired* magazine article by Chris Anderson, where he mentioned its use by Amazon and Netflix. Anderson later wrote a more in-depth book called *The Long Tail: Why the Future of Business is Selling Less for More* (New York: Hyperion, 2006).

Long Tail means that a larger percentage of people will buy lots of different items than will buy a small number of popular items. This is made possible in part by the capability on the Internet to "stock" unlimited items, and the capability for fulfillment companies to be able to manage it.

Now that you understand these core terms, it will be easier for you to understand some of the business reasons for favoring a particular type of app, and then later the art of selling them.

BUSINESS REASONS BEHIND REVENUE MODELS

Obviously, you want to make mountains of money. The best approach to this end depends on both your long- and short-term goals for the app, as well as strategy for maintaining it (app awareness, updates, fixes, and so on), which will be the topic of discussion in Chapter 11.

Let's spend some time going over the business reasons and considerations behind choosing which pricing/revenue model to go with for various types of apps. If it turns out that none of these types of apps is for you, Chapter 8 examines the different paid models.

Free App Considerations

Following are some (but certainly not all) of the key business-motivated reasons to make a free game, regardless of whether you turn it into a freemium model:

➤ **You're hoping to generate ad revenue** — This is but one method to generate revenue in a free app, and results can vary greatly. Because of this, generating money through ads should not be the main driving factor in choosing a model; more lucrative methods certainly exist, as you learn later in this chapter.

➤ **You're cross-selling other apps, some of which might be paid** — For example, you might have a series of storybook apps, several of which are free, but a few others with more features and/or tie-in to a license/popular story that are paid. In other words, you might want buy-in to a series or your company's brand awareness (which is a very good thing), or these features could even be unrelated. Essentially, similar to how lite versions behave, you can use this as an advertisement for cross-selling your other apps.

➤ **You have plans for paid DLC** — As mentioned earlier, paid DLC plus free is considered freemium.

➤ **You're supporting the retention of a brand** — Think about the free apps for Google+, Twitter, Facebook, and so on, where customers use these apps and expect a similar app to be free. Your brand may not (and need not) be as popular as these, but it's the same idea.

Similarly, consider these reasons why a free app *may not* be the best idea:

➤ **You have a foothold in your niche** — This can be because of one or more unique features, and, therefore, you can support a paid app better. A model combining paid plus DLC and/or microtransactions is also becoming incredibly popular, but you must be confident in your value and/or marketing.

➤ **Development cost is/was/will be high** — In order to recoup expenses, consider making either a paid app, or paid *and* lite app, or even other ways to monetize (such as DLC or microtransactions and a freemium model, if that is a fit for your app).

Freemium App Considerations

Freemium apps are all the rage these days, and make up most of the top-grossing apps in the App Store for good reason. Customers want to try for free; they want value and they want options. From Facebook to the App Store, if there's one piece of advice that you can take from this chapter, for your average app, figure out how to make it freemium-based or paid with freemium-like features.

Following are some key reasons you should consider a freemium model for your next or existing app:

➤ **Your app can be modular** — You can break down your app into a core experience with enough value so as to be a complete experience. Then, if you're going the microtransaction route, you can think of several things that might enhance the experience that customers can buy. (You learn more about this later in this chapter.) Additionally, if you're going the DLC route, you can think of more significant options to add to your free app that are thought of as extras and not exactly needed, but that could be useful to a great many people.

➤ **You want to generate long-term revenue** — The best way to generate long-term revenue these days (other than by good fortune) is to create a hugely popular app that has incredible brand awareness (consider "Angry Birds," which transitioned off screen to movies and plush toys). The best way to do this is via DLC, subscription, or microtransaction.

➤ **You have an existing app that isn't yet freemium** — This works best when you have at least a reasonably successful app within your niche, simply because you'll already have the user install base to take advantage of and/or spread the word about your new updates. However, it would be questionable to start making freemium content for an app that wasn't already doing well, unless you believed that this might somehow turn around sales (which, in most cases it won't). It's better to start with a new app in most cases like this, and develop according to the model. There are many examples of this in the App Store, one of which you learn more about later in this chapter.

Certainly the freemium model is incredibly popular and getting more so these days. But there are several reasons you *may not* want to go that route, including the following:

➤ **Existing value regarded as low or near minimum** — If your app is already stripped down to its essence — meaning that, if you took away a few features, there wouldn't be enough value to compel people to use it — then adding more expense to create freemium content may not be the best option until you first increase the core value. For example, consider a simple Twitter app, where the core experience doesn't have a lot of bells and whistles, and is simply to tweet. It's maybe the best at what it does — intuitive, responsive, aesthetically pleasing — but there's not a lot of anything else. Because of that, you have a fair active user base, but it's nothing exceptional yet, mainly because there are other apps that do what you do adequately, but also a bit more, making the overall value of some other apps higher.

You have two main paths if you want to eventually go freemium for long-term revenue. First, create the very best "feature #2" and offer it as an in-app purchase, in which case users might not react so favorably, or with high conversion rates. Another (better) option is to update for free with a few more in-demand features (responding at least in part to customer review needs, or some new unique features the competition has released) to increase the core value of your app so that now you have the very best tweet functionality, along with some of the other useful features competition may or may not have.

The idea is that you listen and respond to customer needs, providing more value for free, which increases word of mouth and virality. Once you stop seeing recurring missing feature requests in your app reviews (for example, "good but it needs/could use XXX"), you can feel confident that you have enough core value to start requesting money for new in-demand features.

➤ **You have premium content** — If your content is not easily duplicated, and you have a good foothold on your niche, a potentially better option would be pricing it in premium territory (which is examined in more detail in Chapter 8). This does not mean that you can't also add on freemium-like features, but if customers are paying $9.99 and up for your app, in most cases, unless your grip on the niche is secure for a while, most or all of your content should be built in.

One example that bucks the trend is premium navigation apps such as those mentioned earlier in this chapter. Because they are recognizable brands with a near monopoly in the niche (likely because of funds needed to develop that sort of sophistication, along with brand recognition), you can afford to offer not only a base package with region-based content at a premium price, but also offer additional DLC packs for additional cost.

➤ **Your app is feature-based, not content-based** — According to a smashapp .com blog article, converting users to an unrestricted full version is generally not very successful with the only motivation being the removal of ads, or if it is "feature-hobbled." It's also much easier to create a freemium app if your app is content-based — that is, if you can restrict content instead of features, because new content is typically much easier to create than new features.

One way feature-based app developers get around this is to create a "free" and fully functional version, but offer an upgrade to the "full" version that may remove ads, *as well as* offer addition content in the form of "skins" for their apps. For example, consider "Calculator for iPad Free" (that's its actual name, which makes use of keywords in its title) shown in Figure 7-4.

For many, it's a handy app that has all the functionality available, except for a banner along the bottom upselling you to its full version.

FIGURE 7-4: "Calculator for iPad Free" is full-featured, but offers removal of ads and additional skins for a full version

Lite App Considerations

There is only one key reason you would want to consider a lite version of your app:

➤ **You have a paid app** — As you have seen, lite apps are free and restricted versions of paid apps. What's not quite so obvious, however, is that, though supporting a paid app with a lite version can be very important, it *becomes more important the higher priced your paid app is*. For example, as shown in Figure 7-5, if you have a premium-priced app, it becomes almost a necessity.

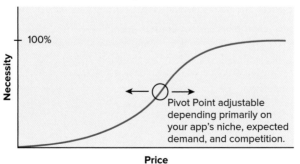

FIGURE 7-5: The higher the price, the more necessary it becomes to release a lite version

With "Archetype," initially released in only its paid version at $2.99, the development team at first heavily debated whether to also release a lite version. It was finally decided fairly early, however, to price it in the mid-premium price range (given the value in unlimited multiplayer gameplay) without a lite version. In hindsight, it definitely helped, because development would have been delayed even further in creating another restricted version in parallel (which should be a big consideration). The team ended up hitting the sweet spot in terms of the unique features the game offered at the time. Releasing it any later may have had drastically different results, given the unpredictability of the market, and what the competition was doing. If development time is not a consideration for your app, then strongly consider supporting any paid version with a lite version. Ten months after release, the price of "Archetype" was dropped to $0.99 and a lite version named "Archetype: Cadet" was released, which follows the guidelines outlined in this book for lite apps (namely, finding that good value balance and upsell incentive).

Following are some reasons to think twice about creating a lite app, even if you have a paid version:

➤ **You already have a successful or known Intellectual Property (IP)** — In this case, an app/game already is somewhat established, as shown in see Figure 7-6. If this fits your scenario, the necessity is lessened, though it is somewhat still there, depending on other factors. You know you'll already get your base users.

**Skipping the Lite Version
Going Right to Paid**

Likelihood of skipping

Success and Positive Buzz

FIGURE 7-6: Success of a previous IP or positive buzz can lessen (though not eliminate) the need for a lite version

➤ **You have recently released an app that's $0.99** — This price is within the impulse buy-and-try range (but still not free). Therefore, you'll have to judge whether it's worth your development money to create two versions. The exception is if your $0.99 app is not selling well for whatever reasons, some of which have been given in Chapter 6. If that's the case, following are your considerations:

> ➤ Make it free and find another route to revenue (such as ads or possible DLC/microtransactions).

> ➤ Possibly support it with a lite version, if the cost isn't too prohibitive, and longevity of the app has the potential to stay current and in demand.

➤ **Quality is in question for your paid app** — This happens to many developers, and may have already happened to you. Maybe that's one of the reasons you're reading this book. For one reason or another — maybe it's a developer who turned out to be more difficult to work with, or less competent than originally perceived — your paid app turned out less polished or optimal than envisioned. On the other hand, maybe you did actually plan a quick-and-dirty app and, for whatever reasons, have decided to make it paid.

When this happens in the video game industry, a demo is not released with the hope of getting as many sales as quickly as possible before word of mouth has a chance to sink in and, thus, help create a hole in the boat that might sink sales. In the same way, a lite version is ill-advised because conversion to your paid version is, of course, likely to be low. This method will likely tarnish your brand's reputation (especially in written reviews of the app), so think carefully before doing this. If this is a concern, it would be better to convert it to free with any fixes/polish updates you can do, and positively spin it in a light that will make you look better to potential customers (that is, the reviews might then imply "this developer is trying or has made some progress").

If you are going free, freemium, or lite with your app, you should now have a clearer picture of the business considerations in order to effectively make a decision on your revenue model. (Chapter 8 discusses paid versions in the same way.) Let's next delve into what the risks and rewards will be for free types of apps.

CONSIDERING RISKS AND REWARDS

Chapter 6 provided an overview of potential risks and rewards, but it bears going into more detail here regarding what you can expect when creating each type of free app.

Free Apps

Following are some considerations for risks and rewards with free apps:

➤ **Ads are unpredictable** — By themselves, ads may serve as a motivator to upgrade to a full version just to remove them. As mentioned previously, the conversion rate usually isn't very high, but when coupled with new content incentives, this can be part of an effective conversion plan. When coupled with the unpredictable revenue generated from using various types of ad networks, this makes it risky to consider free apps if there is no other strategy.

➤ **Cross-selling other apps is rewarding** — Regardless of your revenue strategy, use a free app as an opportunity to cross-sell your other apps, whether free or paid. This can pay off in terms of both brand awareness and direct downloads.

➤ **Expect a slow building of revenue** — Because your app isn't paid, unless it is phenomenally received and supported by ads, you can expect very little revenue in the initial months.

➤ **Less risky because of lower cost** — Because purely free apps are mostly lighter in content, features, and/or scope, they should generally cost less to make. An exception is if you build a system where both purely free and paid apps have the same functionality, but in the paid versions, content is licensed/trademarked, or otherwise offers more premium content.

Freemium Apps

Following are some considerations for risks and rewards with freemium apps:

➤ **Potentially more expensive to develop and maintain** — The cost to create a freemium app is generally higher than it would be when creating another type of app. This is simply because you may be planning on frequent content updates or (logistically and technically) figuring out how to modulize and offer your content. Once your app is released, if it is a microtransaction model and/or DLC, users will continue to be engaged as long as updates continue, which means more cost.

➤ **Lowest business risk not considering initial cost** — Because it's free, a freemium app offers users the chance to try your app and see if it sticks. You'll get more downloads this way, and, assuming you can build it to be engaging (which is explained later in this chapter), you won't have to worry about up and down swings in revenue.

➤ **High downloads and heavy engagement can mean maximum long-term revenue** — When the number of people trying your app increases, and your app is able to engage its users (which you learn more about later in this chapter), conversion of in-app purchases is much higher, thus maximizing revenue.

Lite Apps

Following are some considerations for risks and rewards with lite apps:

➤ **More people try your app** — This is the entire reason to create a lite version, so that more people are exposed to how great your paid and full version will be.

➤ **More development expense** — Though it's somewhat more expensive to support a paid app with a lighter free version, the rewards can easily offset this most of the time.

➤ **Balancing value is risky** — The risk here is being able to carefully balance what you offer as value in your lite version so that it provides enough incentive to upgrade to the full version. If users find that your app provides too much value and stick with the free (not the paid) version, this is what's known as *cannibalism*, because having a lite version (before correcting its value) is eating into the sales of your paid version.

Minimizing Risk for Any App

As they say, if there's no risk, there's little reward. Here's how you can help mitigate risk for any app:

➤ **Create a polished app** — This goes without saying, but isn't always followed. In fact, it's not often followed because of time, budget, or simply not knowing how.

➤ **Have a marketing plan** — Don't wait until two weeks before your app launches to consider a marketing plan. If your marketing budget isn't huge, it really doesn't have to be. Aim for the most exposure in the smallest amount of time during your launch to make as big an impact as you can.

➤ **Have a plan B** — Know how you're going to generate revenue, and have a backup plan should that not pan out the way you hoped. If you are trying out ads for the first time, and it doesn't work, first try working out why and fixing it, then have a general plan for what you're going to try next for your app. Often, this comes down to a combination of marketing initiatives, updates, possibly lowering your app price, or supporting it with other apps. Be *proactive* so that you can better be *reactive*.

➤ **Continuously build your app awareness** — Even if you've released your app, continue building its presence via a Facebook fan page, Twitter page, web page, appropriate review channels, updates, and so on. Don't wait to begin implementing these in parallel.

HOW TO SUCCEED WITH A FREE APP

When you're building a free app, consider how you plan to earn revenue, whether it's through the support of other apps from your company, support of your brand, via ads, or any combination of all three. In this section, you learn how to add required elements to turn your app into a revenue-generating machine, beginning with absolutely free apps.

Free Apps

From a business perspective, regardless of which revenue model you pursue, the key factor in a free app is user engagement. *Engagement* is an important term for any app or game on any platform, but is especially poignant with regard to free apps.

Engaging Your Users

Let's say you're supporting your app via ads. Every time your users use the app and come to one of your ad's landing spots, whether it's on the core gameplay screen or in between screens, one ad gets served. With high engagement (meaning that you have a base of users who frequently use the app on a regular basis), the ads are served that many more times.

When you combine high engagement with short session requirements (meaning that users aren't required to play for more than 5 minutes at a time), the formula becomes a winning combination. The ads are being served much more frequently.

Consider "Angry Birds" as an example. In between each loading screen, you have ads for other Rovio software, or supporting fan pages for the brand. Because each level takes from 30 seconds to 5 minutes to try, users are seeing a great number of ads.

The same logic applies when you're simply cross-selling other apps or your brand. The more users are engaged to come back, the more essential it becomes for them to frequently be exposed to additional promotional links to support your brand (without going overboard, of course).

Supporting Your Brand within Your App

Here are some of the ways you can support your brand:

➤ **Add a "more games" button, the less hidden the better, but not intrusive to gameplay** — For example, don't hide the button in an obscure menu, and, if possible, put it somewhere that is accessed often. "Ninjump HD" hides the button in the Options menu, but it's a fairly simple interface. "Calculator for iPad Free" has the button in the "i" info button, as shown in Figure 7-7. Developer Big Fish Games (discussed in more detail later in this chapter) utilizes two methods. In one, after the first load, it has a giant splash screen that lets you interactively browse other games. In the second, another app named "Game Finder" shows a large selection of games. This app not only finds other iPhone and iPad apps, but also promotes the company's PC and Mac games as well.

Info button

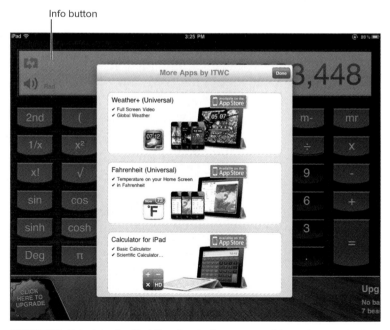

FIGURE 7-7: Calculator for iPad Free has its "more games" list in the popular "i" info button, which some apps use for options

➤ **Add a newsletter subscribe link** — This link will bring up the e-mail right within the app. You should pre-populate it with a nice ad banner of some type, and only require the user to press Send. Now you have access (and the user's permission) to use his or her e-mail to cross-sell your products, which results in an incredibly powerful marketing tool.

➤ **Add some in-game achievements (for games) to keep users coming back** — Though it's true that Game Center (Apple's own social game tie-in) has achievements, they're not quite as accessible — in terms of maintaining style and instant (and offline) access — as if you had them in a game (not to mention that they are a couple of steps away in terms of user engagement). That said, it is highly possible Game Center's achievements will evolve eventually, perhaps even into something that allows you to utilize your theme or skin, so it may be worth using Game Center for future proofing. Two sets of achievements can co-exist for your game quite happily (think tabs).

➤ **Implement Game Center (for games)** — This is a no-brainer if you have a game. Game Center support allows for your game to be seen by "friends" that you add, has support for achievements, and you can easily see what your friends are playing, which further promotes virality. For example, if Fred has played your game and has 20 friends (none of which have your game), and a few of those friends check out what games Fred has, they will come across yours, its overall rating, and its price, right from within Game Center, as shown in Figure 7-8.

➤ **Add your website name to your splash page** — On one of the initial loading screens, place your website link under your logo. That way, users can remember where to go when they need support, or want to find out what sort of community or other apps you might have.

FIGURE 7-8: Apple's Game Center is a necessary social feature to include in any game

Creating a Compelling Icon (Important)

This goes for all apps — free, lite, freemium, paid, or premium. It is absolutely essential for you to nail the app icon for any app. It should be these things:

➤ **Relevant to your app** — This means, for example, not including princesses on a premium business app.

➤ **Readable** — There should be nothing you cannot make out, no abstract jumbles, and any text must be absolutely legible. Enlarged iPad icons make this easier to accomplish.

➤ **Highly polished, even if your app is not** — Users will think this is indicative of the polish and quality of your app.

➤ **Different than your paid version** — This could be a color change for writing the word "Free" on it for a lite version, then removing the change for the paid version. If you make the distinction, however, users will immediately feel extra value if the paid version is slightly "upgraded" in some way.

Remember that icons can sell apps. If there's any part of your budget not to skimp on, it's the development of a proper app icon, and it doesn't have to cost much to begin with.

Asking to Be Rated

Again, this pertains to all apps, free or paid. It is speculated that app ratings figure into an app's popularity, not just downloads. Therefore, if true, the more ratings you have, the better. It's also already been suggested that a great competitive research tool is to go by the number of ratings to unofficially determine app popularity.

In any case, add a button somewhere that is a call to action about rating the app. With "Mahjong Towers Touch HD" for iPad, it was slightly disguised with the clever "More Mahjong HD" rather than the typical "Rate this app," as shown in Figure 7-9. Yes, of course you want more — who wouldn't?

Considering Ad Placement

Where to place your ads within your app can be crucial, not only to maintain usability, but to determine where to find the best engagement and most frequently hit spots without causing an interruption to the experience. The ads should be noticeable, but also unobtrusive, and as engaging as possible.

In a game, a good place would be somewhere constant during gameplay (if achievable), but obviously not if it is distracting enough to diminish engagement with the game, or hamper gameplay in any way. In a normal app, placing an ad somewhere during normal heavy use would be best, again without being disruptive to the main functionality.

Lite Apps

Because lite apps are built for one main reason by definition — to support a paid app — let's go through an example of great implementation ("Mahjong Towers Touch HD" by Big Fish Games), and touch on the main points.

FIGURE 7-9: Mahjong Towers Touch HD has a "rate this app screen" built into the app with a little additional incentive to give it a high rating

> *The reason for using this particular example is that it was made by a developer with (one would assume) a fairly high production budget that had time to maximize and tweak the upsell/cross-sell method, and have other games in a repertoire to support. "Mahjong Towers Touch HD" has been distinguished as the Number 1 free app in the iPad App Store. Essentially, this developer has been doing very well in the App Store with almost across-the-board well-received games (mostly lite plus paid models) because of high production and presentation values.*

Limiting Your Content

Probably the biggest hurdle to overcome when creating a lite app is figuring out what to restrict from your paid app. How do you balance out value and prevent cannibalism of free content at the expense of buying your paid app? "Mahjong Towers Touch HD" does this beautifully in a number of ways.

High Engagement for Limited Content

"Mahjong Towers Touch HD" (or MTT for short) is a tile-based puzzle game where you try to clear each board, which is presented in a new layout. MTT is themed off of the zodiac, and has 12 major areas, one for each sign, plus a bonus unlockable area once all the signs are completed. As shown in Figure 7-10, for each sign, there are 15 different layouts, and the user is rewarded with 1, 2, or 3 stars as a measure of their success on completion. It's very similar to the reward system in "Angry Birds" (and many other games) in this respect.

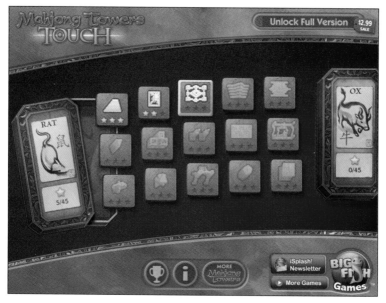

FIGURE 7-10: High engagement for limited content provides a big incentive to purchase the full version, as in "Mahjong Towers Touch HD"

This game is successful because a session is roughly 3–10 minutes, depending on layout and player speed. After completing one layout (which is not too difficult, given the user has access to hints and reshuffles, at a cost), the next is unlocked.

The mystery of unlockables (especially when there is some impact to gameplay, and even if just an aesthetic change) is a huge incentive in games for the user to continue to uncover. In this game, typical Mahjong players are already familiar with multiple layouts, so that in itself is not enough to get excited about. But the method of unlocking is something to drive addictiveness and engagement.

High Value for a Fraction of Content

Whether free or paid, users expect a certain amount of value for their time. In a lite app, the value should represent what the experience would be like if you purchased the full version.

In MTT, the star system of measuring a player's success is an additional incentive to keep replaying the levels. For example, after (and sometimes while) unlocking all the levels, many players — especially the "completionists" out there — will be further compelled to go back to previously played ones in an attempt to fill up each area with three stars. What should be going through many players minds is if this fraction of content provides this much value and entertainment, imagine how much the entire game would provide.

MTT lets you scroll through each of the zodiac sign areas, expand the layout section, and click any one of the levels. But only the first area (15 levels) is accessible in the free version. Not only is the interface unique because this all scrolls left and right within the track (making great use of touch controls and space of the iPad), but the user is able to experience all that the full game would provide, rather than just be provided a bulleted list or inaccessible buttons (as in many games).

Having a Strong, Consistent Call to Action

When upselling your paid version, you'll want to have your button, text, or banner prominently displayed without being overbearing. Users should also be able to access your upsell in several different ways as they use the lite version.

For example, MTT displays a large upsell button on the top right. It's also built into the theme's style. When clicked, the App Store popup appears, and the user can immediately buy the app. Likewise, there are other ways the player can get to this. When players click on any of the levels in subsequent areas, they get the new popup that contains both a "learn more" button and the larger call-to-action button, which takes them right to the purchase, still within the app.

When players attempt to unlock any new area in MTT, then tap to "learn more," they are treated to a full-screen ad, but it's not just static. Instead, whenever any movement is made, a fanned-out visual wheel of levels rotates along with their fingers, showing them interactively some of the different layout styles and backgrounds (in this case, one for each sign of the zodiac, as shown in Figure 7-11).

FIGURE 7-11: As an example of interactivity within your own upsell ad, moving your finger around spins the wheel of level layouts

Contrast this with the static screens found in most apps. Implementing at least a little interactivity or even animation in your own static upsell or cross-sell ads can be one thing that differentiates your app, and should be highly considered. Not all apps (especially serious ones) need to do this, but, if it is feasible for you, you would likely see an increase in conversion.

For example, consider the static screen for "Fruit Ninja HD," as shown in Figure 7-12. Currently, the Buy Now fruit is animating as all fruits do, so the user is not any more engaged than normal. However, it would be very easy for the programmers to make this a game. Imagine how fun it would be if the Buy Now fruit were tossed up slowly as an option, just as other fruit does during the course of normal gameplay. When clicked, it could initiate the purchase. It could repeat every few seconds after falling back down off screen, making the user wait in anticipation of it coming back up again. It's touches like this that will make your app stand out.

FIGURE 7-12: The Buy Now button in "Fruit Ninja HD" is cleverly placed and animating, but there may be a cheap way to make this even more compelling

Lite App Summary

MTT is a great example of a content-based game. A system is in place that could easily be expanded, making additional layouts available as DLC for a cost. But there is a reason the developers likely won't do this. Their brand has a pattern of releasing high-quality standalone games with good value, leaving players wanting more, and knowing more is around the corner. This, plus the fact that the game is highly themed, improves presentation (at least for this app), and makes it a little more difficult in this case to think of alternative options for DLC that fit with the theme and don't seem tacked on. It's better just to reuse what code they can, reskin the graphics, add some new features players have wanted (via feedback), and call it "Mahjong Towers Touch 2 HD."

If you have a feature-based app, the process is the same, except that instead of limiting content, you might provide time-based or use-based limitations on features, allowing users to explore the full range and experience the value, but not forever.

Let's now turn to how to implement ads into your app.

Supporting Your App with Ads

According to a `mashable.com` article, in 2010, mobile ad spending was $87 million, and expected to reach nearly $900 million by 2015. In essence, in-app ads in mobile apps are staying for a while. In the same article, Rovio (makers of "Angry Birds") estimated that, by the end of 2011, they will be bringing in $1 million per month in revenue on the Android platform alone via in-app ads.

In-app ads are relatively easy to implement, and are one of the main ways developers can support a free or lite app with additional revenue, sometimes significantly depending on user engagement with your app and how well targeted they are with both the intended demographic, as well as the platform.

Though you could also place ads on paid or premium apps (as "Angry Birds HD" did by supporting its own brand, resulting in a big customer backlash), it would generally be ill-advised because of their intrusiveness and negative effect on things such as value, customer reviews, and likely overall rating. That said, if your app is as big as "Angry Birds," you can afford to ruffle a few feathers, so to speak.

When ads are used in conjunction with a lite app, it can mean an additional incentive to upgrade, with the promise of removing the ads. But, as mentioned earlier in the chapter, this alone is not usually incentive enough to justify paying for an upgrade.

Insights into Usage

In July 2011, Mobclix (`blog.mobclix.com`) released research statistics that provided a few meaningful insights into app usage and advertising patterns.

➤ The most time spent on apps for iOS and Android users occurs in the late afternoon (4 p.m. to 6 p.m.) and evening (9 p.m. to 11 p.m.).

➤ The morning (8 a.m. to 11 a.m.) is the time most users are most engaged with ads.

➤ App usage is highest on the weekends, at 38 percent of overall time spent.

➤ Of the top 100 free apps, 82 used iAd as one of their ad networks. (Yes, it is possible to use more than one network to maximize your fill rate, as explained later in this chapter.)

➤ Of the top 100 free apps, 56 used analytics tools to help with campaigns.

➤ An amazing 67 of the top 100 free apps used a *mediation* solution provider such as Mobclix, AdMarvel, Admeld, and Nexage. (Mediation is where multiple ad networks are used at once to serve ads.)

Ad Terminology

When shopping for ad networks, it's important that you are familiar with the terminology they'll be using to lure you in. In case you're not completely brushed up on current Internet marketing terminology, or if this is your first experience with ads, following are a couple of key terms to be familiar with:

➤ **eCPM** — This stands for *effective cost per thousands* (with the "M" standing for the prefix "mille"). This is the overall amount you would earn by showing 1,000 ads, and is used as a comparison tool between different ad networks. Some pay out higher eCPM than others, all things considered, but it is not the only important factor. Beware of ad networks or exchanges who tout this number as an end-all be-all. Though it's very important, it may not be accurate in the sense that if you don't have a fill rate to go with it, it could mean just about anything.

➤ **Fill rate** — This is shown as a percentage, and is the number of ads that are actually shown, divided by the number of ads that are requested from a network. Surprisingly (or, perhaps, unsurprisingly if you are already familiar with how they work), ads don't always show up on request, so the rate is not 100 percent. This is either because the time for the ads to actually display is limited (that is, users skip through them faster than they can be displayed), or, for whatever reason, the ad server doesn't have an ad to give you. Heavy engagement ads such as ones that might be displayed via iAd require some time to be displayed, and are targeted. Thus, they may not be available every time.

Choosing an Ad Solution

Because you have many choices (see Appendix B for a larger list), choosing an ad network can be a daunting task. The most popular current ad networks for iOS are Admob (the largest), and, of course, Apple's own iAd. But many other viable solutions exist as well. The key with any ad network is both in eCPM (that is, how much you're earning per 1,000 impressions), and increasing your ad fill rate with targeted content.

Single Ad Network Solutions

Admob and iAd are examples of *single ad network solutions*. Of the two, iAd has been reported to have lower fill rates, but also potentially one of the highest payouts that many developers are happy with. If 82 percent of the top free apps are using it, it is certainly worth looking into as one of your first solutions.

Mediation or Exchange Solutions

As shown in Figure 7-13, Adwhirl (owned by Admob) is a *mediation tool* that allows you to use several ad networks and prioritize between them based on your success metrics. An ad *exchange solution* such as Mobclix claims to mediate between developer and ad networks, and provide access to more analytic data than does a mediation solution. They also offer one payment, as opposed to the different payments from separate networks that you might find in a mediation solution.

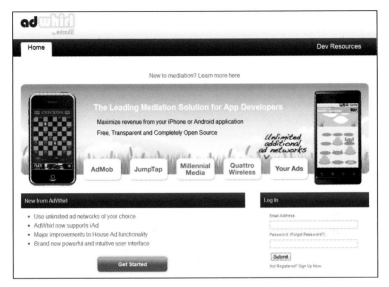

FIGURE 7-13: Adwhirl is an app aggregator (or mediation solution) that can help maximize your fill rate and optimize your campaign

As new ad networks and business models are evolving, it is worth doing some additional research to look into mediation and exchange solutions. But for the average app, given the open source nature and general developer high marks for an ad service, this book would first recommend starting the process by taking a look at a mediation solution such as Adwhirl.

The Offer Wall

The *offer wall* is a single destination within your app that offers the users choices of advertisements in exchange for virtual currency. Basically, you get paid and they get paid based on the clicks to the leads to any of the advertisements, many of which are trials or subscriptions. In 2011, there were reports that Apple is now rejecting apps like this altogether because of a conflict of internal rules.

Ad Implementation Tips

When you've decided to implement ads, here are several suggestions that will help maximize profits:

> Use an ad mediation tool such as Adwhirl so that your fill rates and priorities remain high.

> Ads won't pay unless you have high engagement with your app (that is, returning users on a frequent basis so that you can get those ads served).

> If you can do the same, people have had good success using iAd first, then, should no ad be served (fill rate issues), fall back on something like Adwhirl so that fill rate remains high and iAd is always served first. It is worthwhile to note that Adwhirl does now support iAd as well. So, depending on how it

is implemented and how much you can target toward iAd first, this solution may still be worth looking into.

➤ Use analytics tools whenever offered to examine and reorganize your ad campaigns as necessary. New metrics to pay attention to where available are: where users tap, pinch, swipe; whether they take advantage of any of the interactive bits; and which ones.

➤ Target your ads to the medium. For example, try to make use of touch controls, GPS, the accelerometer, or gyroscope, to better engage your users. This also applies to creating your own ads for supporting different apps within your brand.

As you have seen, a free app is actually a great revenue opportunity cleverly shrouded in the nebulous non-revenue term "free." It is an opportunity to market your other apps, earn revenue via ads, and provide overall brand promotion.

Next, you learn all about the exciting business model of freemium apps, and what key ingredients to add in order to make your app a success.

HOW TO SUCCEED WITH A FREEMIUM APP

Freemium apps represent one of the most profitable new business models in the App Store. The freemium model (via microtransactions) caught fire in Asia several years ago, and has since been the East's number one source of revenue for interactive games and media. The numbers speak for themselves.

In July 2011, the company Flurry (`blog.flurry.com`) reported that of the top 100 games, 61 percent of all revenue in January 2011 came from premium games, and 39 percent from freemium games. In just six months, this shifted to 65 percent freemium, and only 35 percent premium.

Another report the same month (again from a study by Flurry) revealed that games accounted for 75 percent of the revenue of the top 100 iOS apps across all categories, and that 65 percent of these were freemium. The overall number (as of this writing, and likely expected to get higher, perhaps even much higher) is that nearly 50 percent of the revenue of the top 100 iOS apps come from freemium games.

One of the most poignant insights in the article was centered on the average price point for a transaction. At the time, this was $14 spent *per transaction* by consumers, on average, for every freemium transaction. At first, this seems very high, but further evidence was provided. In the under $10 category, transactions clustered around $0.99, $4.99, and $9.99, which is no surprise. However, what was surprising was that less than 2 percent of all transactions were at $0.99. Furthermore, 71 percent of all transactions were from the under $10 category, 16 percent from the $10–$20 category, and 13 percent from the over $20 category. As a matter of fact, 5 percent were purchases greater than $50.

The research raised the question of why so few relative customers were willing to pay $0.99 for a transaction when that is the most popular price point for paid apps. The insightful answer from Flurry GM of Games, Jeferson Valadares, was that there is a different mindset when making an in-app purchase. For in-app purchases, you are deciding *whether to spend*, not on *what* or *how much* to spend. In other words, once you make the decision to spend, the amount makes less of a difference.

This is especially true with most of the microtransaction models, in that value is typically presented as "higher price equals higher value," and, therefore, many people opt for the higher value option.

The same study provided a bit more useful data as well. The number of transactions was inversely correlated with revenue generated. That 71 percent of transactions were under $10, it accounted for only 31 percent of the total revenue generated, while the meager 13 percent that were $20 and over transactions accounted for just over half of all revenue earned, or 51 percent. The take-away was this: Have a range of freemium options when feasible, from the $0.99 option to possibly up to the $100 option, and let the users decide what the best value option is for them.

Let's now look at the various types of freemium monetization methods, or available options, depending on your app.

Microtransactions and the Long Tail

The Long Tail represents a more recently publicized, highly successful business strategy (in certain cases) that is based on offering lots of different options to consumers, rather than just a few of the most popular. It is mainly used with the Internet, via fulfillment companies, and through digital distribution — pretty much anywhere unique goods or services can get to the consumer affordably.

It is called Long Tail because it is based off a curve that looks something similar to Figure 7-14. Because of the ease of getting products to consumers within systems that allow for affordable delivery, it becomes much easier to offer the world and get *all* potential customers to flock to you to pick and choose, than it is to offer just the popular items and get good sales, but only from the customers who are interested. A common example quoted by one Amazon employee was that Amazon sold more books today that didn't sell at all yesterday, than they sold today of all the books that did sell yesterday.

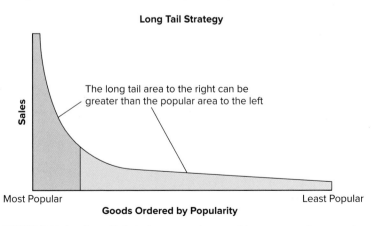

FIGURE 7-14: In a Long Tail strategy, more is earned from many unique goods as a whole than from a few popular goods

A Long Tail success in the game industry is Steam, which has been by far the leader in digital game distribution. At first, it offered up only the most popular games, and then opened up to a more diverse set of games. Now it offers not only almost any new game for digital distribution, but also showcases vast numbers of indie titles.

It happens that, for apps, a microtransaction-based revenue model (especially when paired with the common virtual goods freemium model) falls neatly in line with the Long Tail strategy. Games like "Farmville" and "Smurfs' Village" are a given, because they typically offer hundreds of assets at different virtual currency prices from which users may pick and choose.

To utilize this strategy in your app, whenever you have the capability to offer options to customize the experience in your app, don't just offer what might be considered the most popular. Rather, offer a more diverse selection so that all users can pick and choose something they like. Of course, there's a balance to find in knowing what will seem overly greedy to the consumer. But that assessment is best made when first judging the value of your own app. Whatever you choose to sell individually, make each piece distinct, and something that would appeal to at least one type of consumer.

Viable Ways to Monetize

As discussed earlier, the freemium model depends on providing something for free, and then limiting the use or availability of content or features in some way until the user pays for it. This is usually done in two ways — via DLC or microtransactions — and there are many creative ways to make use of them. The following sections provide lists (absolutely not all-inclusive) that may be of use to you in order to spark ideas for your app(s).

> *The following lists were compiled in part using data from the top 100 grossing apps as of this writing.*

DLC Examples

Following are examples of DLC:

- ➤ Levels
- ➤ Modes
- ➤ Characters
- ➤ Theme packs
- ➤ Texture packs
- ➤ Sound packs
- ➤ Voice packs
- ➤ Animation packs
- ➤ Editing tool

- Databases
- Charts and graphs
- Proprietary information packs
- Add-on features
- Other apps

Subscription Reasons

Following are reasons to use subscriptions:

- For simply using the app
- For news updates
- For propriety information
- For continuous support
- For technical help
- For questions answered
- For streaming services
- For access to specific groups
- For sharing
- For communication
- For networking
- For accessing certain features

Microtransaction Examples

Following are examples of microtransactions:

- Offering multiple tiers of virtual currency (the most common example)
- Removing ads
- Buying a full version
- Offering individual/packs of features
- Offering virtual goods (characters, clothing, in-game tools, weapons, items, and so on)
- Using themes/customization options
- Providing game aids (such as the "Angry Birds" Mighty Eagle that lets you skip levels)
- Providing power-ups (health, energy, boosts, and so on)
- Offering achievements
- Adding modes
- Adding gadgets
- Adding sounds
- Adding animations

➤ Offering donations to developers

➤ Offering more usage of the app (rather than subscription, could be time-or use-based)

➤ Offering store savings (purchase for percent discounts on actual or virtual goods)

Implementing a Virtual Currency System

Virtual goods can be anything from new wallpapers for your i-device background, to clothing to customize an in-app avatar, to purchasable weapons or power-ups in a game. They don't have to be permanent, but can be consumed and repurchased.

The way virtual goods are bought within the app is almost always virtual currency, though many apps simply offer them for real-world money. Virtual currency is simply a representation of real-world or imaginary currency of some sort (diamonds, coins, smurfberries, "bux," and so on), and is almost always bought with a real-money purchase.

Virtual currency (also known as *premium currency*) is one of two types of currency found in these games. Although some use more types of currency, generally that is not needed. It is almost always paired with a common type of currency such as coins (also virtual, but not what's being referred to in this case) that you earn by doing routine tasks within your app.

This model is great for revenue because it allows users to purchase common and required virtual goods for the common currency they earn, then "save up" or outright buy virtual (premium) currency in order to make premium purchases, which typically allow you to be more unique or progress further or faster in the world of the app.

Let's look at a good example of a freemium game using virtual currency, and one in which the author of this book is very familiar with in the name of research — "Smurfs' Village," an often Number 1 grossing title (at least on iPad, and fairly high on the iPhone) by Capcom Mobile, developer Beeline.

Earning Common Currency

"Smurfs' Village" (SV from here on out) is all about customizing your village from its humble beginnings to a Smurf Mecca. There are many such games like this on the App Store, most all of which utilize virtual currency. The way to earn the normal currency (or gold coins in SV) is to plant crops or flowers, wait until they are ready to harvest, and then tap them for both experience points and gold. Experience points (xp) let your village go up levels, which gives you access to more stuff, and more gold lets you buy that stuff, which you can then place in the village to make it prettier (or, in the case of the usual "featured" villages, more cluttered).

Figure 7-15 shows the choosing of a flower to plant. Note the gold in the upper left (around 30,000), the duration of the harvest, gold paid to plant it, gold earned when finished, and xp earned. The user has many options here, and some require the unlocking of certain premium content to be able to plant.

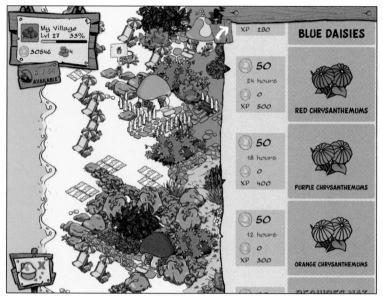

FIGURE 7-15: Choosing what to plant depends on how much time you have to wait around — if you don't harvest, they wither

Earning premium currency *does* happen in SV, but it's dished out in a very clever way so as to only occur on level-ups, and very occasionally at random given by a certain character. This lets users have just enough to see the benefit, and maybe buy one or two buildings by the middle/late game, but not much more. If you want the premium buildings/characters/critters, you'll have to pay.

Common Items Cost Common Currency

About 80 to 90 percent of all items in the game can be bought using common currency, or gold, as shown in Figure 7-16. The remainder can be bought with the premium currency called smurfberries. With gold, you can buy paths, landscaping, flowers, and crops to plant, and critters to place on the land.

Premium Items Cost Premium Currency

As shown in Figure 7-17, the SV store is simple and straightforward. There is a tab for buildings and other structures, plants and paths of all kinds, and the smurfberry premium tab, where most everything there costs smurfberries. This is where you'll find the Smurfs themselves (or rather their buildings — they come and roam around for "free" once you buy the building).

Premium Currency Buys Common Currency

Because the world in SV can hold an incredible number of items, and options are almost endless, the player eventually runs out of gold, whether from planting xp-favorable crops that don't earn much gold but do offer accelerated leveling, or by filling up the world with items. Therefore, SV (and other games like this) provides the option to purchase common currency with premium currency, as shown in Figure 7-18.

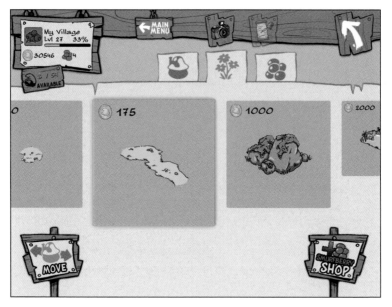

FIGURE 7-16: Common currency (gold coins) can buy most of the things in "Smurfs' Village," but not much of the real fun stuff such as characters

FIGURE 7-17: Paying with premium currency is the only way you can buy more land to expand your village

FIGURE 7-18: Common currency is expensive in terms of premium currency in "Smurfs' Village"

Note that the price of large amounts of gold is expensive in premium currency, because what you're really paying for in this game is time. If players were able to buy premium currency with common currency, however, the model would fail, not only from lost revenue, but also because any sense of "premium" would be lost (and you may as well have just started with one currency). If a system like that were implemented, then the gold cost of premium currency would likely be very high.

The Virtual Currency Game Flow

As a revenue system, SV can be summed up as follows.

1. Players plant and harvest for gold and xp, causing their village level to increase, which unlocks new items and allows them to plant more crops.

2. Players may accelerate this process using premium currency.

3. Players buy virtual goods (using common currency) to place into the world.

4. Players are exposed to premium goods, some of which actually provide gold and xp via mini-games.

5. Players get more attached to the virtual world, but don't have enough for the cool stuff.

6. Players examine the list of premium currency options because they spent it all accidentally accelerating things that really didn't matter.

7. Players mull it over and choose the best value option, typically one of the higher price ranges.

8. Players go on a smurfberry shopping spree, buying up several premium buildings, expanding land, accelerating crops where needed, and eventually running out of smurfberries.

9. Players are more invested than ever, and start to get into the higher levels.

10. Players get friends to gift items and have a "village envy" feeling, or the need to compete for the best virtual utopia. This incentive (or whatever else is rationalized) drives another purchase of premium currency, and thus the cycle continues, as long as there are frequent new items to grab, land to expand, or until interest finally wanes.

It works generally the same for other virtual currency games, too, in that there are a myriad of ways to earn common currency. But users must buy premium currency. The more invested you are in the game (and common currency helps you become so), the more incentive there is to buy the premium stuff.

Succeeding with the Freemium Model

The freemium model is taking over the App Store, and not just in games, but in variations for all apps via creative use of in-app purchases. Though that alone is not reason enough to adopt it, and, in fact, may be an incentive for exercising *some* caution or exploration of other viable options, there are many merits to the system if implemented properly.

SUMMARY

This chapter took a look at some of the important terminology used in creating apps (mostly revenue related) and went in-depth into the reasons for and against choosing either a free or freemium business model. Most importantly, it went into how you can leverage in-app purchases to enhance and maintain longer-term revenue for either type of model, from DLC to microtransaction, and from subscriptions to virtual currency.

If there were one takeaway from this chapter, it would be to strongly consider finding ways to support your free apps with in-app purchases. In the end, if you choose to call this "free + paid content," or "freemium," that choice is yours. At least now, though, you know several methods to accomplish the task.

Chapter 8 launches into the differences between low- and higher-priced paid apps (called premium apps), and goes into a lot of the same considerations that were discussed in this chapter, but using paid models and examples.

Creating Paid and Premium Apps

WHAT'S IN THIS CHAPTER?

➤ Learning how to decide on lower or higher priced paid apps

➤ Thinking about paid apps using the paid app mentality

➤ Discovering the higher value of a practical app versus an entertainment app

➤ Learning about the main risks and rewards involved in paid apps

➤ Learning how to succeed in putting together any paid app

➤ Understanding ad placement in your lite apps

As in any free market (well, generally free), the App Store has its trends and shifts in price, technology, store rules, and app features. Because it is relatively new, there are bound to be more subtle and not-so-subtle changes that affect the entire balance of app diversity. For example, the App Store in its infancy saw paid apps come out relatively high-priced, then rapidly fall until today the average price of a paid app is just around $2, with most apps either free or at $0.99.

A few interesting trends are now emerging as dominant themes in the App Store. One is the relatively large shift to the freemium model, which was examined in detail in Chapter 7. Another is the dominating use of in-app purchases as alternative revenue in both free and paid apps. And a third is more subtle, but still present. It's the confidence in the market that customers are willing to pay for quality.

Though the beginning of the App Store saw a rush to undercut and be competitive, many developers are now settling into a comfortable premium price point, and supporting it with in-app purchases. According to a July 2011 report by Piper Jaffray, the average paid app price increased 14 percent in 2011, versus an 18 percent decline throughout 2010. Despite the shift toward free or freemium, paid and premium-priced apps are here to stay, and can be a profitable venture if a good fit for your app, especially when supported by a lite version.

This chapter examines the reasons for choosing a paid app, risks and rewards, as well as how to make your app succeed in its niche.

BUSINESS REASONS BEHIND REVENUE MODELS

Free-to-play (freemium) and apps using in-app purchases may be taking the App Store by storm. But there are many reasons you may want to consider a paid app, especially because being paid and having in-app purchases are most definitely not mutually exclusive.

As such, you should be aware of some of the warning signs. According to 2010 research by Flurry/Pinch Media (and from just reading forum threads by developers such as on iphonedevsdk.com), the App Store is extremely top-heavy with regard to number of downloads of paid apps and the revenue generated. For example, this study revealed that the number of downloads in the top 10 percent of popular apps was roughly eight times that of the number of downloads in the top 20 percent. By the time you got to the 50th percentile (average app popularity), you were looking at 70 times less downloads than those in the top 10 percent, and 2.5 times less than those in the top 20 percent.

What does this mean for developers? Unless you aim for at least the top 20 percent of popular paid apps (not including in-app purchases), or you have other methods to filter users to your app (such as other apps on this or other platforms), your chances of sustained revenue are significantly reduced. The good news is that this study and others like it do not take into account in-app purchases, downloads of associated lite versions, or their conversion rates.

Essentially, there are a number of ways to mitigate low sales and increase the chance that your paid app will be able to maintain steady, profitable revenue. After all, should the rather well-known statistic that 80 percent of all small businesses fail within the first five years be a deterrent to a new business owner? The answer, of course, is "no" — as long as the business owner has a good plan and can separate from the norm. How to do that is what this chapter is all about.

Two Types of Paid Apps

It may have caught your attention that the title of this chapter implies a difference between paid and premium apps. While some believe a paid app is a paid app, and would even substitute "premium" as a synonym, there are, in fact, two main ways of going about making successful paid apps. The *inexpensive* paid apps and the considerations involved are different from the *premium* high-priced apps and what's needed to support them at that higher price point.

For the purpose of illustration, this book refers to the two types of paid apps as follows:

➤ **Non-premium** — These apps are typically priced under a certain variable threshold, depending on device.

➤ **Premium** — These apps are priced at and above a certain threshold.

These price thresholds change over time, are mostly determined by numbers of downloads or particular niche, and are mostly subjective. But what really matters is the way they're built, which is to fit certain expectations. Though, on the surface, it may appear that the difference is just price, it's a bit more complicated than that, and knowing what to deliver at these two rather subjective (yet distinct) price points can be called the *paid app mentality*. This is discussed later in this chapter in the section, "How to Succeed with Paid Apps."

Entertainment versus Practicality or Education in Price Point Determination

Figure 8-1 compares initial price point justifiability between entertainment apps versus apps that have some usefulness or practicality in helping you advance in everyday life. In other words, are you using the app to be temporarily entertained until its value is depleted, then move on, or are you using an app to get things done to help you be more efficient, achieve more, or learn?

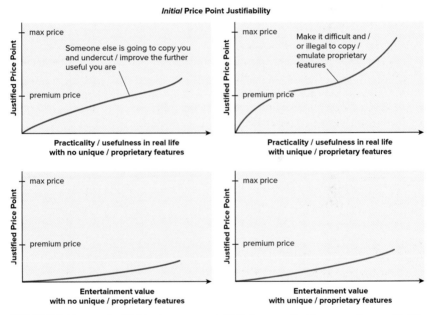

FIGURE 8-1: You can justifiably charge more initially for apps that have greater practicality than entertainment apps, even at high levels of entertainment

As you can probably guess, apps that focus on the latter can fetch much higher initial prices on average, which is why games (though valuable for escapism) generally are at the rock bottom in terms of initial price. The devious developer catch, of course, is that these same low-priced entertainment options can also fetch huge per-transaction in-app purchases because, once you become invested in the world/character, they are actually helping you to more quickly "achieve" a practical something in-game via your character.

In the end, you see a game like "Smurfs' Village" (an entertainment-only app, or, specifically a casual freemium model) sitting at or near the top of the iPhone and iPad charts for top-grossing apps for quite some time.

Non-Premium Paid App Considerations

Let's now consider the following business reasons for why you might want to build a non-premium priced app:

➤ **You have a higher budget** — Often, one of the first impulses when making a high-budget title is to make it paid, usually in order to recoup expenses more quickly. Though this is possibly the right call, take some time to consider reasons for whether or not it could make more sense to go free with in-app purchases. Many of the highest-grossing games and apps are now using the free plus in-app purchase (or freemium) model. This model was examined in Chapter 7.

➤ **You'd like to generate immediate revenue** — Sometimes this is for stakeholders, and sometimes you're just looking to make a quick buck. Either way, this is usually only possible with both a paid app and a strong launch.

➤ **You can support it with a lite version** — If the lite version of your app is ad-driven, this is even better, because that can be an additional in-app purchase incentive to upgrade to your full and paid version.

➤ **You have one or more unique features** — This can partially justify the cost, but only if your features can be perceived as in-demand and not a copy of another app's features. For games, it's rather tricky, because most features are fairly unique. So, for games, gauge the genre and how you're making it different from competitors.

➤ **You have little to no competition in your niche** — The difference between this and the preceding point is that you may have an idea that hasn't yet been done, or, perhaps, a new hybrid game genre, or, perhaps, there are only a few other paid competitors. Though this is sound reasoning, be sure to support your app with a lite version, unless you have a monopoly on a certain in-demand feature and can guarantee visibility for both your app and downloads. If that's the case, you may want to consider going premium.

➤ **You can identify one or more in-app purchase possibilities** — Supporting your app with in-app purchases is one of the best ways to sustain long-term revenue in today's App Store, as long as they aren't part of the core experience. However, be aware that (for paid apps in particular) the core experience should be complete, and any further purchases should be carefully considered as extras, not pieces that still need to be bought in order to make up the core experience. If that is the case, then it should be free.

➤ **You have other apps that can feed visibility of your paid app** — Once you start developing multiple apps and achieve a steady flow of users through them (for ad placement and other cross-sell opportunities), it's easier to justify a few of them as paid. You'll see one example of this later in this chapter in the section, "How to Succeed with Paid Apps."

➤ **You have the potential to lower price when sales slow** — You can always go down as far as free to spike your existing sales curve.

➤ **You have the potential to stand out from free apps as being more valuable** — Because free apps are becoming more popular, a paid app in the right niche might capture a segment looking for something with a little more potential, and not using common upsell to in-app purchase methods.

Now, following are a few main reasons that may give you some pause when considering whether to create a non-premium paid app:

➤ **There is less risk for a free app** — If you're unsure that you have the unique features, content, polish, marketing push, potential visibility, or incentive from your lite version to compete with the paid competition, it could be better to come up with a plan to release in-app purchases along with a free or ad-supported app, or else keep it low at $0.99. Essentially, if you've cut costs or quality, consider a free (or nearly free) model, unless you have a competitive edge.

➤ **Your app integrates with another platform's proprietary features** — If you already have a PC/Mac or web app — for example, Pandora "Internet Radio" or "LogMeIn," which lets you access your files remotely — depending on its practicality versus entertainment value as well as competition, consider either free or premium instead. In the case of "LogMeIn," its features are difficult to emulate, and because it already has a strong user base, it went premium. In the case of Pandora, it went the opposite way, releasing for free for a few reasons. It's geared for entertainment, the web app is mostly free (or cheap) anyway, and it has strong competition.

➤ **You face more complexity** — Especially if this is your first app, tying it in with a lite version can be more complex and cost more in the end than a similarly featured free app.

➤ **$0.99 apps along with lite or free versions can do well** — If you want the benefits of a paid app — in particular, immediate revenue on strong sales and the possible perception as a high-quality brand — then making your app $0.99 can be easier to digest once users are minimally invested in your free and lite app.

None of the negative reasons for creating a non-premium app are meant to deter, just to give you reason to carefully consider whether to go paid at all or free. There is no right answer, and it all depends on what you're offering, compared to the potential demand and existing competition.

Let's now look at factors to consider for premium apps, which, according to the rough guidelines presented earlier and the most current info from 148apps.biz, account for anywhere from 10 to 15 percent of all active apps.

Premium Paid App Considerations

Making the decision on whether to create a premium app is something you'll want to do as soon as possible, because there are clear expectations as to what a premium app is expected to provide. Here are some of the main business reasons for choosing to do a premium app:

➤ **You have a uniquely marketable feature** — This is the number one reason you might be able to succeed with a premium-priced app. Are you working with a popular license? Are you using proprietary information/features that can only be found in your app? Do you have a unique educational spin on traditionally difficult material? Whatever your selling point, when you're in premium territory, you should have something that adds a level of advancement or unique utility for the user.

➤ **You are supporting your other platform app** — "LogMeIn Ignition" (a top 100 grossing app on both iPhone and iPad from LogMeIn, Inc.) is a great example of this (see Figure 8-2). They have a popular free PC/Mac app named "LogMeIn" that allows remote access to your files and can be upgraded to the Pro version, which can get relatively expensive per year for multiple computers. Their associated "Ignition" app (on both i-devices) is currently $29.99, and allows access to your PC/Mac via your mobile device. So, whether you're using their free or Pro versions, this mobile version can sync with them. What's interesting about this is that there is no lite or free version. Obviously, their core business is the computer version, and they're supporting it with their mobile version. However, could they be missing an opportunity (however small, relative to their bigger business) to cross-sell their computer version, too?

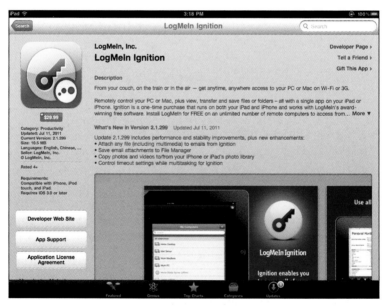

FIGURE 8-2: "LogMeIn Ignition" is a great example of an app developed to support another-platform application or service

➤ **You will deliver exceptional value** — Let's say you've created a game, you're in premium territory (but likely not too deep into it), and you offer an unparalleled game experience for the device, both long and full of lasting value. Perhaps you might simultaneously be educational or tied in with a more expensive platform app or software. If the app you've created isn't a game, your value is measured strictly in its utility to further the user's efficiency or learning, period. *Remember, the key consideration is initial price here.*

"Smurfs' Village," though free to play, has a $99.99 option for its virtual currency as an in-app purchase, which demolishes the prices of most premium apps, and is yet an option many users choose because of the relative value over other lesser-priced options. Plus, this is a currency that actually runs out, so there are some users who take advantage of this option multiple times.

➤ **Future price drops can stimulate sales** — This can be seen as a "defensive" maneuver, a better-safe-than-sorry approach. Though this tactic can come in handy should sales sour, it is recommended not to use this as your overall strategy, or else you'll lose focus on what makes your app special and worth downloading in the first place. Instead, focus on bringing out your unique qualities and making sure you have a polished, bug-free app.

➤ **iPad has great potential for premium apps** — If you're planning on releasing for iPad, not only does the marketplace have significantly less competition, but given the rise in tablet popularity, as well as the increased functionality, there are some real opportunities for producing premium apps.

If you're not solidly delivering on one of the first three previous points, you should strongly consider a different price point.

Let's briefly move on to potential risks and rewards before diving into what to include in your next paid or premium app.

CONSIDERING RISKS AND REWARDS

When people are required to pay before they play, there are certain expectations that differ along the continuum of price. The higher the price of the app, the more value it is expected to contain, often at the expense of entertainment. After all, virtually no one is going to pay $999.99 for even the best game. But if your app helps a user pass the bar exam, as in the "BarMax" app (by BarMax LLC), there may be some interest.

This is the reason games are priced lower than other apps. Although some forms of entertainment are expensive, in the end, if it's just entertainment, there are always nearly infinite options (many free, no less) that can accomplish virtually the same result. The same is not true with other types of apps such as productivity or utility apps, because these apps help you move forward as a human being. They give you points in real life, not just in the virtual world.

Let take a look at some of the main common risks and rewards for either meeting customer and niche expectations or not at these two price points.

Non-Premium Paid Apps

The most common price point for any paid app by a considerable margin is $0.99, currently making up around 28 percent of all apps (according to 148apps.biz). It's been said that this falls into impulse-buy territory, but the keyword here is "buy," and, therefore, it's a lot more risky (relatively speaking) than a free app. True, once you make the decision to purchase, it's not much of a decision to go with that price point. But as shown in the freemium example in Chapter 7 where the average per-app transaction was a surprisingly high $14, the difficult thing for the consumer is not how much to spend when the decision has been made, but whether to buy in the first place.

When making a non-premium paid app, consider this consolidated version of risks and rewards prior to diving in:

> ➤ **Number of downloads will be lower** — This is why you counter it from your other apps with a free/lite version and other cross-selling methods (if possible). Some developers (such as Backflip Studios with their "NinJump HD" game) have done away with the "lite" moniker, because it has the potential to turn some customers away who are too familiar with what a lite version means.

> ➤ **Revenue can be spiky** — If your app only exists on paid revenue and not in-app purchases, as explained in Chapter 6, you can expect revenue and sales to be similar to a roller coaster ride.

> ➤ **There will be more competition** — Let's face it, the more premium priced your app is, the less competition you'll face. Ensure that you do competitive research on all price points with similar features, not just within your projected price range, most especially free!

Premium Paid Apps

Aside from being able to see large spikes in profit, the main goal with a premium app will be to protect your original content and features so that they cannot be easily copied, and to do that will raise its complexity level and thus overall cost. What this typically requires is an initial investment in creating a system that is difficult to emulate, or via trademark, copyright, or patent. You will likely either have this system in place via a proprietary other-platform app or process, or need to build it into your premium app to begin with. Therefore, both the largest risk and reward when taking on a premium app is in its potential cost because of the complexity and earnings derived at the price point.

HOW TO SUCCEED WITH PAID APPS

Paid apps have higher expectations from users than free apps. It's these expectations that make up the *paid app mentality*, and there's a different mentality for each type of app, both non-premium and premium. This section elaborates on some of the expectations introduced in the section, "Business Reasons Behind Revenue Models," earlier in this chapter, including a great example that utilizes a lite app with ad support in addition to in-app purchases.

The Paid App Mentality

You wouldn't expect much success by taking any old free app and suddenly deciding to make it paid if it doesn't meet essential niche and customer expectations for its new price point. Therefore, rather than being differentiated only by price point, non-premium and premium paid apps should be defined by a *separate mentality*, or way of thinking about the expectations involved at a particular price point.

Take a premium app, for example. The amount of dissonance from your actual price point to whether you are offering a truly "premium" app in terms of niche and customer expectations can, in large part, determine its success. This goes for polish, support, content available, in-app purchase options, and so on.

For the purpose of a point of reference, let's establish that non-premium paid apps on iPhone will be anything from $0.99 to $2.99 (with $0.99 being by far the norm), and premium apps will be anything from $3.99 on up. It truly depends on the target device, though. For iPad devices, it's not uncommon to see apps at $4.99 and, therefore, it's a bit of a gray area as to what's premium and not premium. For iPhone apps, that would almost always fall into the premium category.

Non-Premium Mentality

For a non-premium paid app, the mentality should consist of the following development guidelines, any one of which could be applied to other revenue models, but when taken as a whole, make up the non-premium paid app mentality:

➤ **Unique feature(s) not found on competing apps** — You must be better at offering comparable features at the same price. Additionally, you should be offering something uniquely tied to your app, whether it's in aesthetics or functionality.

➤ **Increased support and post-release updates** — In most cases, updates are critical for user retention. Even before purchase, seeing that your app has recently been updated can be a huge factor in a purchase decision, and provide good rationale after purchase. For example, updates tell your customers that you care about product quality, and will be around to fix bugs and sort out other issues as they arise, with hopefully some new updates, or new features added in for good measure. Even if you have a monopoly on the current market for your unique feature, unless you offer good support, your customers will be very ready to drop your app in a heartbeat as soon as something similar or better comes along. Customer loyalty is driven by support.

➤ **Increased polish from free (not freemium) apps in the same niche** — Adding polish to an app or game means all the things you do in order to smooth out the rough edges, and can also mean going above and beyond what an average app does. Polishing an app (or any piece of software) is an art in and of itself. Here are some guidelines for polish, which would also be recommended for any type of app, but especially paid apps, where expectations are somewhat higher:

> ➤ Add proper user interface feedback for all button presses and other actions.

> ➤ Ensure that there are no critical bugs (such as the worst kind — crash bugs). Test on multiple devices and iOS versions, and make these your highest priority. Next, move on to gameplay or functionality bugs, and then graphic, text, and audio bugs.

> ➤ Spare no expense on your app icons, and make your lite version and paid version significantly different. (This doesn't have to be completely different, but could be shading or some extra touches.)

> ➤ Improve speed and responsiveness of functionality. Actions and their responses should be instant and not "laggy."

> ➤ For games, ensure that all controls are tweaked to be the best they can be. Tweak for the casual, not the hard-core users. And don't forget to add support for alternative control schemes.

> ➤ Ensure that your Quality Assurance (QA) team has a test plan that, aside from all functionality, includes testing integration with social apps like Facebook or Twitter; lite app integration and its ad support; in-app purchases in both lite and paid apps; and that "rate this app" functionality works.

➤ **Not ad supported** — Paid apps are expected to be free from ads, or else you can expect customers in the rating section of the App Store to rise up with pitchforks and pop at least a few of your stars.

➤ **Lasting value, exceptional entertainment, or practical value** — One of these three is needed for a non-premium paid app. For a premium app, remove the entertainment part and add "exceptional" to the first and third requirements.

➤ **Knowing why you are charging more** — For the typical paid app, other free options are generally available. So, knowing what makes yours special and worth money is important. The answer to this will be how you create your keyword-rich feature list in the App Store description area.

➤ **Having a longer-term retention plan** — Try to figure out a way to monetize your paid app for in-app purchases and at least periodic content updates to keep people using it longer. This will smooth out or increase revenue, and help to ensure that it lasts as long as possible.

➤ **Knowing when to drop the price** — There is always a point when you won't want to keep bailing water out of a sinking ship. This would be akin to continually spending money on updates before trying something more drastic such as a move to free. Keep an eye on slowing sales, and stagger updates. As soon as updates are no longer producing the type of sales spikes you want to see, consider dropping the price. First, try a time-limited basis, then wait a bit, and then go free if needed, promoting it as a positive philanthropic action.

CONTROLS FOR THE CASUAL AND THE HARDCORE

The development team didn't add gyroscope controls in "Archetype" because they didn't consider it a high enough priority for launch. Soon after release, however, several reviews were asking for this type of support. These were from hard-core users to be sure, but nevertheless, sometimes the vocal minority must be addressed, or their reviews can influence casual purchase decisions in a negative way. The team added in the controls during one of the early post-launch updates.

The way movement and rotation speed was tweaked in the three-dimensional (3D) shooter for "Archetype" was to provide a min speed, max speed, and default values. The user would be able to set these from 1 to 9 in Options, with 5 being the default. However, the default wasn't simply an average of the two, because that would have been too fast for a casual user. Instead, the programmer gave the team a range of possible values to test, from impossibly slow to impossibly fast. When the team provided these three values, it then averaged the low-to-default values for the 2, 3, and 4 speeds, and then averaged the default-to-max values for the 6, 7, and 8 speeds. The reason the default was a bit slower than, say, some of the team would have wanted was to maximize precision for the casual user, because negative feedback would have ruined the game (in which fine control was critical).

Premium Mentality

Because apps in the premium price range vastly outnumber games, the prevailing mentality mostly applies to them. However, there may be a point when an entertainment app or game offers something truly unique and unparalleled, and, therefore, you might be able to charge premium prices.

The premium mentality consists of the following guidelines:

➤ **Secure, original content** — With a premium app, you're offering something no one else has access to (or should have access to), or can easily duplicate.

➤ **High practicality or usefulness** — Again, the higher the value toward a user's own advancement, the more he or she is willing to spend. Entertainment-only apps usually need not apply.

➤ **Support with in-app purchases** — Downloads are going to be much lower than a low-priced or free app. Just because you're premium priced does not mean you can't have extras to help even out revenue, as long as they aren't part of the core experience customers are paying for. Consider subscription-based, in-app purchases for significant content or support updates. Consider paid DLC via in-app purchase that adds optional value to some premium content. Remember, of course, the core value must be extremely high in the first place.

The key goal for the typical premium-priced app is to lay an earthquake-proof foundation for a feature monopoly based on your niche, then work on keeping your customers happy and loyal. Competitors will find it tougher to emulate something that takes a lot of effort and research, and not worth the investment. Big fish eat little fish, so turn yourself into a big fish.

Integrating Your Lite Version

As mentioned in Chapter 7, in almost all cases, it is well worth it to support a paid app with a lite version. There simply are too many alternatives for customers to risk money on an app that may not deliver, because it's becoming a common technique for apps that lack polish to release as paid, and also be unsupported by a lite version in the hopes of luring in some amount of sales. For most lite versions, ad support for revenue from your unpaid version, more downloads, and hopefully balanced content incentives will ensure maximum conversion to your paid app.

This section looks at an example of a top 100 app from Backflip Studios, and what they've done with the popular "NinJump HD Deluxe" non-premium paid game on iPad. It is currently selling for $1.99, and supported by a lite version named simply "NinJump HD." The reason this particular example is used is that it touches on important aspects of a paid app, from utilizing ads to adding in-app purchases at a later date where none existed before. In addition, the potential areas where it has room for improvement will be noted, whereas this is much more difficult to do with an app that is already at Number 1.

The Paid App Upsell

"NinJump HD" is an incredibly casual action game if my 3-year-old is any indication. It features extra-vibrant colors, fantastic art presentation — especially animation — and fantastic simple control. Although the interface graphics aren't quite up to the same level of polish as the rest, it still fits with the theme, and is very user-friendly with minimal big buttons and icons.

Chapter 7 explored the example of a Number 1 lite game named "Mahjong Towers Touch HD." Therefore, to further illustrate specifics of the upsell method, this section uses "NinJump HD" and its numerous upsell points as another good reference.

Not including the ad at the top (which rotates with other apps, and is discussed next), Figure 8-3 shows the upsell placement in four spots within the app. The number "1" indicates the game-over screen. The number "2" designates the main menu, which periodically changes color and background just like an ad to draw attention. The number "3" indicates the Options screen, and clicking this button takes you to the separate in-app purchase landing page shown in Figure 8-4. The number "4" is the button that links to the scrollable cross-sell list of other apps in the Backflip Studios catalogue, including "NinJump HD Deluxe." Note that each upsell point is in an area that sees heavy use.

FIGURE 8-3: "NinJump HD" (the lite version of the paid app, "NinJump HD Deluxe") has four static upsell spots in heavily trafficked areas

The key points to remember when placing upsell pitches for your paid app are to find unobtrusive areas of heavy traffic, and make each pitch slightly different. Note that in the images, each upsell is not using the same graphic or text. As much as possible, you'll also want to get metrics about what is the most successful method of conversion, and try different things to see if you can improve on it. Chapters 10 and 11 provide much more information about turning metrics into actionable results.

Next, let's go more in-depth about ad placement and strategy in a lite app. Chapter 7 provided an overview of ad servers, and, in the following examples, you'll see specific placement techniques used in "NinJump HD."

Ad Support

"NinJump HD" has four main types of horizontal banner ads (the most common type being in the vertical position). The first is several different graphic versions of the "NinJump HD Deluxe" paid app. These rotate in with the other ads (see Figure 8-5 and Figure 8-6). Remember from the discussion in Chapter 7, the goal of ads is to have a high fill rate of targeted ads so that users are always presented with one when able.

The second group of horizontal banner ads features several ads cross-selling other apps by the same studio, often in multiple graphic options as well, as shown in Figure 8-7. This is something you should do as soon as you get any other apps for your brand.

FIGURE 8-4: By clicking to Remove Ads in "NinJump HD," and hitting this landing page, buying the paid version is now an in-app purchase, rather than an App Store download

FIGURE 8-5: Every time users access the "NinJump HD" lite app, they'll see ads served at the bottom

FIGURE 8-6: Create alternate versions of your upsell ad, because this will draw more attention

FIGURE 8-7: Don't forget to cross-sell to your other apps in your ad rotation

As shown in Figure 8-8, the third type of ads is actually other games served as affiliates, targeted to this demographic. Note the promotion of "Zynga Poker" by Zynga and "Tap Zoo" by Pocket Gems. Clicking these ads takes you out of the app and directly to the App Store.

FIGURE 8-8: Affiliate ads can generate revenue as well, even if they're for competing games

The fourth type is interactive ads, likely served up by iAd (discussed in Chapter 7, and shown in Figure 8-9). These ads are highly animated and polished, and you can interact with them without taking you out of the app. There may be other types, depending on how many ad servers they incorporate. Oddly enough, this iAd requires users to rotate the canvas to a horizontal position in order to interact with it, though the native app was in vertical position. Perhaps that's considered an additional interactive element.

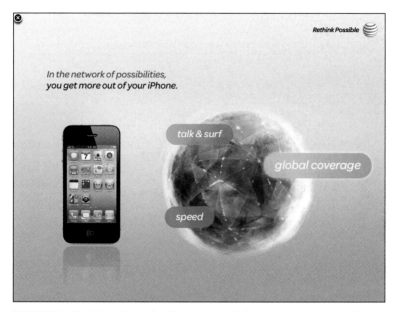

FIGURE 8-9: iAd interactive advertisements can keep users engaged and in the app

Lastly, "NinJump HD" doesn't just place ads on the main menu. Instead, as shown in Figure 8-10, there's a large banner at the top of the main gameplay screen that does the same thing, yet doesn't obstruct gameplay, which is critically important. As you also saw with the calculator app in Chapter 7 (with the banner along the bottom), ads should not be obtrusive, but be placed in areas of heavy traffic and not interfere with the main functionality. Also worthy of note is that the apps promoted on the main gameplay screen are ones offered by Backflip Studios (not iAd or affiliate-based), and do not change during gameplay. Only when users fall to their doom is a new ad served up so as not to be too intrusive. Again, however, the developer is offering many versions of the same ad with different graphics.

FIGURE 8-10: "NinJump HD" ensures its new ads on the main gameplay screen are served up only during the game-over screen so as to remain unobtrusive

Adding In-App Purchases

Because in-app purchases can be critical in sustaining revenue over a longer term, let's look at how "NinJump HD" went from a paid-only solution to paid-with-a-single-microtransaction app.

The goal in "NinJump HD" is simply to climb a wall as high as you can go. Sometimes stuck to the wall are shield bubbles that activate automatically when touched, and can protect you from one enemy attack. Backflip Studios used this mechanism to essentially allow users to buy their way to higher scores via an in-app purchase before and during the game, and then activate them at will. As you can imagine, the game can go on for a long time, and users encounter cooler stuff the higher they go. Backflip Studios hopes, therefore, that a high score will be enough incentive to buy this resource that will eventually run out.

Note that the various purchase options currently only go to $24.99. Though this may seem like a lot of money, as illustrated earlier in this chapter, with an average per-user per-transaction fee of $14, having an option for a $49.99 and $99.99 might actually work well for them, because these are price points that would convert because of their value. For example, 500 shields could cost $49.99, and 1,500 shields could be $99.99.

As with upselling your paid game, it's important that you make new in-app purchases as visible as possible. In the case of "NinJump HD" and "NinJump HD Deluxe," Figure 8-11 shows how Backflip Studios added the option to purchase shields nearly everywhere: on the main menu (see "1" in the image), the gameplay screen ("2"), the game-over screen ("3"), and the Pause menu ("4"). This is not always viable for every app, but the figure shows one way it has been done.

Expanding to future updates, later in-app purchase options for the "NinJump" series might be the option to purchase new levels. They have four already, so customers may not complain too much if there were a fifth for purchase. However, one thing to balance it out might be a simultaneous free update of different blades you could unlock via your scores or number of times played. They could then add the incentive to unlock a certain blade only within one of the in-app new levels that have been purchased.

FIGURE 8-11: Both the lite and paid app of "NinJump HD" utilize a new in-app purchase in various areas

DLC FROM PAID TO FREE

Sometimes, there's a balance with perceived value versus greed. In the case of "Archetype," on release, the developers had about six levels of death-match action. They felt like that was enough, and really wanted to add more paid DLC to the existing paid game. In a huge update a few months post-release, they offered paid DLC with a Capture the Flag (CTF) mode, more levels, and a slew of other enhancements for $2.99, the same price as the original app. Also, around this time, the app itself went to just $0.99, which, as evidenced in iTunes user reviews, conflicted many users who expected either less costly DLC, or all updates to be free. With any DLC, even for apps with extreme value already, you will have a vocal minority who believe any updates should be free, or less than you're charging.

Within six months after the paid DLC update, it was difficult to get enough users to adopt the new mode because of a lack of players, and hence make it worthwhile. As a result, shortly after this, the paid DLC went free.

With DLC, especially in the case of multiplayer DLC, be careful that content doesn't require other users to also buy it in order to view or enjoy it. In hindsight, better perhaps would have been free CTF integration and different DLC options, such as a new focus of appearance-like packs or non-gameplay affecting armor microtransactions. After all, it was part of the team's mission for the game to differentiate by not allowing users to buy progress, because a competitor had that market covered.

SUMMARY

In the last three chapters, you've learned about the risks, rewards, and ways to create an app using most of the main revenue models, including the current top-grossing freemium model.

The central point to remember is this: Monetize your app regardless of its main revenue model or initial price to utilize sensible in-app purchases if possible. Unless you're one of the few developers who are supporting a larger other-platform business, app, or brand, figure out ways to monetize it, sustain its position, and drive traffic to it using smaller apps and some of the social networking tips provided in Chapter 10.

Chapter 9 dives into some of the ways Apple has been successful with its approach to everything from intuitive user experience to customer support, app polish, and more.

Adopting Apple's Approach

WHAT'S IN THIS CHAPTER?

➤ Learning what makes Apple's apps different

➤ Thinking about user experience as Apple does

➤ Discovering how Apple adapts its apps to the iPad

➤ Recognizing Apple's influence in top apps, and utilizing these techniques to improve your own

On May 9, 2011, according to Millward Brown, Apple passed Google to become the "world's most valuable brand," increasing its brand value by 859 percent from 2006 to an estimated $153 billion. Google, according to the report, was a distant second at *only* $111 billion.

And, at the close of market trading on August 10, 2011, Apple passed Exxon Mobile as the world's most valuable company in terms of market capitalization, at roughly $337 billion. Later that month, Steve Jobs retired as CEO, with no business dragons left to slay.

> *To design something really well you have to get it. You have to really grok what it's all about. It takes a passionate commitment to thoroughly understand something — chew it up, not just quickly swallow it. Most people don't take the time to do that… The broader one's understanding of the human experience, the better designs we will have.*
>
> — STEVE JOBS

Apple's resurgence into the mainstream began in the late 1990s with the buzz-worthy iMac, available in several trendy colors as an all-in-one media system for the masses. Though it didn't catch on as much as Apple had hoped, it was profitable enough to keep it around in its many iterations. Even back then, Apple's approach to design (from hardware to software) was to retain simplicity, keep it ultra-user-friendly, and make it elegant. Apple's packaging was (and still is) second to none, and all this helped maintain an air of exclusivity when owning an Apple product. Apple's next device did catch on, and likely in a greater way than even it could imagine.

The first iPod music player was revealed in 2001, which started Apple's monopolization-by-great-design of the music market, a trend that continues to this day, and perhaps foreseeable into the future. It also helped to accelerate the already rapidly dwindling presence of retail music stores, and with iTunes, usher in a new age of digital downloading. What Apple did with the iPod was to fuse traditional button controls into a novel scroll wheel with a central input button and an approachable menu-driven interface. It was a lot like what Sony did with the Walkman back in the early 1980s, but also found a way to distribute all the music under one umbrella.

In 2007, Apple's portable domination branched and flourished with the release of the iPhone and iPod Touch, which revolutionized portable music players once again with natural multitouch gestures, a sleek icon-based interface, and the support of the market-leading App Store.

As of this writing, Apple is in iOS 5, and if tradition continues, the fifth generation of iPhones and iPod Touches, as well as the upcoming third generation of iPad, will no doubt push the iOS envelope further. While technology and software continue to change rapidly, one thing that doesn't is Apple's approach to design.

Sometimes it's enough to have a great business plan or idea, then capitalize on it in the most efficient manner, make your money, and move on. This chapter is for those who, for whatever reason, want to go the extra mile and infuse your app with the "secret sauce" that few apps attain — or at least look into what it takes to get there.

INFUSING AN INSANE AMOUNT OF CARE

In 2008, a presentation by Apple's Senior Engineering Manager Michael Lopp at a South by Southwest conference (SXSW.com) provided some insight into the oft-mysterious design processes at Apple. They illustrated the extent of the care and thought that goes into Apple's products, as well as each individual feature. Although, given more limited resources and budgets, exactly adopting the following methodologies isn't practical for most companies, each of the insights does provide a glimpse into how Apple is able to foster unusually tight design decisions that, most of the time, work well both functionally and aesthetically.

➤ **Pixel-perfect mockups** — By pixel-perfect, Lopp explained that for every interface feature or dialog, there was a mockup that could be deemed final. Though, admittedly, this would take an enormous amount of work and time up front, his reasoning was that it removes all ambiguity, and results in less reworking later on because of unseen additions or unclear direction. This does not mean mockups cannot then evolve as new features are added, or redesigned, along with product changes. However, at any given stage, they are ready with implementable, functional design.

➤ **10 to 3 to 1** — As opposed to what Lopp explained was the more typical "seven to make three look good" approach to creating mockups, Apple's designers build ten uniquely functional and/or aesthetic mockups for any feature, pared it down to three, and then chose the strongest from those.

➤ **Paired design meetings** — Throughout development of an app, design teams at Apple have two meetings a week. One is for brainstorming and ideation, and the other for production, or how to achieve the things conceived in ideation. The production aspect is a great counter to feature creep, because if a creative idea doesn't have the wings to get it through implementation, the idea won't survive. It's this creative, open-ended thinking until the end that allows for the best possible product.

➤ **Pony meetings** — Every two weeks, designers let the decision makers (usually senior management) in on new directions being explored in order to maintain visibility. This, in turn, provides them with buy-in and influence, both to thwart what may otherwise have been a direction the team pursued in vain, or to pursue promising features.

The takeaway here is that, as much as possible, putting care and thought into each aspect of your app can usually catapult it, regardless of its "ideal-ness," somewhere above average for an app in your niche.

Treating User Experience as King

From the earliest Macintosh home computer, Apple has aimed to create as-simple-as-possible, refined, and intuitive user experiences, both for hardware and software.

Our DNA is as a consumer company — for that individual customer who's voting thumbs up or thumbs down. That's who we think about. And we think that our job is to take responsibility for the complete user experience. And if it's not up to par, it's our fault, plain and simply.

— Steve Jobs

As an example, compare two different approaches for productivity software: Microsoft's Office Suite (Figure 9-1) and Apple's iWork Suite (Figure 9-2). Not to knock the PC giant — the newer ribbon interface is pretty easy to work with, and the software is both capable and powerful — but let's face it, Microsoft does throw every option under the sun into the interface.

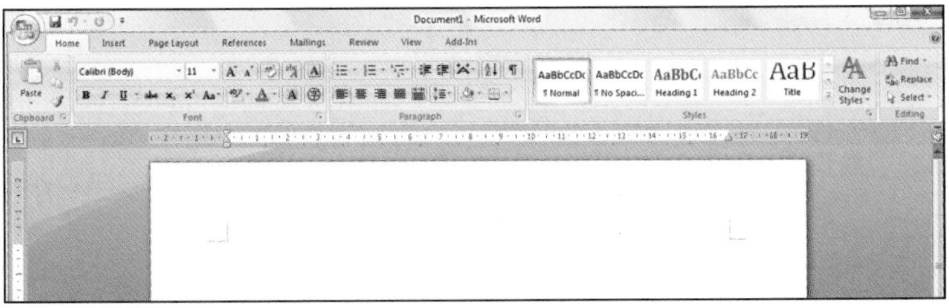

FIGURE 9-1: Microsoft Office 2007 utilizing the newer "ribbon" interface — functional and powerful, but not exactly first-time-user friendly

That's perfect if you know what you're doing, but as an experience or for casual word processing, the more user-friendly and aesthetically pleasing of the two is fairly obvious. Their markets are different, and so is their approach to user experience, though let it be said that Microsoft, on the whole, continues to improve. You can simply look at the improvements in Windows 7, the Zune HD interface (Microsoft's portable MP3 player), completely overhauled Windows 8 interface, Windows Phone, and its search engine, Bing.

FIGURE 9-2: Apple's iWork '09 "Pages" interface, with fewer, larger icons, broader categories, and easier to assimilate

The type of transformation by Apple of most computer tasks to user-friendly design has a lot in common with Google's simplistic/minimalistic approach, and, in general, to the established Web 2.0 movement that began several years ago (and continues to evolve). It can be said that Apple paved the way for this type of simplicity, and for reasons mostly not software-related, did not get adopted by the mainstream until the iPod took off. Today, because there is real momentum behind the user experience "movement," it is best if apps start adopting many of the approaches people are starting to accept as standards in mediums such as web design, app design, software, and hardware.

One of the most essential reads for creating an app can be found at none other than the Apple Developer Site's library (http://developer.apple.com/library/ios/navigation/). It is called the *iOS Human Interface Guidelines* and embodies all of Apple's prior standards of app design, while providing specific examples using the iOS interface.

Within these guidelines, there is a lengthy and practical section on user experience, which does a good job of summarizing not only Apple's approach, but overall knowledge gained in the user experience (sometimes called UX) industry as it applies to app design. If you can implement some of the following approaches, you'll at least be able to keep pace with your competition, and perhaps move ahead of them in terms of user experience, which will reflect in reviews.

➤ **Maximize user feedback** — Provide every button press, gesture, or action with appropriate feedback to signify the user has performed an action. Responsiveness should be as close to 1-to-1 as possible, meaning instant.

It is highly recommended that you put extra polish especially on feedback, so that, in every part of your app, users are getting feedback in one way or another. Things as simple as a small jiggle animation for a button press, or an extra piece of custom animation that users aren't accustomed to, can add *significantly* to the overall experience and set your app apart.

➤ **Top-down approach** — The top of the screen is most visible, simply because of how users hold the device (whether iPhone or iPad). Users scan from top to bottom, so place the most frequently used information near the top, and from general to specific as you go lower.

➤ **Instantly understandable** — Because most people do not read tutorials or rules, or any large block of text, it is imperative that you make the app as easy to navigate and learn as possible. To achieve this, limit controls and clutter, and be consistent with standard app iconography, controls, and gestures.

➤ **Don't make users fiddle with settings** — Settings should be optional, and apps that require that users input information or set up their experience before trying it out are much less likely to be used.

➤ **Add metaphors when appropriate** — Consider implementing metaphors (as discussed in Chapter 6) to make your app more intuitive and easy to digest by comparing actions with physical things users already know how to do,.

➤ **Large enough icons and buttons** — One of the main problems with small devices (and this goes back to regular cell phones) were the too-small buttons, which led to mistakes. In the same way, it can be frustrating (especially in an app that depends on it — like a calculator) to have buttons where the accurate press rate is anywhere below 90 percent. Ensure that all targets can handle fingertips. Sometimes, if there is extra space, it's recommended to make tappable "hotspots" even bigger than the visible button, especially in cases of heavy use (such as in a corner).

Although Apple hasn't always succeeded at every step (especially in the area of mainstream adoption of its computers), there can be no denying that it consistently endeavors to further the user experience. Figure 9-3 shows just how far back Apple's influence has gone.

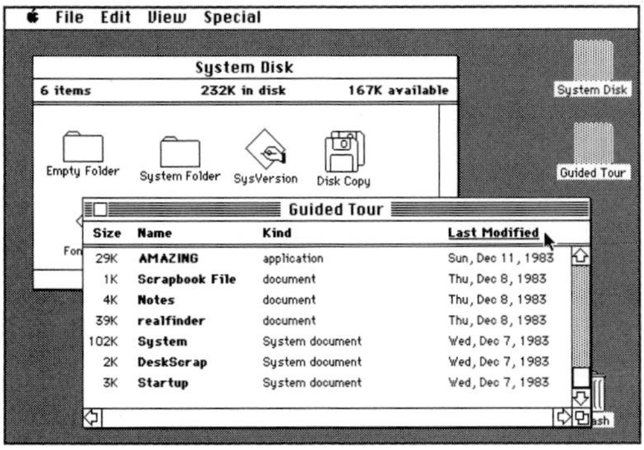

FIGURE 9-3: The early Macintosh "windows" interface helped define operating system standards to this day

The Little Things Matter... More Than You Think

User experience is based on minute details, or the sum of the parts that make the whole experience seem intuitive and engaging. If one thing is missing, it can throw off the entire user experience, especially if that one thing is used often. In fact, apps that don't wrestle with the user for getting things done are often successful *because* users don't have anything to complain about. In other words, it just works.

Getting apps to that stage, however, requires some extreme attention to detail. Consider this quote from the *iOS Human Interface Guidelines*:

> A great user experience is rooted in its attention to detail. It's essential to keep the user experience uppermost in your mind as you design every aspect of your app, from the way you enable a task, to the way your app starts and stops, to the way you use a button. Discover the guidelines that influence the look and behavior of your app, in matters both general and specific.

Let's look at a great example of a native iPhone and iPad app that features Apple's attention to detail: iTunes. Whether browsing for new music or movies, iTunes features a highly graphical, user-friendly experience with amazing feedback for your actions, as shown in Figure 9-4. In other words, when you browse using iTunes, you're not using an app, but are engaging in a great experience.

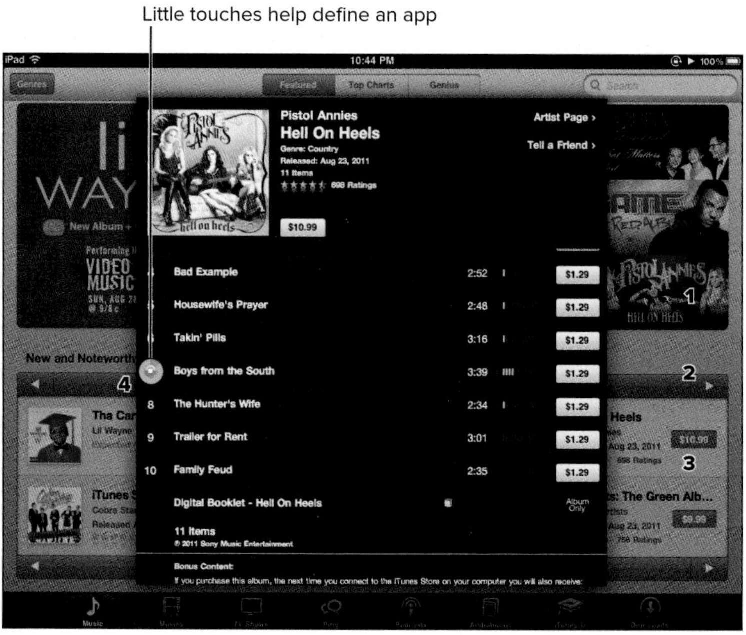

Little touches help define an app

FIGURE 9-4: iTunes features a multitude of small touches that result in an engaging and fun user experience

Here are some fantastic examples of what Apple does to accomplish this:

➤ **Contrast** — The iTunes store interface concentrates on what is most important. Apple uses muted grays and off-whites in the background and text so that all the vibrant color is used for actual products. This makes them more enticing.

➤ **Animated feedback** — This is a more intuitive (and engaging) form of feedback, because the user is able to see actions morph into results. As indicated with the number 1 in the Figure 9-4, tapping on any album cover animates, rotates, and scales up a pop-up window so that it's in front of you. It's almost as if you are looking at the back cover, and is a really slick and fun way to bring up a pop-up window. Likewise, clicking anywhere off of the pop-up window reverses the animation back to the icon that was originally clicked. At the top of the pop-up window is a preview pane, and the bottom features gesture scrolling for more content.

As indicated with the number 2, tapping the category's right and left arrows doesn't just bring up a new list of albums. The button highlights, and the entire set of six albums scrolls to the left as a new set scrolls into view. It's more intuitive this way, because if a new set instantly appeared, it would require the user to keep an eye on album artwork or prices (or something in that category) to notice any change at all.

And, as indicated by the number 3, tapping on any price animates the button to change color (green, as in "go," which is a subtle cue), shape (it elongates to the size of text needed), and text (buy song, buy app, and so on — a strong call to action).

➤ **Extra feedback** — Apple did not need to do this, but it makes the experience that much more engaging. As indicated by the number 4, when tapping any song or track number, the square tile next to the song name smoothly flips around to display a forward-thinking animated icon that enables you to see that it is loading this song briefly, a visual animated duration without any time text (unlike most web app previews), and that you can stop it. When tapping the tile anywhere, it swivels around and stops. It's fun and engaging, and goes a long way toward defining what makes using iTunes different from other similar apps.

➤ **Consistency** — If you're browsing music or audiobooks, you get the same interface and same feedback. If you click a book title or album title, a preview pop-up window rotates into view, and you'll get more information.

When creating an app, try to put your own finishing touches on a few elements that allow you to engage the user in a different way than your competitors. This is a way for you to increase the value per action or session. In the next section you see how and why Apple further increases value by homing in on customer needs and expectations.

Value-Added Benefits
(Go Farther Than You Think You Should)

Barring bugs and technical problems that inevitably creep up (hopefully in QA rather than post release), customers stop complaining about your product (for the most part) when they feel the value presented matches their expectations, and these, of course, rise with price. This can be a balancing act, unfortunately, because customer expectations vary widely.

One way to tackle this value challenge might be to use the 80/20 rule — add enough value to satisfy 80 percent of the customers, while leaving the remaining 20 percent with at least partially unfulfilled expectations. In terms of value, however, this technique won't work because the "vocal minority" can actually have significant influence on your app when its rating starts to falter, and negative reviews appear.

Two things Apple does in its design process help to solve the problem.

First, it *focuses*. In the *iOS Human Interface Guidelines*, Apple suggests an overall "definition statement" for the same reasons provided in Chapter 5 for your controlling idea. Under this umbrella, and in order to help build this definition, Apple provides three important steps:

1. **List all the features your users might like.** Here, your aim is to create a list (in bullet form) comprised of all the tasks you expect users will do. These can be short descriptions, such as "creating lists," "getting recipes," or "comparing prices."

2. **Determine who your users are.** This is another bulleted list of the most important choices your users make when engaging in behaviors related to your app. For example, in Apple's recipe example, it lists the following:

   ➤ Usually cook at home, or prefer ready-made meals

   ➤ Committed coupon users, or think coupons might not be worth the effort

   ➤ Enjoy hunting for specialty ingredients, or most likely to use basics

   ➤ Strictly follow recipes, or use them as inspiration

   Apple suggests narrowing this list to the three most important characteristics before moving on, because in the next section, it explains that *"great iOS applications have a laser focus on the task users want to accomplish."*

3. **Funnel Steps 1 and 2 into your application definition.** Take the features you created in Step 1 and filter them using your audience definitions in Step 2. Again, pare them down to your top three features, and use them to make your application definition statement. Apple's recipe example is, "A shopping list creation tool for thrifty people who love to cook."

Second, as stated earlier in this chapter in the section, "The Little Things Matter...More Than You Think," Apple *considers*. It takes the small (seemingly insignificant) things and turns them into engaging user experiences, which, in turn, are value-adds for the app or piece of software.

For example, many users enjoy browsing for new music using iTunes on iPhone and iPad simply because of its elegant and well-thought-out little touches. Contrast this with the Amazon MP3 downloads area (www.amazon.com) in which Amazon offers a great selection (and no digital rights management), but the interface for sampling songs is still somewhat embedded in old web design, and leaves much to be desired aesthetically. User experience is part of the choice users make as to whether to continue using an app, despite a potential practical benefit advantage of a competing app.

If you hone in on user expectations for the bulk of the value, as well as take the time to consider how these features are implemented as Apple does, you're much less likely to have the odd reviewer put a dent in your app's reputation. Don't focus on how many features you have. Instead, focus on implementation in accordance to the primary user expectations of your app.

Let's now look at one of the most important aspects of any top consumer goods (virtual or real), and one in which Apple has had to evolve. After all, a poor reputation for caring about customers doesn't go well with a top product you want customers to buy.

Customer as King

Apple's reputation for customer service didn't used to be stellar or geared toward friendly Apple Store clerks who took appointments and concerns on a one-to-one basis. Times have changed. Just visit any Apple Store these days, or contact Support (as a customer, not a developer), and you'll find (for the most part) they've learned to shift their overall brand image and public perception to that of a friendly neighbor.

In May 2008, *Consumer Reports* released a report indicating Apple was at the top of both desktop and laptop tech support. Its in-store Genius Bar was said to have "the best troubleshooting by far." In 2009, Forrester Research ranked Apple Number 1 in customer service versus all other PC makers, according to its index. Good customer support is paramount to maintaining an app and keeping loyal customers, and will also be discussed in detail in Chapter 11.

Apple's retail stores go a long way toward maintaining the customer experience. In a *Wall Street Journal Online* (www.wsj.com) video interview in June 2011, Apple's 326 stores at the time had more visitors per quarter than Disney's top four theme parks get in a year. Breaking that down further, roughly 80 Apple Stores were getting the same amount of traffic that Disney's top four parks were getting. To top that off, sales per square foot per year were $4,400, compared with Tiffany's $1,100.

According to the interview, it's all planned to the smallest detail. Apple's core customer service approach is based off the A-P-P-L-E acronym:

➤ A — "Approach customers with a personalized warm welcome." This is something you may consider doing within your app via the user's initial entry.

➤ P — "Probe politely to understand all the customer's needs." Offer a solution on the user's first time in your app, such as a tutorial, small walkthrough, single called-out help screen, and so on.

➤ P — "Present a solution for the customer to take home today." Give your customers an enticing jumping-off point to explore your app.

➤ L — "Listen for and resolve any issues or concerns." Offer your customers easy access to support from within the app.

➤ E — "End with a fond farewell and an invitation to return." Provide incentives to return, such as high scores, an easy way to save progress or sessions, unlockables, dynamic content, and so on.

This is not to say Apple doesn't have a thing or two to learn. In 2007, roughly ten weeks after the launch of the iPhone, Apple announced the discontinuation of the 4 GB model and reduced pricing by $200 for the larger-capacity version. This caused enormous customer backlash from those who recently had forked out $599, and resulted in Apple shares declining 6 percent. As a Band-Aid, Steve Jobs announced a $100 Apple credit to loyal customers, and, if the prior iPhone was purchased within 14 days, customers were getting a full $200 refund.

While this move somewhat alleviated the problem after the fact (though that $100 was still going to Apple), it's indicative of something that should have been done outright — that of rewarding customer loyalty. If Apple had announced a rebate and support of its existing customers at the time of the price drop, much of the damage could have been averted. In the same way, if you have an app with long-time customers, rewarding them for their loyalty from time to time can help retention and positive image for your brand.

When you set up shop on your web page or even within your app, follow Apple's example and offer top service and support, because, all other things being equal, good word of mouth on support can bring in more customers. Chapter 11 discusses more on how to maintain effective support.

Apple also does one other thing exceptionally well — converting apps to the proper device. Let's go over some of Apple's core design methods for porting apps to iPad, which supports higher-priced apps, but also comes with different user expectations.

ADAPTING APPS TO IPAD

Apple is an expert when it comes to converting apps from Mac to iPhone/iPad, as well as from iPhone to iPad. From its Number 1 selling Pages on iPad to Safari to the Mail app and Game Center, Apple knows that it's not simply a matter of scaling up or down graphics to meet a new resolution. It's a matter of delivering an improved experience that matches the larger size and, ultimately, the way people use the device, which is different for iPad than it is for iPhone.

This section is devoted to tips on how to maximize your app's value when converting iPhone apps to iPad, or even building an app from scratch on the device.

➤ **Consider primary use** — iPhone apps are meant for people on the go, whereas iPad apps can feature a bit more depth or complexity, because users are typically more stationary.

➤ **Orientation opens up on iPad** — For iPhone, your orientation is usually locked in, depending on content and use. However, on iPad, because of the greater resolution and space, your app should allow for either, if possible.

➤ **Keep core functionality consistent** — Though you'll have more space to add icons, only do so if required (streamlining is still recommended) and keep the relative positions of icons the same.

➤ **Reduce full-screen transitions** — More space provides an opportunity to keep sections of the screen consistent, while updating only those sections that need it. According to Apple's *iOS Human Interface Guidelines*, to best keep users focused on the task, make use of a split screen, as well as pop-up and pop-over elements. Pop-up elements come up in a specific location, and pop-over elements are similar, but directly tied to size of the UI available when activated.

In Figure 9-5, a split screen is used to add another navigation pane on the iPad to reduce menu switching. The iPhone *Settings* menu is at bottom right in the same image. Note the use of what Apple calls the navigation bar (with the text "General" at the top of the right pane in the image), which is used to navigate shallow menus. For the iPhone, each screen must be a sole entity with a single navigation bar for going back through menu levels.

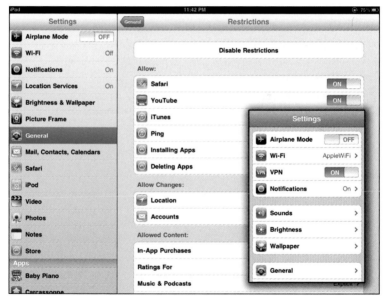

FIGURE 9-5: iPad can make use of another menu to quickly go between root-level menu options, whereas iPhone users are generally used to moving all the way in, and then back out of any particular menu

As shown in Figure 9-6, pop-up, and pop-over elements should be interactive and reduce the need for full-screen transitions, keeping users just a tap away from where they were prior.

➤ **Add more graphic detail to main elements** — Though it is sometimes not practical or within the budget to have two sets of completely different detailed art (apart from just the resolution), it is important that you make the App Store icon, as well as main elements in your app or game, have visibly different levels of detail. This is because there is already a premium mentality about iPad apps that is reflected in the average iPad app price. This would include retina-display–enabled iPhone or future iPad apps as well.

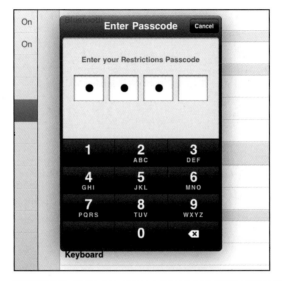

FIGURE 9-6: Make use of pop-up (and pop-over) elements when possible to keep people working on the same task without full-screen switching

Next, let's look at an example of a series of apps that have applied the Apple design philosophy.

CASE STUDY: TAPBOTS

Tapbots is a company and brand that has developed a "suite" of practical and paid apps branded around one theme — cute robots that each performs a core feature exceptionally well, and usually with a highly polished, intuitive interface.

Let's take a look at some of the design strategies Tapbots has used to be successful in its niche with generally exceptional reviews. Specifically, let's look at its current latest app, "Tweetbot," released April 2011. You might think that with all of the Twitter clients available, the niche could be overly saturated already, but Tapbots makes use of its existing brand and reputation to break into a popular niche.

High-Contrast Branding

Taking a look at the Tapbots web page as shown in Figure 9-7, you see an Apple-like simplicity and branding with grays and whites against vibrant color, placing the importance on the product. This is not uncommon for Apple-related or OS X–related web pages, and shows that it can be applied to app branding as well.

FIGURE 9-7: The high-contrast and user-friendly web page for Tapbots demonstrates the professional type of app you would be buying

Figure 9-8 shows an array of the icons for current apps offered by Tapbots, each (except for "Pastebot") recognizable for being branded around the Tapbots robot theme. Having a tight, unified brand provides consumer comfort that if you enjoy the current selection, you can expect more of similar quality or consistency. Furthermore, each icon is generally recognizable for its functionality, or, in the case of "Convertbot" (a conversion utility) and "Weightbot," an engaging icon or interface. "Tweetbot" has improved from the earlier apps.

FIGURE 9-8: Polished App Store icons help sell an app and, in this case, tie in with the theme of a brand (cute robots from Tapbots)

Refined, Responsive, Simplistic Interface

Everything offered by Tapbots is fluid, provides instant animated feedback, makes good use of standard iconography, and features large, tappable icons, and thoughtful graphic touches everywhere. Simplistic interfaces can be designed to hide depth, and this is precisely what "Tweetbot" does.

As shown in Figure 9-9, the Settings menu is laid out with unique radio buttons and simplistic, user-friendly text. Combined with the ever-present bottom navigation bar for instant access to any main function, this helps make the app fun to use. In the end, it may not be quite as full-featured as some other Twitter apps, but it is fairly robust with features, while at the same time providing valuable ease-of-use, reduced clutter, and hidden depth (that is, screens show only what is necessary, and provide simple icons to unlock depth when needed).

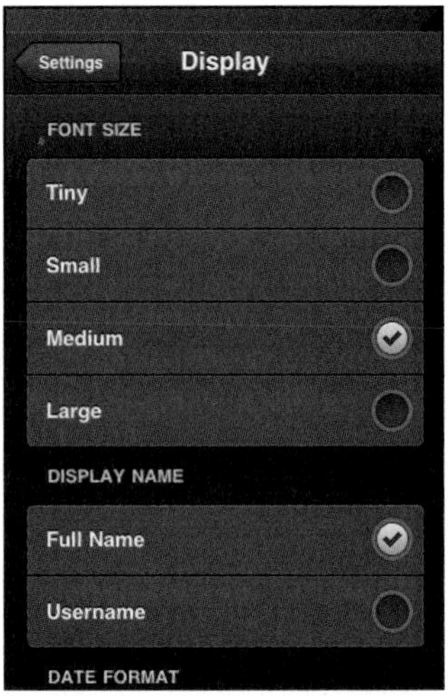

No Transitions

The "Tweetbot" app is almost entirely comprised of one large menu that seamlessly flows in and out of various functions, partly because of the ubiquitous, customizable navigation bar at the bottom that provides a starting point, as well as the upper-left navigation bar to get you back to a previous menu level. There are almost no transitions to new full screen interfaces that do not appear to be a new, integrated pop-up covering your last known place. "Tweetbot" makes heavy use of the navigation bar and popover elements (as shown in Figure 9-10) so that users almost never see a loading animation.

Standard Conventions

As shown in Figure 9-11, "Tweetbot" uses iconography seen in other Apple apps and Twitter clients, as well as zero non-standard navigation, keeping the app easy to use, but with exceptional layout and intuitive button placement. In this respect, it follows general design rules and human interaction principles. For example, when viewing the default page of someone you are following, the most relevant information is at the top, while scrolling down is possible for more in-depth information and choices.

You might argue that the Tapbots apps have not been overly popular yet, and, therefore, the approach is not one that can (or should) be modeled exactly. However, some of that is likely caused by other factors such as pric-

FIGURE 9-9: The Settings menu in "Tweetbot" is simplified because of its user-friendly, concise text, large checkmarks, and lack of clutter

FIGURE 9-10: Almost anywhere within the app is within easy reach from the bottom navigation menu, which can be prioritized to the user's preference

ing, marketing, or the lack of a lite version for any of the Tapbots apps. Also note that "Tweetbot" is within striking distance in its niche (within the top ten social apps) and has exceptional user review feedback, a vindication at least for its design.

What should be taken from this case study is that the Tapbots has a solid reputation now for the amount of thought that went into creating each aspect of this and most of its other apps, especially in the way of button placement, streamlining (simplifying) the interface, and lack of transitions, helping to keep you in the apps seamlessly with little to no loading. Apps like this are fun to use, and do not have to be as full-featured as other apps in order to be more desirable. Have the right features, and do them well.

SUMMARY

It's sometimes easy to forget that Apple has its roots in great design and user experience, given its current corporate presence and popularity. Hopefully, now you can take some of the lessons Apple has to offer and strengthen your current and future apps with these in mind.

FIGURE 9-11: None of the screens in "Tweetbot" feature much clutter, and almost all relevant information uses a top-down approach

The purpose of this chapter was not to put the Apple design or customer service method on a pedestal as unquestioningly the right way to build hardware or software — after all, unless you have Apple's virtually unlimited resources, leadership, time, and talent, it's not always practical. Rather, the goal of this chapter was to encourage you to take targeted cues from an ultra-successful company with a proven track record for elevating user experience and form design, and mash them into actionable ideas that can help any developer in creating a stellar app.

Chapter 10 looks at one of the final pieces of the puzzle prior to release — how best to integrate the social networking phenomenon within and outside your app to engage and retain users.

Riding the Social Networking Wave

From a business perspective, social media is all about marketing. It's another way to directly impact proliferation and sales of your product by engaging and interacting with your target audience (in this case, apps), but it can work for most any business. *Social media* means unique channels where users can directly communicate with others (one-way or two-way), via direct message or chat, Facebook wall or newsfeed posts and notifications, tweets and re-tweets on Twitter, LinkedIn, the old-fashioned (but still heavily relied upon) e-mail, and other social platforms — both general and targeted to a specific niche.

In June 2010, Admob reported that roughly 50 percent of iPhone users discover new apps via word of mouth, which included social media recommendations. Though the report did not break down further which social media channels were used, it matters little, because a diverse and targeted approach would still be highly recommended.

This chapter provides a head start into utilizing all the social facets that are available to you as a developer of any type of app or game, in order to both promote traffic, and sustain user interest from within.

FOSTERING THE ULTIMATE VIRAL MARKETING: SOCIAL NETWORKS

Two social networks dominate the current social media market: Facebook and Twitter. Because of the sheer number of users across all demographics, it is essential for any out-of-app marketing campaign to make use of these, and, when possible, to do so in-app as well.

At its core, *viral marketing* is any method of acquiring users that provides more than one *additional* user for every new user acquired. There was a catchy Faberge Shampoo television commercial in the 1980s that featured Heather Locklear saying, "It was so good I told two friends about it. And they told two friends. And so on, and so on..." — all while the screen was dividing up into smaller and smaller squares with new faces. Viral marketing is like that.

The good thing is that viral marketing doesn't completely depend on just one channel any more. In fact, to maximize those areas that are overachieving and to tweak areas that need improvement, it's good to utilize as many channels as you have the time and resources for. If you can utilize all your channels, and the end result is that your overall cost per new user (all social marketing costs including YouTube videos, websites, support, Facebook fan pages, Twitter campaigns, and so on) is less than their expected lifetime value or expenditure, then your campaigns are paying off, regardless of the viral component. The terms *cost per user acquisition* (CPA), *customer acquisition cost* (CAC), and *lifetime value per customer* (LTV) are most often used.

This book won't delve too deeply into metrics, because other books are available that can cover that subject in much better detail.

Integrating In-App Networks

Currently, the four largest in-app social networks (primarily for games) are Apple's Game Center, OpenFeint (www.openfeint.com), the Plus+ network (spoken as "plus plus," at www.plusplus.com), and Facebook (putting a link here would be ridiculous). This section examines the benefits of using each, and why most games should consider using Game Center. Unfortunately, for apps, there is nothing like this yet, though you might expect Apple or a third party to be working on something that could more socially integrate all types of apps (game or non-game).

Game Center

In June 2011, Apple noted that 50 million users were using Game Center, the native social network that is integrated with all iOS apps post version 4.0. However, older iPhones and iPods (which aren't compatible with the newer iOS) won't be able to run it.

Game Center's primary appeal is that it offers in-game achievements across friends, one of the main incentives to drive retention in games (and, in the future, most likely many apps as well — achievement rewards for common tasks).

Game Center differs substantially from OpenFeint and Plus+ in a couple of key areas:

➤ Apart from being an API that users can implement with a game, Game Center is also a native iOS app (see Figure 10-1) that users can open and manage their friends on — out of the game — rather than a separate interface to manage friends that is called from within-game in OpenFeint and Plus+.

FIGURE 10-1: In Game Center, you manage your friends and games from within its own app

➤ Game Center currently provides much less social connectivity functionality while *playing* games, such as finding new friends or seeing what they are up to. However, Apple is evolving Game Center, and will no doubt improve this over time. In fact, for the app itself, iOS 5 brings a number of new changes, including the display of achievement notification banners, adding a profile picture, friend recommendations, and seeing what friends of friends are playing, among other things.

When deciding whether to use Game Center, you should consider some unique pros and cons.

Unique pros of Game Center include the following:

➤ All newer i-devices come with it by default.

➤ Apple continues to update and improve its social connectivity.

➤ Game Center has the most current active users (not including Facebook, which is mostly externally driven).

➤ Game Center includes an integrated search right within the App Store, which none of the competitors can match (see Figure 10-2).

➤ Game Center has auto matchmaking and excellent multiplayer support.

➤ Users can make purchases right from within Game Center (which is a big deal).

FIGURE 10-2: Game Center integrates with iTunes, giving it an edge over its competition

Unique cons of Game Center include the following:

➤ Apple is slow to implement social connectivity features within games themselves, other than typical multiplayer features.

➤ Communication outlets within the Game Center community are currently low. For example, there are no forums, and it has limited profile information, message, and search/find friend functionality, especially when waiting in lobbies to join games.

➤ It has limited to no current cross-platform gaming.

➤ Its visual appearance within an app is not currently integrated into the visual style of the app, which decreases immersion. Note that the other major social game networks have the same problem, and are in need of more re-theming possibilities.

To sum up, mainly because it is native to iOS, Game Center has great multiplayer support, and you should strongly consider it for games. But you may want to also consider adding another social networking capability (such as OpenFeint or Facebook) to supplement it for social connectivity reasons.

It is possible (or worthwhile) to use multiple social services within one game. However, keep in mind that more services aren't necessarily better. Requiring users to jump through the hoops of registering your app, or jumping from one service to another, can be a barrier to both entry and use. Nonetheless, this might be a good option in instances where you want to support Game Center, but need more social connectivity, such that as found in OpenFeint. Later versions of OpenFeint even have Game Center integration, so that users can share achievements over either platform.

Other cases where you can use multiple social platforms at the same time include the scenario of adding friends. In the world-building, free-to-play game "We Rule" by ngmoco shown in Figure 10-3, you can pull friends in from Twitter, Facebook, as well as Plus+, making it easy for users, depending on which platform they use most frequently. This type of integration also causes very little back and forth between platforms.

FIGURE 10-3: "We Rule" from ngmoco uses Plus+, Facebook, and Twitter

OpenFeint versus Plus+

The main differences between these two platforms is in the number of users (OpenFeint has more), social features, and implementation. For the most part, Plus+ is falling behind in the race, and because Game Center is becoming more popular and adding social features (slowly but surely), this book tends to recommend the OpenFeint platform over Plus+. Following are a couple of the important areas of consideration:

➤ **Ease of use** — Although Plus+ has a more traditional and colorful layout (as shown in Figure 10-4), it has fewer options, and so is somewhat easier for the user to navigate. On the other hand, as shown in Figure 10-5, the

OpenFeint icons are numerous, and it is easier to get lost within the screens (though they do have a standard "back" navigation bar throughout, which you can use to cycle back to the main menu).

➤ **Social integration** — OpenFeint is clearly ahead of every competitor on this front, with live chat and messaging, forums, and Facebook and Twitter links for most everything, as shown in Figure 10-6. Because of this, you should use OpenFeint, though this is offset somewhat by the sheer number of games (many of which are not worthy of a download).

FIGURE 10-4: The Plus+ network uses an aesthetically pleasing layout that is easy to navigate

Facebook

Because of its massive adoption, Facebook should be a part of your app in some way if possible, whether utilizing Facebook Connect (discussed later in this chapter) to be able to add friends, or being able to share achievements or post something to your wall. Non-game apps, of course, should rely on Facebook over any other platform, unless you have a specific social platform that relates better to your app, such as what YouVersion (www.youversion.com) does with the "Glo Bible" app (www .globible.com). In the end, it is possible for Facebook and other networks to co-exist peacefully.

FIGURE 10-5: Because of all the functionality in OpenFeint, users make heavy use of "back" button navigation

FIGURE 10-6: OpenFeint uses a custom, streamlined layout that contains a lot of functionality

Building Achievements, Medals, Badges, and Other Rewards

Game achievements are the cornerstone of user retention. They provide players with a sense of progression and goals over multiple sessions, and rewards for achievements can provide even further incentives to try to complete the game.

The best example of achievements found today in a social-like network is on the Xbox Live Arcade (XBLA) platform. Every retail game must feature 1,000 points worth of achievements, divvied up typically between 20 and 40 individual ones, some worth more points, and some less, depending on the developer's design.

Any user of XBLA can instantly (from within a game) call up a friend's achievements and compare. This is a huge incentive to compete. After this system was such a success, Sony implemented Trophies for its PlayStation Online Network, which hasn't had quite the success (mostly because of social implementation) as the XBLA counterpart.

Enter Game Center, OpenFeint, and Plus+. These networks are capitalizing on creating shared achievements between friends and across games, so that users can compare total points earned. If you have a game and are not yet using achievements or some sort of goal-based rewards, you probably should, even if it remains in your game-only network of friends, because it will help drive future retention and engagement.

The best way to create achievements is to spread out the time it takes to complete them, creating sets of achievements that can be earned fairly quickly, as well as those that take progressively longer and are more challenging to complete. You should even add achievements for the hardcore gamer that can only be earned with sweat and tears.

> In "Archetype," the team created a set of in-game achievements named Titles, which were based off experience points. These could be seen as a badge while in the lobby and in games, and, in a way, represented your skill and devotion. There was also a complete set of medals that could be earned via gameplay in each game (for example, kill five enemies within seven seconds). Experience, in turn, was dependent on winning or losing, and medals earned. These ideas weren't new to the genre, but were required for the type of user to ensure longer retention. In addition, the "Archetype" website featured leaderboards, player profiles, and search functionality, so players could stay invested in their progress out of the app as well.

Aside from bragging rights that most achievements provide, further incentivizing them can be a smart move to drive better long-term retention. Not every achievement needs to unlock something, but it provides further goals to aspire to. For example, in "Fruit Ninja" and "Fruit Ninja HD," the game features not only Game Center and OpenFeint (tied together) achievements, but another set of in-game achievements that unlock various rewards, such as new swords or backgrounds, as shown in Figure 10-7.

FIGURE 10-7: Achievements in "Fruit Ninja" unlock various in-game rewards, which is great for incentivizing long-term retention

Now, let's take a look at the current king of social media, Facebook, and what developers can learn from Facebook's successful apps.

TAKING CUES FROM FACEBOOK

Prior to Facebook, multiplayer gaming, chat, and even monetization was taking off, especially in Asia. Facebook took the ideas in MySpace further by tightly integrating it all in one place. See what your friends are up to and provide your own quick updates, find friends you forgot you had, develop and become invested in your user profile, share and tag pictures, and, eventually, game and compete with friends.

Because social gaming 2.0 (not just multiplayer and chat) was born and evolved via Facebook, and especially skyrocketed in popularity (thanks in large part to Zynga and other innovative social strategic gaming companies), the art of developing a social app is now a science. It may be an imperfect science still full of new discoveries, but it is also a rapidly changing process-and-metrics-driven marketing phenomenon with the potential to turn any intellectual property from unknown to globally known virtually overnight. How is this possible? Friends.

Everything Is More Fun with Friends

Developers of Facebook apps have learned the fine art of turning what would normally be single-player experiences ("Farmville") into socially driven games. Displaced friends along one side of many games provide that sense of community and competition (even while playing solo) that would otherwise not be there. This friend presence (combined with frequent opportunities to share your experience, gift, and receive friends' items, as well as to visit your friends' worlds) provides an atmosphere almost as if they were there playing with you.

The fact that they normally are not doesn't matter, and can actually be better, because there is less pressure for competition, and more room for surprise and anticipation. Logging back onto a social game to see the progress of friends or to receive new gifts and responses lends an element of long-term retention to apps.

Just what elements to provide in your app to provide this, however, is something that will need to be constantly monitored, tweaked, and measured.

It's All about Metrics — Tweak Values Early and Often

Number 1 Facebook developer Zynga is known for taking a heavy metrics-based approach to game design, which is one of the reasons its games are immensely addictive and popular.

Brian Reynolds, chief creative officer, provided this company insight during an interview with IndustryGamers (`www.industrygamers.com`):

> *[T]he numbers give us an idea of roughly what kind of feature to do because there are some kinds of features that are more likely to drive people to pay, or to drive people to stick and come back a lot, or to invite their friends, or things like that. So, you can kind of aim a feature at different things or different combinations of things, but then you still have to have someone to be creative to make it cool and to make it fun and to make it fit into a long-term story that makes sense to people. So, I think that the metrics are something that help us make the games better.*

In February 2010, at the DICE Summit in Las Vegas, Reynolds said that, for Zynga's game "Mafia Wars," up to seven different tutorial experiences ran in parallel. "We learned all kinds of stuff about what it takes to get somebody to become a regular player. We went down to three, then one, and that one was totally counter-intuitive to what we thought the tutorial should be like."

What he is referring to about going down different paths is called *split testing*, or *a/b testing* (both are synonymous). This is the most common method for analyzing two sets of data that two sets of random samples experienced, all other things being equal. Split testing is immensely useful for everything from testing whether product landing pages have impactful text, to banner ads, and to user engagement in games and other apps.

Any time that you can take advantage of split testing, you should — which also means getting involved in analytics for your app. The more things that can be quantitatively measured (whether in handy charts and graphs, or solid numbers), the easier it will be to take action.

Three of the leaders in analytics for both Facebook and iOS apps are AppData (for measurement and trending of Facebook apps — www.appdata.com), Kontagent (for full analytics — www.kontagent.com, see Figure 10-8), and Flurry (for full analytics — www.flurry.com). The core value in split testing is in taking the best approach, then pairing that approach with another alternative, and testing it again. That way, each process can evolve until you have the best possible, heaviest engagement, or profitable experience.

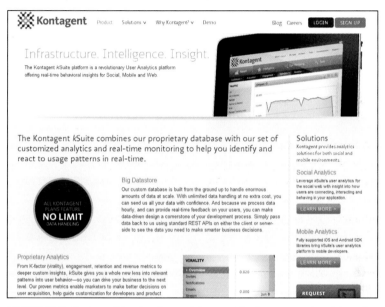

FIGURE 10-8: Kontagent is a leading metrics provider for apps and social media

For example, following are some split test examples in apps:

➤ Determining which keywords work better for searches

➤ Measuring user engagement of your app past certain barriers such as tutorials or even the main menu

➤ Determining how long users stay in your app

➤ Pricing for in-app purchases versus sales

You can split-test most anything these days, and should. In December 2010, Albert Lai (simplyalbert.blogspot.com), co-founder and President of Kontagent, provided seven important social metrics that should be measured:

➤ **Customer Acquisition Cost (CAC)** — He said that CAC is currently from $1 to $4 and trending upward because of big brands entering the advertising ecosystem, driving costs higher for the smaller developer.

➤ **K-factor** — The *k-factor* is how viral your app or product being measured is. That is, for a k-factor of 0.5, you are bringing one "free" new user for every two users you acquire. At a k-factor of 0.2, you'd be bringing in one free new user for every five users acquired. For an app to go viral, you must have a k-factor greater than 1.0, preferably at least 1.2 for faster and sustainable viral growth.

➤ **Sessions per user and average session length** — A *session* is how long users stay in your app at any one time. A higher user engagement usually means longer session length, which is good all around, especially if you're into monetizing. Lai said that Kontagent was seeing 10+ minutes and 1.7 to 2.2 sessions per user per day in its most successful apps.

➤ **One-day + One-week retention** — Take a look at how many users are coming back to your app after their first time. In addition, measure how many are coming back one week after their first use. This can be enhanced, Lai says, using a/b testing on game mechanics.

➤ **Average lifetime per user** — Focus on the engagement loop (in other words, the psychology of what makes a user want to come back). And, Lai says, end with a reminder to come back. For apps, this can be as simple as push notifications, but should be inherently embedded into the game mechanics.

➤ **ARPU, ARPPU** — This refers to average revenue per user (ARPU), and average revenue per paying user (ARPPU). Both of these, according to Lai, are trending upward as companies are learning more about virtual goods' models. These can be measured through revenue per daily active user (DAU), transactions per DAU, and dollars per transaction.

➤ **Percentage of paying users** — As production and acquisition costs rise, it is important that more users are of the paying kind, especially for freemium models or those with DLC. Acquiring users via targeted marketing is key. The typical paying user rate, Lai says, is roughly 1 percent to 3 percent of total users.

When you develop an app, you'll have access to Apple's built-in iTunes Connect data as well. However, although handy for a few statistics, you should strongly consider signing up with a third party to be able to track most anything and everything in a degree of depth that Apple doesn't currently (and may never) provide.

IGNORING FACEBOOK CONVENTIONS

There are a lot of things you can learn by picking up a book on Facebook monetization, but all of them don't necessarily translate well to iOS apps, nor do iPhone users expect the same type of experience they can get on Facebook. Usage patterns are different, session times on iPhone are shorter, and people expect more entertainment in shorter bursts for their time (as proven by the low price of apps and heavy competition in most niches). The exception to this would be the iPad, because session times are more on par with using a PC, in addition to the resolution offered.

For iOS devices, however, the much better graphic processing power, in addition to user expectations compared to that of games in Flash (which have traditionally lower expectations in terms of polish because of the sheer number of them and graphic capabilities), result in different user experience expectations. Following are two examples of Facebook conventions you should consider ignoring altogether, or special-tailor them to suit your audience on behalf of the iOS user.

Waiting Is Not Fun

Many of Facebook's most popular apps are built on a monetization model that makes users wait for currency and progress rewards from their various virtual world objects. For example, in "Farmville" (and almost all other apps like it, including "Smurfs' Village" for iOS), the main driving incentive for earning game currency and experience toward new levels is having to wait for your planted crops to grow, in real time. Even the recently released "Sims Social" has implemented this into its monetization scheme when none of the previous PC "Sims" games had any sort of mechanism like it.

What this does (and is not necessarily fun) is drive user retention to come back and "harvest" these crops when they are ready for the rewards, then plant/build more and repeat the process. Some games do it slightly differently, but the method is the same — making users wait in real time for rewards.

Although this is a smart (though increasingly ubiquitous) way to drive retention, if you have elements like this, you must also look to drive user engagement within the app to extend session times for things other than simply planting and waiting for rewards. Things like social engagement, mini-games, customization of the world, actual gameplay or character progress, and more, are valuable engagement tools that can be used to offset the rather mundane mechanism of planting and waiting.

Fortunately, "Sims Social" also does this in spades; thus, that's one of the reasons it is so popular. In other words, be sure that this type of mechanism, if implemented in your game, is only a small portion of your overall retention dynamic.

No Forced Friends, Please

In 2008, Facebook had a problem. Many games and other apps were essentially forcing users to add friends in order to progress. To get to the results of some quiz, poll, or prize, users were often forced to add a certain number of friends just to skip. Some games started the trend of requiring a certain number of friends to expand land or further advance. The main problem was not so much in asking a friend to play or "be a neighbor," but rather it was that the asking became what is known as *friend spam*. Your wall would get flooded with friend requests and free gifts encouraging you to play their game.

While Facebook put a Band-Aid on the problem by requiring a skip or cancel button, the practice of requiring friends (understandably for the viral effect) has become almost a study in how to find loopholes in the law of whichever platform you're monetizing on.

Enter iOS apps. As Apple moves Game Center more toward open social networking conventions and communication outlets, it will be very tempting to see what early advantages you can glean. But keep in mind that overuse of mechanics that rely on adding friends can be just as big a turn-off to users as those that don't utilize friends at all.

The virtual currency-based freemium game "Smurfs' Village" takes a positive (yet subtle) approach to this aspect. Friends can provide *some* advantages to your built-up village, and gift you with the occasional item that you cannot find without them. But there is never a requirement that you add friends in order to get even a significant portion of value back. For example, none of the items for sale require X number of friends to buy. It's supplemental and additive, rather than part of the core experience.

You should find ways to incentivize social behavior and make use of viral channels without relying on it, instead of forcing the issue. When asking a user to share his or her achievements, consider providing a free benefit to all those who might see the post. In other words, consider combining gifting and promotion to provide both bragging rights and incentives for other users, and not just in a competitive way.

In Figure 10-9, "Sims Social" (which is a relatively newer, but highly popular Facebook app) does this with all of its sharing prompts. And, speaking of promotion and rewards, this provides a good segue to the next section.

FIGURE 10-9: "Sims Social" for Facebook combines rewards for everyone for each share opportunity

REWARDING USERS FOR PROMOTING YOUR APP

One of the best ways to promote your app (other than it being extremely awesome on its own, worthy of immediate praise and 5-star ratings) is to incentivize your users to proliferate the Internet and their own friend lists to extol its virtues, or ask for free virtual swag. How exactly is this accomplished? Offering tangible rewards is one good strategy with varied methods of accomplishing it. Another is offering a sense of community that can build organically around your app.

Gifting with Virtual Objects, Free Stuff

In psychology, there is what's known as the *rule of reciprocation*. Give someone something for free, and most people will feel strongly obligated to not only accept the gift, and when doing so, feel obligated to return the favor. It's one of the core persuasion techniques used by sales people in all walks. How many times have you walked past a person or kiosk giving away free stuff (pamphlet, trinket) only to try your best to ignore them because you know all too well that if you accept it, you're inviting them into a conversation about something you're probably not interested in?

The rule of reciprocation is also true for apps, especially as proven so successfully in Facebook, albeit with some amount of conversion loss. For example, not being face to face with a sales person provides some anonymity, and not being there to accept in real time means there will definitely be conversion rate problems. Still, the rule retains some of its effectiveness, and ways have evolved to mitigate loss.

You should split-test some of the following to determine what works best for your app:

➤ **Targeted gifting** — This remains a traditional approach for most games, and, because Zynga (the metrics powerhouse) continues to use it, that must mean it still has merit. Picking a friend to give a virtual gift makes it more personal, especially if the gift itself is valued by the friend (which can be virtual or real-life practical). When you see a flower pot appear in your "Smurfs' Village," it shows who it's from and there's some small amount of guilt if you don't reciprocate in turn. In "Zynga Poker," users can target other users to gift chips, as shown in Figure 10-10.

FIGURE 10-10: An example of targeted gifting in "Zynga Poker"

➤ **Competitive gifting** — Offering up a gift to the first user who claims it encourages friendly competition.

➤ **Gifting to all** — Conversion rates for reciprocity won't be anywhere near 100 percent, but some significant portion will react. Usually, this is combined with sharing an achievement, as in everyone gets a reward if they take a peek at your app.

➤ **Emotion-based gifting** — This is a clever method to tempt users to buy into a "story" by appealing to their emotions. If you've played "Farmville" or "Frontierville," you know how it works. Essentially, as shown in Figure 10-11, a surprise occurs, such as an injured or lost animal, and you share this event with your friends because you don't want to see it lost or hurt. In this case, the key emotion would be sympathy. Similarly, when the event appears to other users, they also have a sympathetic need to buy in and help out, thus completing the chain. This occurs most often in games, but could be something fun to add in socially oriented apps (for example, friend X or friends need your help to accomplish Y). The key emotion in this case does not always have to be sympathy; jealousy, greed, empathy, fear, surprise, anger, joy, love, and so on, are all candidates. The more social you make the event, the more dominant the emotion becomes.

FIGURE 10-11: An example of sympathy gifting in "Frontierville" appeals to the emotions of users

➤ **App-to-person gifting** — Gifting need not apply only to person-to-person gifts, but app-to-person as well. When users enter your app or game, consider giving them something in return. If it is an app, you could include a useful notification or stat, and, if a game, some reward. Popular Facebook portals and games utilize this to encourage you to come back after an absence. One popular way is free spins in a casino style to provide a currency reward bonus.

Gifting does not have to apply only to games either. Sharing a picture in Facebook is a form of gifting. Even tagging another's post or comment with a "like" or "+1" (a public statement that you endorse the comment) is a form of gifting subject to the rule of reciprocity.

Gifting in-app with virtual objects is the most common form of gifting, but certainly not the only way. There's another gigantic social marketing trend that has emerged in the past year, which is that of incentivizing users to both "like" your Facebook Fan Page in exchange for a real-world or virtual gift (personal or collaborative), or become a follower of your Twitter stream in exchange for insider information such as discounts or first-to-know knowledge about the brand.

One of the proven success stories in this regard is that of the Dell Outlet (shown in Figure 10-12), Dell Computer's Twitter account that offers discounts exclusive to followers of @DellOutlet. In 2010, Dell made more than $6 million in sales just from its Twitter feed.

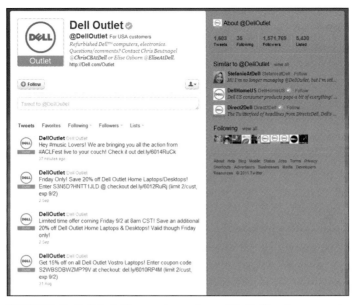

FIGURE 10-12: Dell Outlet has made great use of its Twitter stream, earning millions in sales via follower-only discounts

Providing Users with a Sense of Community

As users become engaged and retained with your app, the heavier they become invested, the more social options become important for expressing and sharing their experience. One of the ways to tap into this desire and enrich their experience is by building a sense of community, either within the app, or, more commonly, outside of it.

When heavily engaged, users will often *remain* engaged with your app, even when unplugged from it. They'll think about going back to it, make plans to do so, and figure out how most efficiently to use it, all within their minds. Exploring or sharing their experiences of using the app is one outlet many users enjoy engaging in. One of the most popular ways to achieve this is to build up a brand site where users can not only explore this app, but others from you as they become available, assimilate your brand as a whole, and engage in a forum for expressing their needs.

Sometimes, without this, one of the first places to go and vent issues is in iTunes, where any frustration might be expressed in a negative review. If your site has a brand presence instead (even if just support), users might go there to seek fixes to their issues, rather than taking the easy route of complaining, and likely then breaking their retention for good.

SOCIAL INTERACTION AS FEATURES

When marketing your app, bullet points count, especially in the App Store description and for reviewers. To that end, what you can and cannot market as valuable social features should be noted.

Features versus Extras

As you've seen, social promotion of your app is important, but throwing in Facebook Connect or (as in iOS 5) the capability to Tweet events or share achievements does not make your app a "social" app, or encourage users to download it on these merits alone. Neither does the capability to promote it via e-mail, though it is a feature most apps should have. These types of social interactivity are extra features that can both help promote and extend its value, but they hold little value as bullet points for marketing these days, because they are both simple to do, and most apps feature some sort of social connectivity (or are trending that way).

Social *features*, on the other hand, are meant to be marketed and called out in your App Store description, whereas social *extras* might be the last bullet point, but certainly not the first. A social feature would be the capability to directly go head-to-head against or play along with friends, in-game chat or message, share photos, or collaborate. As you're developing your app, see if you can implement social features that provide more marketing mileage, versus social extras, which should be included, but are generally less meaningful.

Because apps with a form of competition, cooperation, or collaboration are becoming more frequent (take a look at all the Web 2.0 apps that feature collaboration), let's take a look at some of the ways to accomplish this in your own app so that they can stand out as key marketable features.

Setting the Stage for Users to Compete

Social gaming started with multiplayer features, which have been around from the earliest systems. Multiplayer features have, of course, evolved so that players can play remotely (the next big innovation), then chat, and now groups of friends can compete or co-op (play cooperatively) together with live chat or video, or even as artificial intelligence (AI) entities.

Multiplayer gaming has become so ubiquitous with most every game that games without it are often penalized in reviews. For example, the successful Action/RPG Indie hit "Torchlight" from Runic Games (which can be considered a more casual "Diablo") released in late 2009 as a single-player only experience. Critical reviews were overwhelmingly positive, except for the one levied against a lack of multiplayer or even co-op. "Torchlight 2" includes multiplayer capabilities.

For iOS devices, currently the four social gaming platforms described earlier in the chapter can help you accomplish this: Game Center, OpenFeint, Plus+, and Facebook. As stated earlier, unless you have specific needs or are already enmeshed in Facebook, OpenFeint, or Plus+, it makes sense to provide at least Game Center support in most new games, but there are cases where you will want multiple options.

To provide the best experience, you have important considerations for specific types of games. Let's look at some of the key variations and conventions for implementing competition or cooperation in iOS games. Because literally dozens of combinations and hybrids of genres exist, the following list can be combined or mixed to suit the needs of your game, depending on genre and features.

Following are some important general considerations:

➤ **Matchmaking** — Whenever pitting one user against another, it is useful to have trackable metrics based on user profile, such as experience earned, win/loss ratios, score, and so on. Many matchmaking algorithms are available out there, so find or create one that suitably matches players of roughly equal skill. It can be frustrating for players to be matched with both a person too high above their skill level and too low, because no challenge translates into boredom.

➤ **Lobbies** — In any venue where you are pairing one or more people against others, it is often useful to have a "lobby" as a waiting room. Game Center features one without a lot of possible interaction between players. You should consider chat and messaging, and possibly other fun interactivity during the waits.

➤ **Leaderboards** — Anything with a score should have leaderboards, in any genre, but they are almost always found in these genres. Game Center and other networks support these, and you can also add your own, though these days it might be best to integrate with one of the main networking options discussed earlier in this chapter.

Following are some multiplayer and social connection possibilities:

➤ **Team-based** — Teams can be a fun mechanism and provide a strong sense of community, especially with direct friends. This is a favorite style in first person shooter (FPS) death match games, and even real-time strategy (RTS). Other genres can make creative use of teams as well.

➤ **Co-op** — Running through a game or level cooperatively is a favorite way to play among many players in everything from FPS games to RPS, but is a little more difficult to balance because of the typical need to design encounters for both single and multiple players.

> *Regardless of genre, games with co-op can feature this in a huge marketing bullet point, because it's not as common as the other methods, in large part because of design complexity.*

➤ **Head-to-head** — Direct competition can be found in almost any genre, from fighting to RTS to FPS to casual and educational.

➤ **Live chat** — This is most often used in FPS or other action-oriented games where it is not always feasible to stop and type, but this will continue to gain more popularity as technology improves.

➤ **Direct messaging and chat** — This is a popular mode of connection in social and casual puzzle games, such as "Words with Friends" by Zynga. It should be considered anytime users are pitted against one another.

➤ **Live video** — This is currently viable mostly only in apps that are centered around the technology, because it can be expensive to implement programmatically, in addition to the casual user not being quite familiar with this yet. Like live chat, this will continue to gain in popularity.

Let's take a look at an example of how "Fruit Ninja HD" has implemented direct head-to-head multiplayer features using Game Center, and subsequently integrated results using OpenFeint in order to share via Facebook or Twitter. That's a lot of options.

First, players are given the standard option of a multiplayer game, and then are taken to a menu of options, as shown in Figure 10-13.

FIGURE 10-13: Multiplayer options in "Fruit Ninja HD" include a couple of head-to-head split-screen modes, as well as an online head-to-head mode

After tapping Online, players get the Game Center pop-up with just a couple of options (and this is likely to be improved in the future) — either play now via Auto-Match, or Invite a Friend. Inviting a friend uses the same dialog, and you are able to select from online Game Center friends. In this example, Play Now is chosen, as shown in Figure 10-14.

When a match is found, players are taken to a splash loading screen with easy-to-digest rules, and then the match begins after a short countdown. As shown in Figure 10-15, in this game, players take turns swiping their own colored fruit all on the same screen, and get subtracted points if swiping the wrong color. (It looks like the author is losing this one.)

When the battle is finished, the results screen shown in Figure 10-16 appears, where an option to rematch is provided, as well as social options to share results.

Finally, the player can tap the social button with Twitter and Facebook icons, and is taken to OpenFeint's social page for sharing. Now, if "Fruit Ninja HD" didn't have OpenFeint, the developers could have opted for Facebook Connect or the

Twitter API to share the news instead (though, in iOS 5, as explained in the next section, Twitter functionality has changed).

FIGURE 10-14: Game Center's current and rather sparse lobby will likely be the target of improvement in future versions of iOS

FIGURE 10-15: Head-to-head battle in "Fruit Ninja HD" using Game Center's Auto-Match feature

FIGURE 10-16: The results screen in "Fruit Ninja HD," with rematch and social options using Twitter and Facebook

PROVIDING THE TOOLS FOR USERS TO CONNECT

This section goes into detail about how to drive virality and social engagement from within and outside of your app. One of the easiest ways to accomplish this is with Facebook Connect and a few lines of code. Note also that Twitter functionality is currently in the midst of a large overhaul in the way Apple handles it in iOS 5, which is examined in more detail next.

Implementing Facebook Connect and Twitter

Facebook Connect allows you to draw from the hundreds of millions of other Facebook users to connect and compete with your friends. It doesn't have the same type of functionality as a dedicated networking platform such as OpenFeint with forums and achievements and the like, but it is a must-have for adding another viral channel to your promotion campaign.

The best way to implement Facebook functionality is using the Facebook Connect API (http://developers.facebook.com/docs/guides/mobile/). This is essentially the injection of C code into your existing Xcode project that utilizes the Facebook API to access user profiles and share information back on Facebook.

For Twitter, in iOS 5, Apple now integrates directly and natively with the device, allowing any app to be able to tweet events or achievements. With this sort of functionality, it will be important to consider adding Twitter as another share mechanism, just as Facebook traditionally has been.

Let's look at a couple of examples of the ways Facebook Connect has been utilized in games and apps.

"Zynga Poker" exclusively uses Facebook Connect for multiplayer features and chat. Note the locked icons in Figure 10-17, representing all of the things you cannot do unless you log in to Facebook.

Similarly, note how the entire game changes once logged in to Facebook, as shown in Figure 10-18. Of course, the developers purposely de-emphasized the nature of the photographs when not logged in to Facebook as an incentive to sign in (and other notifications and touches in the same vein abound). But, nevertheless, the game is built to be played with friends and on a social network.

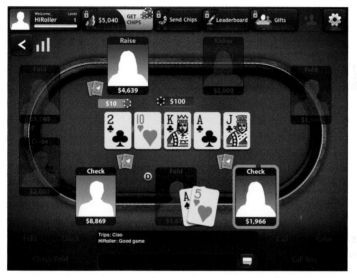

FIGURE 10-17: "Zynga Poker" relies heavily on Facebook for its multiplayer and user engagement

FIGURE 10-18: The entire game dynamic in "Zynga Poker" changes when you can see your friends, and even play with strangers as in real life

An example of an app and not a game is demonstrated in how Amazon's Kindle app functions. As shown in Figure 10-19, it uses both Twitter and Facebook Connect to be able to share excerpts to your Twitter feed and Facebook wall. In Kindle options, users are able to log in to both of the networks.

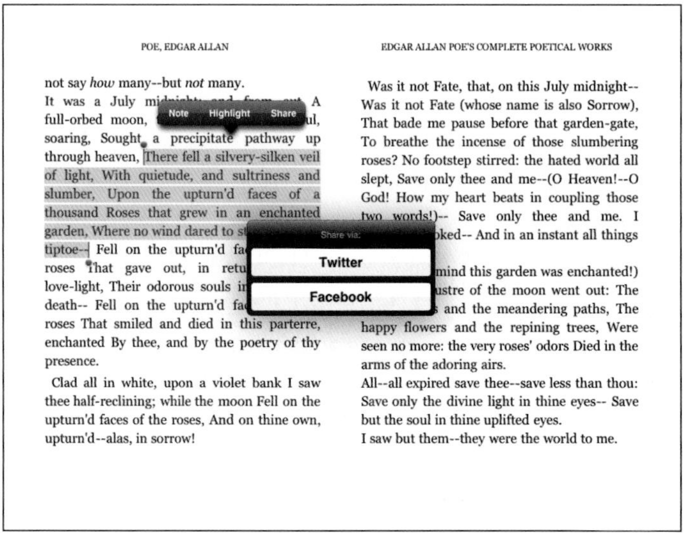

FIGURE 10-19: The popular free Kindle app allows users to share excerpts of books to Twitter or Facebook

In the next section, you learn some techniques developers use for maintaining a social community within the app.

Fostering Your In-App User Community

When users of an app can share and receive information, or communicate with one another while using it, it increases both engagement with your app, and, because people are always full of surprises, encourages users to come back (retention). Here are some examples of how this can be accomplished:

➤ **Integration with a specialized network** — For example, YouVersion (www .youversion.com) is an extensive social network centered around those who study the Bible, and is tightly integrated with a highly polished Bible study app named "Glo Bible" (shown in Figure 10-20). When logged in, users can see the comments of others, and write and share their own notes for virtually any facet of the lengthy tome.

➤ **Use OpenFeint or Facebook to chat and more** — With Facebook, developers can set up chat for friends, and OpenFeint features chat and forums across all apps, and even cross-platform.

➤ **Use leaderboards and achievements** — As mentioned earlier in this chapter, both of these can help foster a sense of community.

➤ **Provide support from within-app** — Allow users to e-mail you with feedback or questions without needing to exit the app, or at least route them easily to your website's support page.

FIGURE 10-20: The "Glo Bible" app integrates with YouVersion, a social network based around study of the Bible

Maximizing Viral Channels

Though this book isn't designed to go into too much in-depth detail concerning social marketing, some overall tips will help accelerate your online presence and help propel your viral growth. Aside from advertising campaigns, the main ways to do this are within your app (discussed earlier in this section), and externally via the Facebook Fan Page, Twitter feed, and YouTube videos. These last three should be a part of every new app marketing campaign (at least until something better comes along).

Facebook Fan Page

Facebook Fan Pages can have millions of fans (those who "like" it), come up frequently near the top of Google searches for various brands, and are excellent ways for users to interact with your brand without going to a separate brand website (as shown in Figure 10-21). The goal for a Fan Page is to provide information to users interested in your brand, thus keeping them continuously engaged. You typically do this by updating it frequently with the latest news about your product or brand.

When a user comes to your page and "likes" it (via the Like button), a notification is placed on his or her wall where other users can see it, thus starting the viral loop. Furthermore, additional content that you post and promote will also appear on their pages. Therefore, your end goal is to get users to "like" your page so that their friends will see their endorsement.

Fan Pages consist of a "landing tab" (which can be configured and will be where users first find themselves, thus making it imperative that this is as engaging and branded toward your app as possible), a wall (where news and user comments can be found that should be updated frequently, along with any other number of sub tabs/pages, including support, contests, quizzes, downloads, and specific information), and interactable pages about different aspects of your app or brand. Finally (and importantly), you can have fan-only content that can be locked until they "like" the page.

FIGURE 10-21: The Coca-Cola Fan Page, the largest on Facebook, was created literally by fans, and has the company's endorsement

There is an art to creating a Facebook Fan Page, and Internet articles abound on how best to achieve it. The following top tips are formed from a combination of the author's research, in addition to the best techniques gleaned from such articles, in no particular order of importance (except for the top recommendation):

➤ **Use Facebook apps to enhance your Fan Page** — This is critical, and cannot be stressed enough. Don't just settle for the default setup. Zillions of add-on apps have been built for the purpose of adding interactivity and helping promote your page. Fortunately, there are also quite a few blog articles that focus on filtering out the best of them, such as an excellent one at `www.socialmediaexaminer.com/facebook-apps/`.

➤ **Auto-post your selected Twitter feeds for wall content** — Apps can help with this, such as the appropriately named Selective Tweets, so that you aren't spamming unrelated information. See `www.facebook.com/selectivetwitter` for more information.

➤ **Have a branded landing tab** — This is another critical element to any Fan Page. In fact, it was reported that the founder of BrandedGlue, Jeff Widman, performed split tests with his company on conversion to fans with and without a landing tab, and found that having a landing tab *doubled* conversion rates (from 23 percent to 47 percent).

➤ **Import your blog's RSS feed for additional content** — A good app to help with this is Networked Blogs at `www.facebook.com/networkedblogs`.

➤ **Incentivize users to become fans** — Offer unlockable content such as downloads, wallpapers, exclusive content, coupons, discounts, or other promotions to entice users to become fans via the Like button. Many pages add a large graphic arrow that literally points to the Like button along with the offer. Victoria's Secret has on its wall an exclusive tab for fans.

➤ **Consider your fans and what is important to them** — This is common sense, but if you over-promote, you run the risk of losing retention. Fans can and will "unlike" your page because of the spam it can post on their own pages.

➤ **Ask for feedback to gain loyalty** — If you are willing to support your app post-release, this can be a great way to gain "street cred" with your fans, because it shows you are a developer/brand who listens and attempts to make it better. Don't forget to take some action on feedback.

➤ **Promote real-world events** — This can bridge the gap between online and off.

➤ **Funnel fans to your Facebook Fan Page throughout your marketing** — This can be through e-mail newsletters, your brand site, blog, anywhere you can link to your Fan Page to increase conversion into fans.

➤ **Hold contests and incentivize with rewards** — The bigger the reward, the more shareable the app becomes throughout social circles.

➤ **Pay for fans** — There are sites in which you can "buy" fans in bulk and fairly cheaply. This can be a good way to kick-start your Fan Page.

➤ **Make use of large profile photos** — Don't just use the square photo. Develop something larger and more prominent. The 200×600 pixels they provide offers a lot of flexibility.

➤ **Update frequently** — Fans will leave if you don't keep your content fresh and frequent. Just how frequent is subject to debate, but once per day to start should be sufficient. You'll eventually want to balance your own posts with those of users, once they start becoming engaged. Remember to keep new information unique and not repost anything twice.

With these tips, you should be able to create (or update) a fantastic Fan Page capable of good conversion rates for your brand. Next up is Twitter.

Twitter

Another large social network with great viral potential is Twitter. Users tend to tweet much more often than they post on their Facebook wall, and with the invention of "re-tweeting" what other users have already tweeted (sort of like forwarding an e-mail to everyone on your contact list), there is a huge potential to get more attention for popular tweets.

Every app or brand should also have a corresponding Twitter feed to reach the most people, and funnel them into your brand's online presence to also include the Facebook Fan Page. Here are some of the best tips for getting more Twitter followers, and maintaining an effective feed for your brand:

➤ **Offer special codes, coupons, or gifts only to Twitter followers** — In the earlier section, "Gifting with Virtual Objects, Free Stuff," the Dell Outlet example was used. This can be a powerful method to incentivize users to become followers.

➤ **Shorten and track tweet links with Bitly** — Bitly (`www.bit.ly`) is a popular link shortener that can turn any link into a manageable length in order to be able to insert it into your 140-character-limit tweets (or anywhere a link is required). Not only that, it provides detailed tracking of click information for each link, including how many times a particular link was clicked. Another popular link shortener is TinyURL (`www.tinyurl.com`), though it doesn't offer the same type of tracking that Bitly does. Metrics are your way to iterate on success.

➤ **Follow those people who are relevant to your brand** — People take a look at who you are following, and you will lose credibility if you follow anyone and everyone, which brings up the next point.

➤ **Don't follow more people than you have followers** — It's counter-productive to seem like you've followed 10,000 people and only have 2,000 followers. Fewer people will follow you if your follow ratio is too high.

➤ **Use hashtags** — A *hashtag* is a more recent and community-driven evolution of Twitter functionality, where you can insert a number sign (#) in front of key-words so that Twitter can make use of the word itself as metadata in searches. To opt-in, you follow @hashtags.

➤ **Buy Twitter followers** — Just as you can buy Facebook fans, you can do the same with Twitter. Remember, this will be part of your user acquisition cost (UAC).

➤ **Tweet relevant and varied information to your users** — Don't go all out with sales promotions. Ration them to about one-third general info about your brand, one-third relevant info about your industry/app, and one-third sales promotions or marketing.

   ➤ Sales and marketing info can include codes, specials, contests, events, or promotion date information.

   ➤ Brand info includes uploading new app pics (`www.twitpic.com`), staff information, support information, customer/client news, and product tips.

   ➤ Industry info includes news, questions (start conversations), asking for suggestions, and re-tweeting information.

➤ **Do a little competitive research** — Find out what others in your niche are tweeting about, and strive to match or do better for your followers.

➤ **Optimize Twitter bio content** — This is indexed in search engines, so optimize for keywords (use the Google keyword search tool — search `google.com` for "Google keyword search tool").

➤ **Add Twitter links to your brand website** — This will funnel potential followers to your feed.

➤ **Add your brand's URL to Twitter** — Cross-referencing your Twitter with your brand page (and vice versa) will result in more traffic to both.

➤ **Optimize your tweets for keywords** — Use the Google keyword tool men-tioned earlier when possible to optimize searchability for your tweets. This is easiest when you're outsourcing your tweets.

YouTube

YouTube marketing is a powerful and relatively recent technique for bringing in new traffic to your brand. The reason it is gaining in popularity is that users simply would rather watch a video than read text. Videos provide passive engagement where users expend very little effort to absorb your brand, app, or message. They can also be incredibly valuable for search engine optimization via user reviews for your app, and a viral promotion technique if you are able to capitalize on a quality viral video.

Following are some tips for using YouTube to increase your viral k-factor:

➤ Keep them short.

➤ Use keyword optimization in descriptions and title.

➤ Link YouTube with your Facebook Fan Page and Twitter feeds.

➤ Share information about your videos on Facebook and Twitter.

➤ Embed videos on your brand's website.

➤ Use humor!

The Hidden Power of Social Endorsing

One of the most prevalent new powers of social marketing has taken a cue from the Digg.com social news platform — that of endorsing a story with your vote. When a user likes your Fan Page, app, blog post (see Figure 10-22), or article, or anywhere you can conveniently add a Like button (virtually endless possibilities, but most definitely at the top of your Fan Page), what happens is that all your friends are able to see that you publicly endorsed it (with accompanying link) and, if curious, will follow it themselves.

FIGURE 10-22: Facebook's Like button and other social media bookmarklets are an easy way to achieve higher virality for your app or brand

This is effective marketing because it increases brand awareness for free, and even better, each of the "like" posts have a small (but significant) footprint on someone's wall. Finally, clicking the Like button anywhere provides almost no immediate feedback other than the counter going up, so users know they are doing something, but the connection that this will land on their wall is often missed. (There have been blog posts about what clicking it actually does.) Sometimes, the pop-up on the Like button can even be incentivized, such as "Be the first of your friends to like this."

Similar to the Like button, the newer Google + social network has its +1 button with a counter that works in the same way, and Twitter has a public counter for counting the number of Tweets that a particular page or link received. The +1's from Google are shown in your profile on a separate page, rather than intertwined within your news stream, and because the network is just starting to see significant traffic, it is not yet as efficient a marketing technique as the Like button.

There's another trend that is just emerging in which a friend's recommendations and "likes" play a huge part. It is social-based searching. Microsoft's Bing search engine has introduced a feature named "Social Search" at `social.discoverbing.com`. As shown in Figure 10-23, whenever you are logged in to Facebook and Bing, search results take into account what your friends have liked and shared.

FIGURE 10-23: Bing's new Social Search engine from Microsoft juxtaposes your friends' opinions and search results

By now, you've seen several ways in which to maximize your brand presence via viral marketing. Hopefully, your app (with or without the support of a larger brand) can take advantage of some of these recommendations (as well as some of your own) and see significant gains in overall awareness, along with a diverse set of channels in which people can find it.

SUMMARY

In this chapter, you learned several valuable techniques for promoting your app from within and without via social networking. You learned about in-app social networks such as Game Center, OpenFeint, and Facebook. You learned which cues to borrow from Facebook, and how to adapt others to work for your app, such as incentivizing friends without being overbearing. You learned how to reward users via virtual gifts, free stuff like discounts, and the importance of a community as a reward for loyalty. And you learned how to use metrics and split testing to improve user engagement and drive long-term retention.

You saw examples of how to implement Facebook Connect and Apple's iOS 5 changes to Twitter integration. You also learned how to maximize other viral channels, such as with Facebook Fan Pages, Twitter feeds, and YouTube videos.

In Chapter 11, you learn how to handle post-release feedback, and plan for future updates and content to keep your revenue streams flowing.

Feedback, Maintaining, and Scaling

WHAT'S IN THIS CHAPTER?

➤ Learning why you might consider a soft launch, and what feedback to look for

➤ Understanding how to take various types of feedback and convert it into actionables for your next updates

➤ Demonstrating that consistent updates is a means of marketing

➤ Understanding considerations when scaling your app for new content updates

➤ Knowing some options for porting your app to other platforms

➤ Learning even more methods for promoting your app post-launch

For most developers, the ride just begins when you see your first app go up for sale. Then comes post-launch marketing (keeping up the buzz), updates, future DLC or other content (paid or free), localization, planning and development of your next app(s), building your brand/app community, and, of course, fixes to problems you never knew about.

One of the biggest obstacles post-launch (and one that can severely drain momentum) is bugs that are caught by your new customers, who then leave feedback on iTunes that reduce the overall rating and lead to less than stellar reviews. As has been mentioned before, it's critical to squash the crash bugs, but a lot of other things can go wrong with your app, or things that people will otherwise leave feedback on. How best to assimilate the feedback and then set priorities to take action is something every developer should know.

EVALUATING FEEDBACK

To be best prepared for your main launch, a good plan might be to release in a smaller market early (which is called a *soft launch*) in order to get more data and make any fixes or tweaks prior to your theoretically more important core launch in a major market.

Soft Launch Preparation

Not all developers can afford to do this, but it's easier if your app uses very little text (or none at all). For example, it's quite affordable to find outsourced localization services that can quickly turn around your app description copy into another language, and be effectively localized.

> *Chapter 5 provides more information on localization.*

Once you're ready with the language and app description/marketing in a selected country, try releasing in one of these markets approximately four weeks (at least) prior to your core marketing launch date. Your app, after all, should already be in a roughly releasable state, and your goal, therefore, will be to concentrate on any unforeseen major bugs, as well as getting as much data as you can for everything else.

An important thing to note for soft launches is that they can save you time to release with a slightly reduced feature set than you are planning on with your main launch. Then you can eventually update all versions to be the same on main launch. In this way, you iterate through the feedback you get, and patch any changes to your current development (or latest working) version, in addition to the live soft launch versions, to gather more data.

Let's look at some of the feedback that you'll be looking for once you soft-launch an app.

➤ **Third-party integration** — Social networks (Facebook Connect, Twitter, Game Center, and other options), should be functioning as intended. Quality Assurance (QA) should ensure this, but launching will prove it, and give you time to make corrections should anything go wrong.

➤ **Servers and databases** — If your app connects to leaderboards, uses servers for hosting multiplayer gaming, or uses large amounts of data with simultaneous users — that is, will suffer any type of load — it's smart to get a handle on what limitations you're facing, and fix them (if necessary) prior to your main launch.

➤ **Performance** — See how (or even whether) users are reacting to performance, feedback, usability, and, if the app is a game, gameplay. If you find significant problems, you'll need to fix and optimize. The most often reported performance problem on iOS (especially for games) is lack of memory.

➤ **Tweak metric tracking** — Learn how your metrics are performing, and whether you have enough data points using your current metrics, or need to upgrade to a more advanced third-party option prior to launch.

➤ **Price and engagement** — See how users are adopting your app at the current price, and track how engaged your users are (average session time, where they spend the most time/money, and retention after a week). See Chapter 10 for more details.

For soft launches, gather as much information as you can, tweak according to the feedback you've received both in metrics and user data, and your main launch will go significantly smoother in terms of the unforeseen.

Main Launch Feedback

If you've decided to forego a soft launch, then, on your main launch, you'll immediately help your odds of smoothing any wrinkles by placing a top priority on the points presented in the previous section. In addition, be sure your App Store description can be held up to scrutiny as being accurate, and your keywords are optimized for search.

On main launch, you may want to set up teams to closely monitor feedback and metrics for a short time so that your team is ready to solve issues as they come up.

A TIME TO ACT QUICKLY

The team for "Archetype" set up schedules for round-the-clock monitoring and play-testing the first week, and made sure the programmers were available any time to fix possible high-priority issues (such as crashes or disconnect issues). After all, the game had several servers worldwide, and users could choose between them, ideally so that there wasn't a shortage of players for the multiplayer-only title. If any one of them went down, for example, it would have been flagged.

About two weeks after launch, the first major issue appeared. For whatever reason, an update binary that did not let users get past the splash screen, and, therefore, crashed for all users, was approved by Apple. During this time, there were many comments in the App Store review section with 1- and 2-star ratings, and large capital letters spelling "CRASH," helping to bring the overall average down, and not looking good.

Traditionally, this is a time when, if no other marketing efforts are helping propel sales, apps can fall off the radar, so it was critically important that the issue was taken care of. To hotfix this, the team removed the app as fast as possible, put in an expedite request to Tech Support, and resubmitted the older version to Apple. They also used Twitter and the Facebook Fan page to keep users abreast of the issue. Then they waited. Roughly two days later, the older version was restored, and comments returned to normal, but not without consequences, namely loss of revenue and some reputation as a competent developer. The mistake did not occur again.

Because it is guaranteed that customers will find new problems (even if they are subjective), it is best to start prioritizing a list and begin considering what to include in your first update, aside from the bugs you are currently aware of. This is to show that you are very invested in the success of your app, and that you listen to the community.

Chapter 3 discussed what types of feedback to look for in App Store competitor reviews. Now it's time to discuss what to look for in your own app.

Taking the Good and the Bad

There's one type of feedback you don't want, and that's no feedback. Any feedback says that you did something right — converted a user to download your app, and further, somehow motivated the user to give you a review, hopefully with a positive experience. If you have very little feedback, what's there becomes more poignant.

Feedback, though, doesn't come only with iTunes reviews. You must pay close attention to other sources. Forums (such as www.toucharcade.com), review sites, and YouTube videos can all be places to check. The types of feedback for each review, regardless of source, can be broken down into the following categories, one or more of which can be found in any review:

➤ **General opinion without support** — This is a general opinion about your app as a whole. It can be akin to saying "great app!" Though these are great to have as a means of promotion, they don't offer any means to improve the app.

> *Be wary of 1-star reviews that trash your app using bad grammar, hacker talk, lots of exclamation points, or ALL CAPS. The frequency of this type of feedback generally depends on the niche. Also, be aware of negative reviews left by your competition. This doesn't always happen, but is an occasional reality in a tight, competitive market.*

➤ **Targeted opinion** — With these statements, users often are targeting a specific part of the whole as the subject of their opinion. "Transitions are slow," "this gun is over/underpowered," "DLC should have been included," and "why are there ads when I paid for this?" are common examples. This type of feedback generally makes up the bulk of user reviews in iTunes, and should be categorized and prioritized (see the next section, "Converting Data into Actionables"). Opinions like this are very useful, especially as a way to gauge parts of your app that need improving. Some of them might also be two types of feedback in one: targeted opinion and a suggested fix, (such as "needs a bigger inbox").

➤ **Constructive criticism** — In this case, reviewers provide reasons to support their opinions. Give more weight to these as individual concerns, and categorize them in a separate place than the others, because, when you make decisions on next steps for updates and content, you can refer back to them for possible do's and don'ts regarding implementation.

➤ **Suggested fixes** — In this case, reviewers suggest a fix for something that, in their opinion, needs improvement. This is most common in professional/ YouTube reviews and forum posts, especially from fans. But you can also find them in iTunes reviews, and with higher frequency for higher priced or productivity apps. Don't be afraid to ask your community what's missing and what they want, especially on your Facebook Fan Page (see Chapter 10) or brand support forum. It may also be a good thing (at least temporarily) to include a "suggestion box" in-app so that users can directly e-mail their thoughts.

➤ **Reports** — The majority of these can be thought of as bug reports. Users will review the app to state that it is now crashing, the latest update fixes X but Y has gone missing, or that they can't access Z, and so on. It is good to monitor these as potential high-priority updates.

➤ **Nothing useful** — These might include exclamations, obscenities, and nothing constructive. Generally, it's best to ignore these as outliers, and focus on information you can be certain of.

How do you compile the various types of feedback, and arrange it in an order that is meaningful and can provide some direction? The next section provides a viable solution.

Converting Data into Actionables

The top priority for updates post-launch will always be fixes to major bugs as they come up. Hopefully, they won't, but there is always some element of risk. These are killers of momentum, especially in professional reviews, and you won't want them to continue to crop up. The next step is prioritizing the feedback data you've accumulated.

Creating a Spreadsheet

One way that worked well for the team at Villain was to use a spreadsheet program (the team used Excel, but Google Spreadsheet — docs.google.com — is also viable for this type of thing) and compile review feedback from the four main sources in the following manner. Figure 11-1 shows a sample of the feedback document used for "Archetype."

1. Create a separate sheet for user reviews from iTunes, one for forum posts (if applicable), and one for professional and YouTube reviews (again, if applicable).

2. For each sheet, create columns for *type of issue*, *specific category*, *wording used* in review, and *suggested fix*.

    a. *Type of issues* are broad categories of app design such as presentation, art, audio, gameplay, and the like.

    b. *Specific categories* are a subset of the type of issue. For example, if the type of issue is "art," the specific category might be "loading screen." This is to narrow down feedback within a broader category to something that can be assigned to the proper team member(s) and worked on.

	A	B	C	D
1	**Reset (re-sort)**	note for Reset button: make sure "select all" is checked in each drop down box		
2	*type of issue*	*specific category*	*exact wording used*	*suggested fix (exact wording)*
12	art	maps	open maps	
13	audio	weapons	better gun noises	
14	gameplay	controls	better controls	
15	gameplay	controls	better controls	
16	gameplay	controls	better controls	
17	gameplay	controls	better controls	
18	gameplay	controls	change controls	
19	gameplay	controls	change controls	
20	gameplay	controls	change controls	
21	gameplay	controls	change controls	
22	gameplay	controls	change controls	
23	gameplay	controls	change controls	
24	gameplay	controls	controls are horrible	
25	gameplay	controls	cut down movement rate	lowered to half the speed
26	gameplay	controls	faster turning	
27	gameplay	controls	remove friendly fire	
28	gameplay	controls	simple controls	
29	gameplay	controls	take off auto fire	
30	gameplay	controls	turn off friendly fire	
31	gameplay	controls	turning, could be a little better	like a continuous turn, without stop
32	gameplay	gameplay	change respawn area	
33	gameplay	gameplay	limited radar	
34	gameplay	gameplay	longer online games	
35	gameplay	gameplay	longer times	
36	gameplay	gameplay	slow down characters	
37	gameplay	gameplay	throw grenades further	
38	gameplay	gameplay	throw grenades further	
39	gameplay	gameplay	to short online	
40	gameplay	security	remove hackers	
41	gameplay	social	more players	
42	gameplay	stability	I get kicked out of games too much even though I'm on wifi	
43	gameplay	stability	stop it crashing	
44	gameplay	weapons	ability to turn off friendly-fire	

FIGURE 11-1: For tracking and analyzing review feedback, a spreadsheet comes in handy

    c. *Wording used* is taking the exact phrase that the user used when referring to the issue. For example, if the sentence was, "I like this game a lot, but the controls are horrible," the key phrase here is "controls are horrible." You should keep this short for brevity and ease of scanning.

    d. Finally, the *suggested fix* column is for those reviewers who suggest a possible fix for their issue. In Figure 11-1, one user writes that "turning could be a little better" and also suggests this fix: "like a continueous turn, without stop." Note the spelling was left unchecked. It is good to use exact wording so that you know what kind of effort or skill the reviewers put into their reviews. Although bad spelling or grammar doesn't invalidate a review, it can decrease its weight in some instances, depending on the offense and wording used. It is best to simply use your discretion.

3. Whereas the iTunes user review sheet should look something like Figure 11-1, with lots of brief statements, the forum feedback sheet demonstrates that posts on forums tend to be a little more verbose, as shown in Figure 11-2. To save time, it is easiest to grab a brief snippet of the pertinent paragraph, one for each issue mentioned in a post. The good thing here is that, though the text might be longer, the issues are still sorted by overall issue, and then a subcategory is used for easy reference.

4. Once you've compiled each of the columns, use your spreadsheet's sort feature to sort by type of issue, then category, and you'll get a very readable, ordered list of issues, many of which are duplicates. It is the number of these that matter.

2	type of issue	specific category	exact wording used	suggested fix (exact wording)
3	presentation	story	Good opening cg animation story. But in game, where's the story?	
4	presentation	story	Umm.. Not sure I follow the whole story of the game. So there is an alien race invading, and we are killing each other on earth? This dosent make sense. Will we later fight the aliens?	
5	presentation	story	There is no story per se, you are training against other soldiers to take on the alien invaders. It's the same core gameplay Eliminate is.	
6	art	animation	Very weak character animations. These are *must have*s I think. Look, I am not targeting this game as a bad guy, just want updates to fix these.	
7	art	animation	Character animations could use some work	
8	art	interface		The only suggestion I have is to work on the menu UI. It really lacks the smoothness that I think would bring the game to a more professional level.
9	art	interface	Problems with the position of the grenade (upper-left) and melee attack (radar display at bottom-centre) buttons unfortunately can't be addressed due to the lack of customisable controls. For example, too often melee attacks were triggered accidentally because of the function's proximity to the analogue sticks.	An option to reconfigure the interface is needed so as to account for individual control preferences. At the very least, alternative control schemes should be offered.
10	art	maps	Maps are great in size, but weak in textures and complexity. Very weak.	

FIGURE 11-2: Forum feedback features more heavy text, but also more constructive criticism

Now that you have a spreadsheet with compiled and sorted user feedback data, it's time to prioritize for your first update using *all* your data, including in-app metrics and your existing update plans.

Prioritizing for Updates

Sometimes it's easy. For example, there may be a few major issues that will take all of your resources just to be able to fix and get an update out as soon as possible. Or, perhaps the feedback you're getting is overwhelmingly directed at one or two issues, either missing, or bug-related.

Your first update (and likely the next few updates) should concentrate on offering excellent support, and show that you are listening to your customers. They're not expecting new content without first exploring the app, and, therefore, the overall goal for prioritizing your first updates should encompass mostly fixes and tweaks in the following order:

1. Squash major bugs or correct major usability issues first. Remember to keep an eye on all feedback so that you can spot these quickly the first week.

2. Address minor (but significant) usability or gameplay concerns such as balance.

3. Perform minor fixes and tweaks to performance or functionality.

Once your routine for updating is established, it is time to start thinking about feature and content updates, in addition to user feedback tweaks and suggestions.

There's no doubt that you may have many ideas about how to improve and grow your app post-launch, perhaps with DLC, new features you weren't able to add and decided to hold off on, or a clear-cut update strategy. With whatever strategy you have, it is important to temper it with the results from user feedback, in addition to any in-app metrics that merit adapting to. Let's look at some of the considerations for prioritizing the user feedback spreadsheet so that you can take into account this type of feedback.

With a lot of reviews, there should be a number of categories of issues (see Step 2 in the earlier section, "Creating a Spreadsheet") that match, in addition to specific comments. You should already have an idea of what some of the important issues for your app are, so now take into account the greatest number of exact matches as potential targets for including in an update.

Next, refer back to the risk analysis table (Table 5-2) in Chapter 5. For each of the top-ten issues with the highest number of matches, do the following:

1. Calculate the expected probability of your team being able to accomplish the task in the timeframe of one of your upcoming updates (as a percentage, 100 percent meaning you can absolutely tackle the task).

2. Estimate the expected potential impact that this change would have (100 percent would be maximum impact) if implemented.

3. Multiply the two percentages together for each issue.

4. The number that results should be a percentage as well.

5. Are there any that are more than 60 percent combined (meaning roughly 80 percent chance of success with at least 80 percent impact)? If so, focus on these first, the highest being the next update (or updates, if small) you should implement. If not, do the same thing with the next ten top issues until you have a clear picture of your next updates.

After you've decided what to include, continue adding to the user feedback data, and every week or two, reassess, removing those issues that have already been taken care of.

Now that you have a clearer picture of your future update plans, let's look at the reasons why updating is much more than fixes and content releases.

MAINTENANCE ISN'T JUST FIXING, IT'S MARKETING

Each time you update your app, users are notified on their home screen above the App Store icon. In this sense, it is almost as good as a push notification, because when users go to the update section, your app and its update description will show up and remain there until they tap it. Users may only see a few lines for each app, so be sure to optimize the first few lines of update descriptions to be your most important, as shown in Figure 11-3.

Frequent updates lend some credibility to you as a developer, especially when these updates are things users have asked for. And the best platform for them to communicate with you is directly, not through iTunes (as useful as reviews can be).

Customer Support Is Key

It is critical to establish a strong brand relationship with your customer. Support is one of the best ways to do this, because when all other things are equal, good support will undoubtedly push your app over the top via word of mouth.

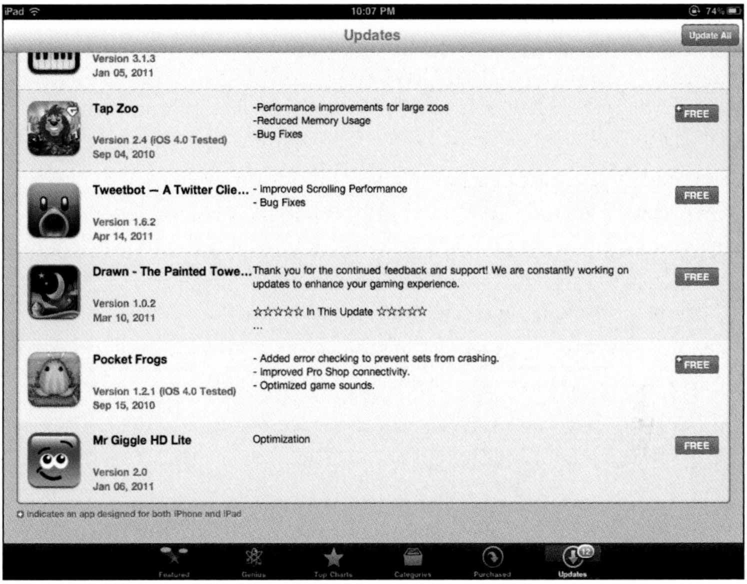

FIGURE 11-3: Users see only a few lines for each update, so make them count

All you need to do is take a look at Newegg.com (the premier online retailer for computer hardware and electronics), and Nordstrom's department stores (whose customer service standards of being able to return anything, even without a receipt, are legendary). Word-of-mouth marketing is powerful, and your brand can certainly benefit from one of the best ways to come by this, which is support. Let's take a look at some of the online options you have for providing it.

App Support Options

The more apps you develop, the more important support for your brand is. Fortunately, you have several ways to effectively accomplish this with relatively minimal effort, apart from time and initial setup. One of the most popular ways is to build an easy-to-use support forum right into your website, or even Facebook Fan Page, as shown in Figure 11-4.

Supporting your website with a plug-in customer support solution is perhaps the most efficient way to bring full-feature support to your brand's web page. One very popular system that can be customized to your brand's identity is Zendesk (www.zendesk.com). It offers affordable pricing and various options, depending on your budget and needs. You can find other options in Appendix B.

Finally, you can choose to have direct e-mail support right within your app. If you do decide to go this route, be sure to follow up with your customer as soon as possible, regardless of the issue. Personal touches are great, and if you can build up a standard library of responses for certain known issues, it can speed up the process.

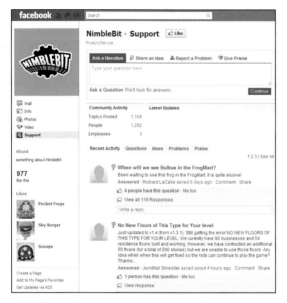

FIGURE 11-4: Nimblebit (makers of one of the top-grossing apps, "Tiny Tower") has a branded Facebook Fan Page with support built in

Always Replying to Customer E-Mails

Newegg.com was built on two things: fast, consistent delivery, and prompt, courteous replies to customer problems, showing a willingness to go the extra mile and eat some cost if necessary to please a customer. As someone who's used them since their early beginnings, the author has seen the countless posts and propagation of a spectacular support mythos that's propelled Newegg to be *the* recommended store for any purchase in the U.S. (and now in Canada), almost by default. Apple is about consistent quality; Newegg is about consistent support.

It may be wise to consider support as a marketing expense, in the same way that many companies offer rebates, or temporary price-reduction promotions on apps. Though it is true that you will lose some amount of money to those who, for rebates, actually take the time to fill out and send in a form — or with apps, those who download the reduced-price version — in the end, the promotion value for new customers typically offsets the cost. The difference, though, between good support and rebates or promotions is that your brand reputation continues to grow with good support. Never underestimate the value of customer loyalty to your brand. Because competition is fierce in the App Store, adding the personal touch of replying to all e-mails and support requests may be the thing that solidifies your company's edge.

An additional benefit with the support tie-in to the App Store is that when you offer excellent support, you can then ask your users to rate your app if they haven't already (providing brief directions on how within your app), and/or ask that they leave positive feedback, right from your brand's support site forum.

One example of this is Truethemes (`support.truethemes.net`), an excellent premium WordPress theme site that offers spectacular support and answers every question in a timely manner. After the inevitable "wow, fantastic support, thanks!" follow-up, Truethemes follows that up with a sincere thank you, and then a request that if the users found the support adequate, to please help get the word out by rating them on the associated download site and providing some feedback. Other users then see these posts when searching for answers of their own, and over time, your brand becomes recognized for it, and will be the first one recommended.

The other part of support is showing that you are willing to listen to feedback and make necessary changes to your app.

Timely Updates

Providing updates as a mechanism of promotion is important in the App Store, for a few reasons. One is that customers typically look at the "last updated" section of iTunes for your app prior to downloading to see whether they are potentially getting an older, forgotten app, or one for which they can expect some support. Another is that large feature/content updates can be further marketed via press release and app review websites. Finally, updates tie into your support presence (as discussed earlier in this chapter) and promote brand/app loyalty.

All updates should occur relatively frequently and consistently. Once every week to two weeks is a good timeline — more frequently at first, and then later, it is okay to increase the duration between them, as long as they are consistent. Timely updates with estimations on your brand's site, Facebook Fan Page, and Twitter feed provide customers with something to look forward to, and can be a means to increase sales — especially content updates.

With all updates, try to include a minor fix or tweak, even if it is only generically phrased, such as "improved stability" or "performance increase." Even the most minor and consistent updates will keep your fans checking, engaged, and loyal.

Because updates involving new content are appreciated by fans, but take more time to implement, carefully consider how you plan to scale your app.

SCALING

Prior to release, you will likely have an idea of at least some of the features and content that you weren't able to include in your app on launch. And, if you don't yet, then post-launch customer feedback can help you add new potential features, as well as help you gauge which of your currently planned updates are a suitably high priority.

Releasing New Content

When you are scaling your app for more content (whether paid or free), you should take advantage of both the metrics that you have gathered (how are people using your app, what are they buying within your app, how long are they using it, and so on — Flurry is one popular company that can help, at `www.flurry.com`) and the user feedback. Once you have a shortlist of new features or content (see the earlier section, "Prioritizing for Updates"), keep in mind some of the following considerations:

➤ Have the users asked for this feature? If not, you may want to consider temporarily shelving it, and creating content that has shown to be in demand.

➤ How well is your app doing? Initial launch metrics will help you decide if it could be worth the expense.

➤ How long will the update take to implement? Keep in mind that your first update should be roughly a week after you launch.

➤ Will the update require users to update in order to sync with another version? For example, in multiplayer games or multi-user apps, can users of the older version still use the app in conjunction with newer versions? Keep in mind that the more casual the app, the less likely it will be that users see or bother with updating frequently. Apps with a large amount of features that are used often (such as tech or gadget apps, and even games) may have users who update on a more regular basis.

One consideration you may not have thought about if you're planning on new content is whether it might be worthwhile to instead expend some of your resources on developing for other platforms.

Building for Other Platforms

At some point during development, almost every developer wonders whether the app could also be suited to another platform. If you are reading this book, you are obviously intending to develop on iOS, but may have also considered the current second-largest app marketplace, which is the one built for Android apps.

Whether you have an existing Android app and want to port it to iOS (or vice versa), note that tools are available that can help you achieve this. Corona SDK (www.anscamobile.com/corona/) is one of the most popular and should be on your list to research, especially if you have not yet begun coding. Another up-and-coming company that may be able to assist you with this is ScoreLoop (www.scoreloop.com/).

Similarly, if you have a Flash app and you'd like it ported to iOS, then Adobe Flash Professional CS5 (www.adobe.com) can export your projects to iOS via a packager for iPhone.

Finally, as HTML 5 picks up steam, you may want to consider development of your apps in web format for use with iOS devices and the App Store. One such technology to help is PhoneGap (www.phonegap.com/).

> *Note that Apple may eventually put into place more restrictions regarding HTML 5 implementation, so be sure to stay updated during development.*

The Future of Your App

The thrill of releasing your first app can be both exhilarating and nerve-wracking. Whether or not you are successful in the App Store on your first try, you can use your initial app(s) as a launching point to build your greater overall brand, and continue to learn and evolve your process so that your future apps are even more successful.

With the right support, consistent updates, community building, metric tracking, and brand presence through promotion within apps and via social networking, you can significantly increase your odds of success. It will always take some amount of money, time, talent, and smart planning, but can certainly be done with almost any app.

Post-launch, the smartest approach to designing a bright future for your apps is to foster their strengths and minimize their weaknesses through aggressive metric tracking in order to help prioritize future updates, cross-promotion, and through your fan base via social media and branding.

Following are some tips for continued promotion of your app post-release:

- ➤ Use press releases for major content updates and milestones (your app has X amount of downloads, and so on). Some good outlets include www.pr-inside.com, www.prweb.com, and www.prleap.com.

- ➤ Submit news to iPhone and iPad blog sites for significant updates and milestones.

- ➤ Get continued YouTube user reviews of your app.

- ➤ Use Search Engine Optimization (SEO) for both your keywords and brand.

- ➤ Utilize social media as outlined in Chapter 10.

- ➤ Provide top-quality support.

- ➤ Upload videos of your app in motion, and use YouTube and your other social networks (Facebook, Twitter, Google+, and so on) for promotion.

- ➤ Promote your videos using a service such as TubeMogul (www.tubemogul.com).

- ➤ Have a branded website and Facebook Fan Page.

- ➤ Run contests and promotions, and cycle them through your social media networks, as well as iOS app blogs.

- ➤ Continue to create buzz about your app via posts on various forums.

- ➤ Use paid search marketing via Google, Yahoo!, and so on.

- ➤ Offer free downloads to reviewers, especially video reviewers or top bloggers.

- ➤ Create Twitter and Facebook functionality within your app so that users can promote it.

- ➤ Participate in forums, LinkedIn groups as experts, Yahoo Answers (answers.yahoo.com), and Wiki Answers (wiki.answers.com).

- ➤ Blog on your brand's website, especially cross-linking with Twitter and Facebook about the industry and your updates.

- ➤ Post positive user reviews on your brand's home page and testimonials page.

- ➤ Offer limited-time promotions and heavy discounts of your paid apps to encourage downloads.

- ➤ Appear as a speaker at industry trade shows, and promote your appearances.

These are just a few of the more popular ways to promote your app and brand as a whole (although countless other ways exist). By utilizing some of the techniques described here, especially taking advantage of social media marketing, your app has a great chance to last significantly longer than it otherwise would have, and, therefore, result in large net gains for your company and future apps as a whole.

SUMMARY

Throughout this book, you've learned how to build, design, and price your next hit app, from initial research and team building, to revenue models, feature selection, aesthetics, social media integration, post-release updating, and, finally, enhancing brand reputation.

It's a lot to take in, but a process such as this is best approached organically with a healthy respect for budgets, timelines, and priorities. Throughout the course of development, new doors will open, and you will never quite know how successful you can be until you go through it all. Remember, it is all about action.

A

Reading List of Recommended Books

I never perfected an invention that I did not think about in terms of the service it might give others... I find out what the world needs, then I proceed to invent.

— Thomas Edison

The two appendixes in this book provide a wealth of further strategies for accomplishing all of the goals laid out in this book, and much more. This appendix, in particular, provides information on books that are recommended reading.

APP DEVELOPMENT

The following books are highly recommended in the area of application development.

Business and Project Management

The following books are highly recommended in the area of business and project management:

➤ *Upstarts!: How GenY Entrepreneurs are Rocking the World of Business and 8 Ways You Can Profit from Their Success* by Donna Fenn (New York: McGraw-Hill, 2009)

➤ For a different spin from this book (slightly more technical and legal), see *The Business of iPhone and iPad App Development: Making and Marketing Apps that Succeed* by Dave Wooldridge and Michael Schneider (New York: Apress, 2011)

➤ *Agile Game Development with Scrum* by Clinton Keith (Boston: Addison-Wesley Professional, 2010)

➤ *Game Development Essentials: Game Project Management* by John Hight and Jeannie Novak (Florence, Kentucky: Delmar Cengage Learning, 2007)

➤ *The Game Producer's Handbook* by Dan Irish (Florence, Kentucky: Course Technology PTR, 2005)

iOS Programming

The following books are highly recommended in the area of iOS programming:

➤ *iPhone Programming: The Big Nerd Ranch Guide* by Joe Conway and Aaron Hillegass (Boston: Addison-Wesley Professional, 2010)

➤ *Cocoa Design Patterns* by Eric M. Buck and Donald A. Yacktman (Boston: Addison-Wesley Professional, 2009)

Design and Art

The following books are highly recommended in the area of design and art:

➤ For design and project brainstorms, see *iPhone 4 Made Simple* by Martin Trautschold, Gary Mazo, and Rene Ritchie (New York: Apress, 2010)

➤ *Tapworthy: Designing Great iPhone Apps* by Josh Clark (Sebastopol, California: O'Reilly Media, 2010)

➤ *A Theory of Fun for Game Design* by Raph Koster (Sebastopol, California: Paraglyph Press, 2004)

➤ For an amazing repertoire of design ideas, see *David Perry on Game Design: A Brainstorming ToolBox* by David Perry and Rusel DeMaria (Hingham, Massachusetts: Charles River Media, 2009)

➤ *The Design of Everyday Things* by Donald A. Norman (New York: Basic Books, 2002)

➤ *The Design of Design: Essays from a Computer Scientist* by Frederick P. Brooks, Jr. (Boston: Addison-Wesley, 2010)

➤ *From Idea to App: Creating iOS UI, Animations, And Gestures (Voices That Matter)* by Shawn Welch (Berkeley, California: New Riders Press, 2011)

Marketing

The following books are highly recommended in the area of marketing:

➤ *Social Nation: How to Harness the Power of Social Media to Attract Customers, Motivate Employees, and Grow Your Business* by Barry Libert (Indianapolis: Wiley, 2010)

➤ *The Old Rules of Marketing are Dead: 6 New Rules to Reinvent Your Brand and Reignite Your Business* by Timothy R. Pearson (New York: McGraw-Hill, 2011)

➤ *Designing Brand Identity: An Essential Guide for the Whole Branding Team* by Alina Wheeler (Indianapolis: Wiley, 2009)

➤ *The Zen of Social Media Marketing: An Easier Way to Build Credibility, Generate Buzz, and Increase Revenue* by Shama Kabani (Dallas: BenBella Books, 2010)

➤ *Likeable Social Media: How to Delight Your Customers, Create an Irresistible Brand, and Be Generally Amazing on Facebook (& Other Social Networks)* by Dave Kerpen (New York: McGraw-Hill, 2011)

CREATIVITY AND INSPIRATION

The following books are highly recommended in the area of creativity and inspiration:

➤ *The Genius Machine: The Eleven Steps That Turn Raw Ideas into Brilliance* by Gerald Sindell (Novato, California: New World Library, 2009)

➤ *The Art of Innovation: Lessons in Creativity from IDEO, America's Leading Design Firm* by Tom Kelly and Jonathan Littman (New York: Crown Business, 2001)

➤ *The Creative Habit: Learn It and Use It for Life* by Twyla Tharp (New York: Simon & Shuster, 2005)

➤ *Zen and the Art of Motorcycle Maintenance: An Inquiry into Values* by Robert M. Pirsig (New York: Harper Perennial Modern Classics, 2008)

Online Resources

You can't depend on your judgment when your imagination is out of focus.

— Mark Twain

This appendix examines some of the most valuable online resources currently available for all aspects of app development. Because companies and websites change all the time, some of these may be out-of-date in the not-too-distant future. Therefore, where relevant, the author provides a useful search term or two to use in search engines like Google or Bing.

RESEARCH AND METRICS

This section examines resources in the areas of research and metrics.

App Store Metrics and Rankings

Following are resources for App Store metrics and rankings:

➤ **AppAnnie (app sales and rankings)** — See www.appannie.com.

➤ **Applyzer (app sales and rankings)** — See www.applyzer.com.

➤ **148Apps.biz (app rankings)** — See www.148apps.biz.

➤ **Top App Charts (app rankings)** — See www.topappcharts.com.

➤ **AppFigures (app sales metrics)** — See www.appfigures.com.

> *Useful search engine terms include "app store metrics" and "app rankings."*

App Usage and Engagement Metrics

Following are resources for app usage and engagement metrics:

➤ **Flurry (full-service app metrics)** — See www.flurry.com. Sites such as this (see Figure B-1) and the following two provide you with in-depth metrics, perfect for split-testing engagement within your app.

FIGURE B-1: Flurry is one of the top in-app metric providers, offering much more depth than just sales data

➤ **Kontagent (full-service app metrics)** — See www.kontagent.com.

➤ **TapMetrics (full-service app metrics)** — See www.tapmetrics.com.

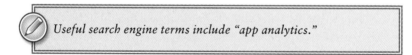

Useful search engine terms include "app analytics."

Website Metrics and SEO

Following are resources for website metrics and Search Engine Optimization (SEO):

➤ **Google Analytics (website traffic tracking and solutions)** — See analytics.google.com. This is a free and recommended way to keep track of most of your traffic needs.

➤ **Google Keyword Tool (keyword research)** — See adwords.google.com/select/KeywordToolExternal. Best just to search for "google keyword tool" to get the link. Paired with Google Analytics, you'll be "SEO-ing" in no time. This is also a great way to do research for your app description and app's keywords.

Useful search engine terms "website analytics."

PLANNING AND COMMUNICATING

This section examines resources in the areas of planning and communicating.

Outsourcing

Following are resources for outsourcing:

> ➤ **Elance (top rated outsourcing)** — See `www.elance.com`. Elance is a premier place to find outsourced talent. Prices are a bit higher than Guru or oDesk, but on the whole, talent may be a bit more reliable as well.

> ➤ **Guru (popular outsource site)** — See `www.guru.com`. Like Elance, Guru is another outsourcing option. Its prices are a bit lower, and you will find more non-U.S. talent here.

> ➤ **oDesk (popular outsource site)** — See `www.odesk.com`. oDesk is the newest general outsource site of the big three. You can find great rates here, a lot of non-U.S. talent, and, like Guru, it isn't quite as full-featured a site as Elance, but is capable and recommended.

> ➤ **Get Apps Done (iOS and other platform outsourcing)** — See www `.getappsdone.com`. Whether you are a developer, or need to outsource to one, this is one site that can help connect the two, primarily focused on iOS and Android developers.

Useful search engine terms include "iPhone app development," "mobile app development," "iPhone outsourcing," and "iPhone developers."

Project Management

Following are resources for project management:

> ➤ **Basecamp (online project management)** — See `www.basecamphq.com`. "Basecamp" (shown in Figure B-2) from 37 Signals is a full-featured, online project-management app, with collaboration tools, file storage, milestones, tasks, and notifications. It's one of the (if not *the*) most recommended online apps out there, but there are other good ones as well. "Basecamp" also features a number of iOS (and other mobile) apps that integrate well with it.

> ➤ **Zoho Projects (online project management)** — See `www.zoho.com`. This is the main competition for "Basecamp" in the area of online project management. Both have their strengths and loyal fans. On the whole, "Zoho" (shown in Figure B-3) appears to be a bit cheaper, but features are also slightly different.

For example, it integrates well with Google Apps, whereas "Basecamp" doesn't at the same level.

FIGURE B-2: "Basecamp" has millions of users and relatively affordable pricing for an online project-management app

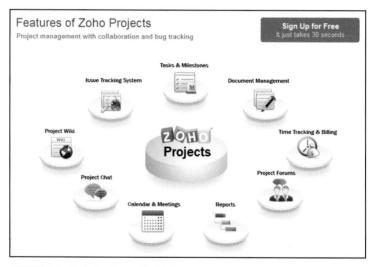

FIGURE B-3: "Zoho" offers affordable pricing and tight integration with Google Apps

➤ **JIRA (paid project-management solution and bug tracking)** — See www
.atlassian.com/software/jira/. This is a complete bug-tracking and
project-management platform. The interface was recently overhauled to be
more "Web 2.0" compliant.

➤ **Bugzilla (open source bug tracking)** — See www.bugzilla.org.

> *Useful search engine terms include "online project management," "bug tracking software," and "online bug tracking."*

E-Mail, Video Conferencing, Chat, and Screen Sharing

Following are resources for e-mail, video conferencing, chat, and screen sharing:

➤ **Gmail (e-mail)** — See www.gmail.com. This is the best free e-mail client. It also integrates well with Google Docs, and all of Google's other fantastic free online apps.

➤ **Skype (instant communication)** — See www.skype.com. Skype is a great way to freely communicate, to video conference, and to share files directly to outsourced and internal teams. It has some premium features as well, such as calling credits and video conferencing with multiple people.

➤ **Mikogo (screen sharing)** — See www.mikogo.com. If you work with outsourced teams, or if you're just lazy and don't feel like walking over to the desk of a teammate, chances are you can benefit from screen sharing. This is a great free option that allows you to log in to a session and use your mouse to click on someone's screen without it affecting them. This is useful when collaborating with large teams or using Skype (that is, having Skype on for voice and "Mikogo" on for screen sharing).

> *Useful search engine terms include "online collaboration" (or "best online collaboration"), "best free communication tools," "free teleconferencing," and "free screen sharing."*

DEVELOPING

This section examines resources in the area of developing.

iOS Development

Following are resources for iOS development:

➤ **Apple and iOS Developer Site (your Apple development portal)** — See developer.apple.com/ios. Well ahead of release (likely when you have the green light on your first app), head to this site (shown in Figure B-4), sign up to be an iOS Developer, and pay the fee for the iOS Developer Program. You'll then get access to all the tools and latest iOS Software Development Kits (SDKs). This is a requirement for all developers, so don't wait, because it can take weeks for approval. Use this site as a launching point to tutorials, guidelines, and managing all your Apple developer devices.

FIGURE B-4: The iOS Developer center has lots of resources and tutorials, and will be a frequent destination during your development

➤ **cocos2D (2D iOS development framework)** — See www.cocos2d.com. This is a full-featured, two-dimensional (2D) development framework, which means that you can use it to build almost any type of app or game as long as it isn't three-dimensional (3D).

➤ **Corona SDK (iOS development framework)** — See www.anscamobile.com/corona/. Also mentioned as a resource in the section "Cross-Platform Development" later in this appendix, this framework provides another way to create great looking and performing iOS apps.

➤ **TestFlight (free testing service)** — See www.testflightapp.com. This is an amazingly easy-to-use and highly recommended beta (or any stage) distribution service. It's free, and individual users can get updates without ever having to sync to iTunes, right within their own simple app. This is a much better way than requiring your team to go through the certification process.

> *Useful search engine terms include "iPhone app development tutorials," "iPhone app testing," and "best iPhone framework."*

Social Game Solutions

Other than Apple's Game Center (for which more information can be found at developer.apple.com), here are a couple of main players for iOS apps.

➤ **OpenFeint** — See www.openfeint.com. This is the best current social connectivity within an app for any platform, including Game Center.

➤ **Plus+** — See www.plusplus.com. Pronounced "plus plus," this is another leading social network, but without some of the live features that OpenFeint includes.

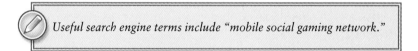

Useful search engine terms include "mobile social gaming network."

Brainstorming and Prototyping

Following are resources for brainstorming and prototyping:

➤ **MindMeister (online mind mapping)** — See www.mindmeister.com. This is one of the best online mind-mapping tools. Mind mapping is great for tracking brainstorms, recording your scattered thoughts, and taking notes from meetings. Once you start mind mapping, it's hard to go back to traditional note taking and lists.

➤ **Freemind (offline mind mapping)** — See freemind.sourceforge.net. This is a wonderful Java-based, free download, and is great for offline use. It has easy-to-remember hotkeys to build new maps surprisingly fast.

➤ **Balsamiq Mockups (online mockup prototyping and wireframing)** — See www.balsamiq.com. This provides an amazing use of current Web 2.0+ technology to quickly prototype new interfaces (see Figure B-5).

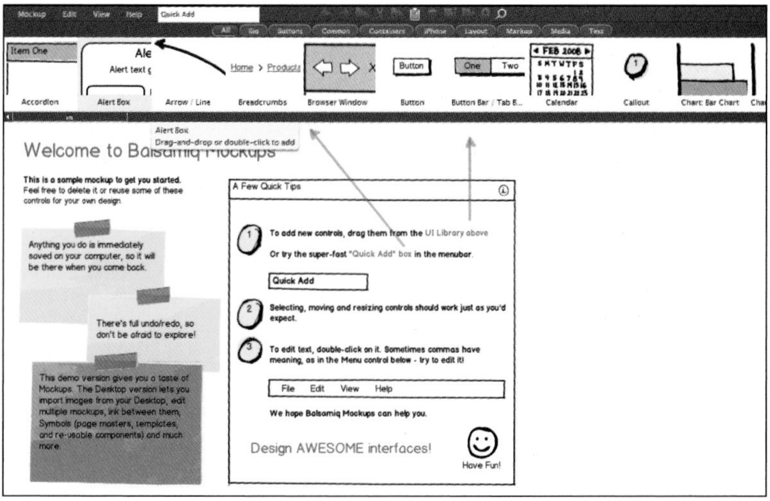

FIGURE B-5: "Balsamiq Mockups" can be used online or off, and has a great user interface

➤ **Mockups To Go (database of UI elements)** — See www.mockupstogo.net. This provides user-uploaded user interface (UI) content for plugging into "Balsamiq."

> *Useful search engine terms include "online brainstorming," "mind mapping," "online prototyping," and "best prototyping tools."*

Documentation

Following are resources for documentation:

➤ **Google Docs (free online office software)** — See `docs.google.com`. When you need simple documents created without all the functionality of, say, Microsoft Office, look no further than the free Google Docs. The single best feature is that you can share the documents with anyone or everyone on your team, giving individual users unique permissions. Google has basic versions of spreadsheets, word processing, and presentation software, and can export in several formats. Once you try it, you'll be hooked.

➤ **Open Office (free offline office software)** — See `www.openoffice.org`. Open Office is an Open Source and free full-featured office suite, comparable to Microsoft Office. It's great if you need something free, and you can export in all the Microsoft formats (though results can sometimes vary).

➤ **Microsoft Office (paid offline office software)** — See `office.microsoft.com`. This provides all the functionality you need in a documentation program, and more, at a relatively reasonable cost. If for no other reason, buy it for Word and Excel, but Presentation and Visio are great tools as well, depending on your needs. Furthermore, in the future, all documentation programs (including this one) will likely move to be "cloud" based. For now though, you can't go wrong.

> *Useful search engine terms include "online document creation" and "online collaboration."*

Cross-Platform Development

Following are resources for cross-platform development:

➤ **Corona SDK (cross-platform development)** — See `www.anscamobile.com/corona/`. These are also mentioned in Chapter 11. Corona is a great SDK to use for iPhone, iPhone, or Android, either consecutively or simultaneously.

➤ **ScoreLoop (cross-platform development)** — See `www.scoreloop.com`. Tightly integrated with monetizing on the Android platform, it also has an initiative to help developers in cross-platform development.

➤ **Adobe Flash Professional CS5 (cross-platform development)** — See `www.adobe.com`. For porting Flash games to iOS, Flash Professional versions CS5 and greater can currently do this.

➤ **PhoneGap (cross-platform development)** — See `www.phonegap.com`. Use this to port HTML 5 apps to the iOS to be able to use on the App Store.

> *Useful search engine terms include "iOS cross-platform development" and "porting iOS to [your platform here]."*

Royalty-Free Audio

Following are resources for royalty-free audio:

➤ **Audio Jungle (paid audio files)** — See `www.audiojungle.net`. This is an excellent resource for low-cost, royalty-free music. Most of it is created by engineers specifically for the site, and sorted based on popularity and need. Chances are you can find some to all of what you need here.

➤ **Stock Music (paid audio files)** — See `www.stockmusic.net`. This is a huge library of good quality audio, and features a simple pricing scheme.

➤ **Non Stop Music (paid music library)** — See `www.nonstopmusic.com`. This has an amazing list of credits, and is one of the leaders in high-quality music tracks.

➤ **Digital Juice (paid audio files)** — See `www.digitaljuice.com`. This offers affordable music, sound FX, and more stock stuff.

➤ **Sample Swap (free sound effects)** — See `www.sampleswap.org`. This provides a fantastic array of free sound effects.

> *Useful search engine terms include "royalty free music" and "royalty free sound effects."*

MARKETING

This section examines resources in the area of marketing.

App News and Review Sites

In August, 2011, ManiacDev (`www.maniacdev.com/2011/08/ios-app-review-sites/`) put together a fantastic list of current news and review sites for promoting your app, very handily sorted by Alexa ranking. Following are the top 30 from that extensive list:

➤ **CNET** — See `reviews.cnet.com`.

➤ **IGN** — See `www.ign.com`.

➤ **GameSpot** — See `www.gamespot.com`.

➤ **MacRumors** — See `www.macrumors.com`.

➤ **Appscout by PC Magazine** — See `appscout.pcmagazine.com`.

➤ **GigaOM** — See `www.gigaom.com`.

➤ **Ars Technica** — See `www.arstechnica.com`.

➤ **Macworld** — See `www.macworld.com`.

➤ **N4G (news 4 gamers)** — See `www.n4g.com`.

➤ **All Things D** — See `www.allthingsd.com`.

➤ **TUAW (The Unofficial Apple Weblog)** — See `www.tuaw.com`.

➤ **Eurogamer** — See `www.eurogamer.net`.

➤ **App Storm** — See `iphone.appstorm.net`.

➤ **TouchArcade** — See `www.toucharcade.com`.

➤ **The iPhone Blog** — See `www.tipb.com`.

➤ **iLounge** — See `www.ilounge.com`.

➤ **IntoMobile** — See `www.intomobile.com`.

➤ **Gamezebo** — See `www.gamezebo.com`.

➤ **AppAdvice** — See `www.appadvice.com`.

➤ **T3** — See `www.t3.com`.

➤ **iPhoneclub (Dutch)** — See `www.iphoneclub.nl`.

➤ **Appolicious** — See `www.appolicious.com`.

➤ **148Apps** — See `www.148apps.com`.

➤ **Maclife** — See `www.maclife.com/articles/iphone`.

➤ **App Gamer** — See `www.appgamer.net`.

➤ **blog do iPhone (Brazil/Portuguese)** — See `www.blogdoiphone.com`.

➤ **Pocket Gamer** — See `www.pocketgamer.co.uk`.

➤ **iSmashPhone** — See `www.ismashphone.com`.

➤ **iPhone Application List** — See `www.iphoneapplicationlist.com`.

➤ **iPhone World** — See `www.iphoneworld.ca`.

> *Useful search engine terms include "iPhone app reviews" and "iPhone news."*

Ad Networks and Affiliates

Following are resources for ad networks and affiliates:

➤ **iAd (Apple's ad network)** — See `developer.apple.com/iad/`. This provides media-rich advertising on any iOS device. It is recommended as one of your free or lite solutions.

➤ **AdMob (ad network)** — See `www.admob.com`. Owned by Google, this is a huge ad network with metrics.

➤ **JumpTap (ad network)** — See `www.jumptap.com`. This is smaller than AdMob, and still one of the larger networks.

➤ **Adwhirl (ad mediator/exchange)** — See `www.adwhirl.com`. Also owned by AdMob (and thus Google), this is an ad-mediation tool that lets you use several ad networks together.

➤ **Mobclix (ad mediator/exchange)** — See `www.mobclix.com`. This is another ad-mediation network with the capability to use multiple networks and bid for ads.

➤ **iTunes Affiliate Program** — See `www.apple.com/itunes/affiliates/`. If you can link to products on iTunes, the App Store, and other Apple venues from your app or website, you can generate extra income via up to 5 percent returns on iTunes purchases. Some developers have used affiliate ad banners for other popular apps as part of their in-app advertising.

> *Useful search engine terms include "iOS advertising" and "iOS affiliate marketing."*

Award Sites

You can promote your app and brand easier by entering competitions for awards.

➤ **Apple Design Awards (award site)** — See `developer.apple.com/wwdc/ada`. Apple picks these from apps on the App Store.

➤ **Appy Awards (award site)** — See `www.appyawards.net`. You can also be featured as its "App of the Week" if you submit an entry.

➤ **Best App Ever (by 148Apps, award site)** — See `www.bestappever.com`. This includes many possible categories of eligibility, and a good presentation of award winners.

➤ **AppsFire Awards (award and recognition site)** — See `www.appsfire.com`. Use the contact page for more information about its awards.

> *Useful search terms include "app awards" and "iOS app awards."*

Press Release Submission

Following are resources for press release submission:

➤ **PR-inside.com (free)** — See `www.pr-inside.com`.

➤ **PRWeb (paid)** — See `www.prweb.com`.

➤ **PR Leap (paid)** — See `www.prleap.com`.

> *Useful search engine terms include "press releases," "press release promotion," and "free press release submission."*

E-Mail Marketing

Following are resources for e-mail marketing:

➤ **MailChimp (e-mail newsletters, some free options)** — See www.mailchimp.com. This highly popular service lets you design and send your own newsletters and get code to insert into your websites. E-mail lists are one of the best ways to reach out to your existing fan base with new services (known as *pushing* them through the marketing funnel). Some others follow.

➤ **Campaign Monitor (paid full service)** — See www.campaignmonitor.com. This is another full-featured mailing and newsletter service with great analytics. This is paid starting at $15 per month (currently).

➤ **Constant Contact (e-mail + social networking)** — See www.constantcontact .com. This integrates well with social media, and is recommended.

> *Useful search engine terms include "e-mail marketing" and "newsletter service."*

Full-Featured Marketing Solutions

Following are resources for full-featured marketing solutions:

➤ **Apalon (mobile development and marketing studio)** — See www.apalon.com/ iphone_marketing.html. In addition to being an outsourced mobile development house, it has marketing plans covering hype, release, and post-launch with multiple tier pricing. There are countless others, as well as individuals and small firms that also do this type of thing, so shop around for something that fits your budget and needs.

➤ **Appency (marketing)** — See www.appency.com.

➤ **App2Market (marketing)** — See www.app2market.com.

➤ **Appular (marketing)** — See www.appular.com.

> *Useful search engine terms include "mobile application marketing" and "iPhone app marketing."*

Social Media

Following are resources for social media:

➤ **Facebook Page Creation** — See www.facebook.com/pages/create.php. You will need a Facebook Fan Page for your app and/or brand.

> *Refer to specific subsections within this section for recommended search terms.*

➤ **Facebook Vanity URL** — See `www.facebook.com/username/`. Once you have 25 "likes" on your Facebook Fan Page (you can buy these, too), you can use this link to change your name to your brand or app's name.

➤ **Twitter** — See `www.twitter.com`. When you've finalized the name of your app, go here to sign up for a Twitter account and start tweeting. You can/should also do this with your brand, in case it's the brand you want to feed into.

➤ **Timely (tweet scheduling)** — See `www.timely.is`. Write your tweets in advance and schedule them so that you can get more done.

➤ **BackTweets (Twitter search analytics)** — See `www.backtweets.com`. Acquired by Twitter, this is a free search engine to look for any URL or @*term*, or hashtag (tags) to see where and when it was "tweeted."

Sharing Toolbars

The following toolbars can be implemented into websites, posts, and more:

➤ **Add This (general social media toolbar)** — See `www.addthis.com`. This is a customizable sharing toolbar to implement most anywhere with analytics (see Figure B-6).

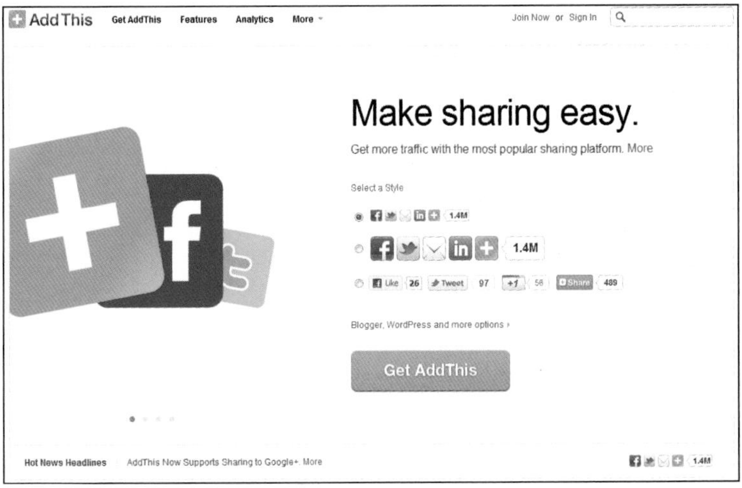

FIGURE B-6: Social toolbars like this one from Add This are becoming mandatory to keep up with social marketing

➤ **ShareThis (general social media toolbar)** — See `www.sharethis.com`. This is similar in function to Add This.

➤ **WP Social (social media toolbar plugin for WordPress)** — See `www.wordpress.org/extend/plugins/wp-social-toolbar/`. This is a fantastic customizable toolbar for any WordPress site.

> *Useful search engine terms include "social media toolbars" and "sharing toolbars."*

Video Marketing

Following are resources for video marketing:

➤ **YouTube** — See www.youtube.com. Tie-in videos of your app with your brand via other social channels.

➤ **TubeMogul** — See www.tubemogul.com. Use TubeMogul to distribute, market, advertise, and analyze your branded videos.

> *Useful search engine terms include "video marketing."*

Customer Support

Following are resources for customer support:

➤ **Zendesk (built-in site support)** — See www.zendesk.com. This is the current leader in customer support platforms (see Figure B-7).

FIGURE B-7: Zendesk offers excellent, high-quality support options for your brand

➤ **Get Satisfaction (built-in site support)** — See www.getsatisfaction.com.

➤ **Tenderapp (built-in site support)** — See www.tenderapp.com.

> *Useful search engine terms include "online customer support solution."*

INDEX